INTIMATE MOMENTS

WITH MY

BELOVED KING

BY

REV. VIVIAN THOMPSON

CO-AUTHORED BY VIRGINIA AH YEE

ISBN NUMBER: **978-0-9797037-0-6**
First Printing, July 2007
Second Printing, October 2007
Publisher: Virginia Ah Yee

Additional copies of this book are available by mail.
Virginia Ah Yee
95-460 Kaelo Place
Mililani, HI 96789

Printed in the U.S.A. by
Morris Publishing
3212 East Highway 30
Kearney, NE 68847
1-800-650-7888

DEDICATION

To my beloved husband

Rev. David T. Thompson

It was a fifty-year adventure working side-by-side with such an amazing man of faith. God had prepared and gifted my husband in so many ways, and David used every gift to preach the gospel. The first and foremost gift was his love for people. David loved people in general, but he was drawn to people of all ethnic groups. He was so interested in people of different languages and cultures. This love led us from a skid-row mission in the heart of San Francisco, to home missions work on the Apache reservation in San Carlos, Arizona, on to Hawaii and the Marshall Islands. God gave David the heart of a pastor and missionary.

His second gift was his communication skills. He loved to study the Bible and especially prophesy. He was a marvelous Bible teacher because he could explain difficult passages with simple and direct clarity. He was a wonderful storyteller—causing the Bible to come alive. He gave his sermons catchy titles, which helped us to remember the sermon for a long time. His greatest joy was to see his students grasp the more difficult passages of the Word of God.

His third gift was his keen and logical mind. David was always thinking and learning new things. He could keep an accurate set of accounting books, figure out a computer program, fix anything that was mechanical, and build anything he put his mind to build.

He planned and built two churches in Arizona with only the assistance of volunteer labor. Then God called us to Hawaii. Our daughter met her husband there while we were the pastors of Naalehu Assembly of God. We built a new church building there with the help of many volunteers. It was during our time in Naalehu that the Lord began speaking to us about a place we had never heard of before—called the Marshall Islands.

The way seemed to be blocked for us to go to the Marshall Islands, so we took on a small church on the island of Oahu in a town named Haleiwa. Ginger and her family followed us there. When the doors opened up for us to go to the Marshall Islands, we sold everything we owned, and we were off on a new faith adventure.

We went to Majuro, Marshall Islands as Bible school teachers. Soon after we arrived, David realized that all kinds of mechanical things were broken down—cars, trucks, motorcycles, and power generators. After classes, David started fixing everything he could with what little parts he could find. The thing that broke David's heart was a beautiful 42-ft diesel cruiser sitting out in the lagoon, unable to move because it had been run without oil in both diesel engines.

He spent two months working on the engines, thinking that the boat would be sold because nobody wanted to take the chance of running it. After finishing the repairs, David took it on a test run to the next atoll. When the Missionary Board saw that he knew how to navigate, they gave him the authorization to use the vessel for the mission work. In the meantime, David had studied as much as he could about navigation—using the stars, marine sextant and charts. Actually, God was giving him supernatural knowledge. God miraculously kept us from getting lost at sea, even when we were caught in awful storms. We took our students to far away islands to build and plant churches.

After our five year missions tour in the Marshall Islands, we returned to Hawaii and were the pastors at First Assembly of God in Kahalui, Maui. David served as the Treasurer for the District office, and I served as the District Women's Ministry Director.

From Maui, we went to Salinas, California and served at Calvary Assembly of God. After retiring from the ministry, David became ill with an enlarged heart. We were able to return to Hawaii where our daughter lives. This was made possible because Rev. William Ashpole asked David to come and set up a bookkeeping system for his church, Faith Assembly of God, in Mililani, Hawaii.

David closed out the church books for the year 1992 right before Jesus called him Home on January 6, 1993. I thank God for the adventures of faith, and even for the sometimes-troubled seas we sailed together.

Vivian and David Thompson

This picture was taken while they were Pastors of
Calvary Assembly of God in Salinas, California

Vivian started her journal of the Song of Solomon during this time

ACKNOWLEDGEMENTS

I would like to thank the many people who have encouraged me to write this book. If it were not for their gentle prodding, I do not think it would have come to pass. I will name a few of these wonderful people.

There was my dear friend Rev. Shirley Kimzey. She took my handwritten notes and transformed them into computer files. This was such a blessing as it made the book readable.

My daughter, Virginia "Ginger" Ah Yee took it from that point. She has spent many months of writing and rewriting. She was able to take my thoughts and make sense of them to the extent of almost reading my mind. With much prayer, research, and most of all the discernment of the Holy Spirit, she was able to say exactly what I had set out to say. Thanks to Ginger's husband, Raphael, who with patient indulgence became a sounding board—listening and assisting with many helpful suggestions on the integrity and clarity of the work.

Several people have assisted in editing. The foremost editor was Kelly Becker who willingly devoted numerous hours in correcting spelling, grammar, and punctuation. She also gave us valuable feedback from the reader's viewpoint. Her words of encouragement were precious to Ginger and me as she shared how the words of this book have blessed her. Others who have added valuable insight were Rev. Barbara Yamashita, Martha Ah Yee, Jonette Fraticelli, and my granddaughter Colleen McClain. Thanks to Mackenzie Yoshida for the front cover photograph.

Above all, I acknowledge the precious Holy Spirit, for He directed me to write these thoughts. The Holy Spirit would not let me put this book away, but He prompted me repeatedly over the past twenty years to put it into print.

TABLE OF CONTENTS

INTRODUCTION

The Song of Solomon has been a deep interest of mine ever since I attended Glad Tidings Bible College in San Francisco during the early 1940's. [1] It has been a question in my mind as to why this subject has not been explored more often in sermons and books. During our last pastorate in Salinas, California, I decided to study the Song of Solomon again and keep a journal. I became engrossed with the Song because it ministered to me in my daily walk with the Lord. As I drew near to Jesus, He drew near to me. I was compelled to share this love story with the Church. While sharing my thoughts with several women's groups, I saw the excitement and devotion it created in their lives. That is how this book was birthed. It has taken many years to develop. I thank many of my encouraging brothers and sisters who have helped me to press on until it was complete.

Solomon wrote over one thousand songs, and of all these songs, this is the only one that has withstood the test of time. It has survived because it is inspired by the Holy Spirit, and it speaks to the Church right up to the end of time. There are many types, symbols, and shadows within the book, which we will explore. I know there have been various interpretations of this book in the past; however, I feel that the Lord would like me to share with His body the thoughts and inspiration which He has given to me. Many of these insights are very intimate between the Lover of my soul and me. They are also based on my experience in church life as a pastor's wife, missionary, and ordained minister.

As you read this book, I pray that you will open your heart to what the Spirit is saying to the Church. As we draw near to the second coming of our Lord Jesus Christ, the words of this song seem to vibrate in the Bride's ears. It is a Word for today. I have heard the themes of this song repeated in our modern day praise and worship songs. The Lord is opening up our hearts and preparing us for that great day when He calls His people home.

I wrote this book as a devotional verse-by-verse as that is the process I used in study and meditation. I recommend that you read and meditate on one verse each day—meditation is an important factor in understanding.

[1] Glad Tidings Bible College is currently named Bethany University an is located in Santa Cruz, California.

Here are some keys to understanding this book:

1. The Beloved, the King, and the Shepherd portray various types of Jesus Christ.
2. David is a type of Jesus as he was a shepherd, a warrior, and then he became a King.
3. David already defeated Goliath, a type of Satan.
4. Solomon, David's son, did not fight the battles. Solomon built the temple, which is a type of the church and the individual members of the Bride of Christ.
5. The dove, the spouse, the fair one, and the friend described by the King represent the true Church and/or the Bride of Christ. The Bride of Christ includes both men and women of the Church. (In referring to "her" in this book, we are referring to both men and women of the Church).
6. The love relationship between the King and the Shulamite woman depicts the relationship between Jesus and the Church.
7. The daughters of Jerusalem are my fellow believers in the Church—the New Jerusalem being our mother. (Galatians 4:25, 26)

Note: While quoting the Bible, I have highlighted key words with *italics **and** **bold print*** to give emphasis to the subject being discussed.

CHAPTER 1

SONG OF SONGS

The Song of Songs, which is Solomon's. Song of Solomon 1:1

Let us look at the author of this unique book in the middle of our beloved Bible. King Solomon was the third king of Israel. He was the most wealthy and powerful king to reign in Israel's history. The land of Israel was at peace after many years of battles. Every day, at the king's table, there was a banquet of thirty oxen and one hundred sheep as well as wild animals and fowls. But the most precious of all his possessions was the fact that, "God gave Solomon wisdom and understanding exceeding much, and largeness of heart, even as the sand that is on the sea shore" (1 Kings 4:29). Out of this great wisdom, he spoke three thousand proverbs and wrote one thousand and five songs. All the kings and queens of the earth respected Solomon and came to him to hear his wisdom (see 1 Kings 4:20-34).

The Bible has many types and shadows. This book, I believe, is a "shadow of things to come" (Colossians 2:17). King Solomon is a shadow of our King Jesus. The key verse in the Song of Solomon is 2:17, "Until the day break and the shadows flee away, turn my beloved." It corresponds with Paul's eloquent words in 1 Corinthians 13:12, "We see through a glass darkly, but then, face to face." Let us look into this mysterious shadow and catch a glimpse of our beloved Jesus.

Jesus declared as He walked on the earth, "a greater than Solomon is here" (Matthew 12:42). He was referring to Himself. Jesus, of course, was much greater than Solomon because He was God in the flesh. His wisdom surpassed that of Solomon's. His glory surpassed Solomon's glory. For Jesus was and is the King of kings and the Lord of lords. The mystery of this song is the beautiful relationship Jesus has formed with His Bride, the Church (Ephesians 5:32). My songs of praise crescendo as the time draws near for my Beloved's soon return. But I am not the only one who is singing: "The LORD thy God in the midst of thee is mighty, he will save, he will rejoice over thee with joy; he will rest in his love, he will joy over thee with *singing*" (Zephaniah 3:17). To think that God sings over me causes me to burst out in the song of the redeemed.

My Prayer: I sing praises to Jesus for He has given me a new song. Deep in my heart, a melody of love and joy rises up into my mouth. This song is eternal. It has withstood the test of time. It is not an earthly, sensual, or carnal song; it is one of love beyond this earth's comprehension. I enter into the Holy of Holies singing this sweet song of praise.

THE KISS OF RECONCILIATION

Let him kiss me with the kisses of his mouth;
Song of Solomon 1:2a

In human relationships, we have learned that a kiss can mean so many lovely things. It is the expression of love that seals the relationship between a man and a woman. I have found in Jesus my true love, and He has filled the longing of my deepest self. He is the Lover of my soul.

Have you heard the famous saying, "Kiss and make up?" When we have a disagreement or a broken relationship with a loved one, whether it be a husband, wife, father, mother, son, daughter, sister, brother, or a close friend, we will put an end to the conflict with a kiss.

Do you remember the moving scene Jesus spoke of concerning the prodigal son and his father? In Luke 15:20 it says, "And he arose, and came to his father. But when he was yet a great way off, his father saw him, and had compassion, and ran, and fell on his neck, and kissed him." This is an example of the kiss of reconciliation.

I have experienced this kiss of reconciliation from my dear Lord. Even as Isaiah cried out, "Woe is me! I am undone; because I am a man of unclean lips, and I dwell in the midst of a people of unclean lips" (Isaiah 6:5)—so I cry out, "Lord cleanse me." He took my lips and cleansed them with His holy fire, and now I am able to look into His dear face and declare, "My Lord and my God." All things are fresh and clean, and I am made like a new babe—born again by the power of His love.

I have learned submission, even as a wife submits to her husband. In Psalms 2:12, we see an interesting scripture about our kissing the Son (Jesus). It always takes two to kiss. It says, "Kiss the Son, lest he be angry, and ye perish from the way, when his wrath is kindled a little. Blessed are all they that put their trust in him." Now that I have experienced the kiss of reconciliation, I do not want to cause Jesus to be angry with me. He loves those who put their trust in Him. Therefore, if I am to please Him, I will submit to His will and trust Him to take care of me.

To kiss the Lord, I must come face to face with Him. He captures my full attention, and I cannot see any other love. I have learned that if I take my eyes off Him and look at people or circumstances, I find myself sinking beneath waves of doubt. The moment I turn my eyes back to His face, He embraces me once more, and I am at rest in His bosom.

Is your life in turmoil as you read this book? Come, kiss the Son, and be reconciled to Him. He loves you with an everlasting love. Are you struggling with relationships that have gone bad? You will find that as you experience His love, you, in turn, will love others.

My Prayer: Lord, I long for our love to become deeper still. I long to feel the touch of Your lips on mine. Your love and pleasure is my greatest desire. Help me Lord to express Your love to others. I know this can only be done as I come into communion with You. Let Your holy lips cleanse my unholy lips, until only love, truth, and praise come forth from my mouth.

BETTER THAN WINE

For thy love is better than wine.
Song of Solomon 1:2b

Not only does the Lord favor us with kisses, but He also pours His love on us. Similar to the way wine warms the heart and makes a person glad, so the love of our blessed Lord fills our cup to overflowing. Jesus displayed His love for us when He paid the price for our salvation while hanging on an old rugged cross.

I remember the blood that flowed from Calvary as I lift the small communion cup to my lips. I remember how my Lord suffered, bled, and died for my sins. I meditate on His great love, which is beyond my human understanding. In my mind's eye, I see that infamous night so long ago, when Jesus held the cup and said, "This is my blood of the New Testament, which is shed for many for the remission of sins. But I say unto you, I will not drink henceforth of this fruit of the vine, until that day when I drink it new with you in my Father's kingdom" (Matthew 26:28-29).

Tears flow down my cheeks as I remember the pain, humiliation, and tremendous sacrifice He made. Then the blessed Holy Spirit reminds me that Jesus has risen from the dead and is now sitting at the right hand of God, His Father, and my Father, making intercession for me (Hebrews 7:25). Not only has He risen, but He is coming back for me very soon. Jesus said that He is looking forward to the day when He will sit down with me and drink of the fruit of the vine again in the kingdom of heaven (Matthew 26:29).

Joy and love flood my heart, and my inner man is renewed. I praise Him again-and-again. The price Jesus paid causes me to rejoice with the new wine from heaven. My cup runneth over. The prophet Isaiah said, " Ho, every one that thirsteth, come ye to the waters, and he that hath no money; come ye, buy, and eat; yea, come, buy wine and milk without money and without price" (Isaiah 55:1). We do not have to pay money for this wine of fellowship with our Savior because He has already paid the ultimate price on Calvary.

My Prayer: Dear Lord, I love You. I thank You for the sweet communion that I partake of with my fellow believers. I thank You for paying the price for my salvation. I long for the day when we will sip of the fruit of the vine in the Father's Kingdom.

OINTMENT POURED ALL OVER ME

Because of the savour of thy good ointments thy name is as ointment poured forth, therefore do the virgins love thee.
Song of Solomon 1:3

In the Bible, ointment speaks to us of the healing of wounds—the soothing of inflammation. This scripture says that the speaking of His Name, the Name of Jesus, is as if ointment poured forth.

When we fall in love in the natural way, one of the first things the girl will do is to match her name up with the one she loves. She will write her lover's name in as many beautiful styles as possible. She will speak it aloud, for she loves to hear the sound. On the day of marriage, she will write her new name on the marriage certificate; thus, she is forever sealing her love for her husband.

Mary, a young virgin, heard the beautiful name of Jesus from the angel Gabriel. Gabriel announced, "And, behold, thou shalt conceive in thy womb, and bring forth a son, and shalt call his name JESUS" (Luke 1:31). I wonder if Mary fully understood that her baby, who was to be conceived by the Holy Ghost, would change this sinful world forever (Luke 1:35). I can imagine her saying that name over and over again during her pregnancy. The sound of His name must have given her peace, during the times she faced humiliation and distress, because her family and friends did not understand what God was doing through her.

In Matthew 25, Jesus related a parable of ten virgins. He tells of five virgins who had a good supply of oil (a type of the Holy Spirit) and five who ran out of oil before the bridegroom came.   These virgins are a symbol of purity and holiness. We develop holiness by keeping our lives full of the oil of the Holy Spirit. As we look for Christ coming, we must keep our hearts burning with His love. One of the ways we are able to accomplish this is to claim His name as our own; after all, we are soon to be married to Jesus, the Bridegroom. Paul realized this as he wrote to the Corinthians, "For I am jealous over you with godly jealousy: for I have espoused you to one husband, that I may present you as a chaste virgin to Christ" (2 Corinthians 11:2).

Our scripture in the Song of Solomon says that the *virgins* love the Lord because His name is as ointment poured forth. We live in a hurtful world. Christians suffer pain, disease, sickness, war, hunger, and malicious accusations. However, the name of Jesus gives us victory, strength, and healing. We are to ask in His name to receive the joy and peace that only He can give. Jesus said, "Hitherto have ye asked nothing in my name: ask, and ye shall receive, that your joy may be full" (John 16:24).

My Prayer: I come into Your presence through Your precious name. You bring healing as You anoint my head with oil. I love to speak Your wonderful names in prayer. Lord, Emmanuel, Prince of Peace, Mighty God, Savior, Redeemer, and my Rock—but I always come back to the name I love the best, *Jesus*!

DRAW ME

Draw me, we will run after thee: the king hath brought me into his chambers: we will be glad and rejoice in thee, we will remember thy love more than wine: the upright love thee.
Song of Solomon 1:4

"Draw me." Is this your heart's cry? Does it seem difficult to draw nearer to God? Perhaps it seems difficult because we have not learned the secret—that it is only through His assistance that we are able to draw close. Jesus said, "No man can come to me, except the Father which hath sent me *draw* him" (John 6:44). Therefore, we need to pray to the Father to draw us closer. There is no prayer dearer to the heart of God than this one, "Draw me." He said if I will draw close to Him, He will draw close to me (James 4:8). He is so anxious for us to draw close. All we have to do is to express our desire to come close to Him.

We must not let anything hinder us from this pursuit of entering into His chambers. In Hebrews 12:1 it says we are to, "lay aside every weight, and the sin which doth so easily beset us, and let us run with patience the race that is set before us." In Bible times, a person did not dare to enter the king's presence without first being invited and preparing oneself in the correct protocol. We prepare ourselves by asking the Lord to cleanse us, by laying aside any hindrances in our life, and by being patient. Patient in that we wait upon Him to move in our lives.

Notice in our scripture that it starts with the singular pronoun, **me**, and then quickly turns to the plural pronoun, **we**. Solomon did not have his pronouns mixed up; the Holy Spirit moved upon him to write it this way. Each one of us has to draw near to the Lord individually. This is a personal experience, but you will find that as you draw close to Jesus, you will not be able to keep it to yourself. You will share your experience with others, and they will begin to **run** with you. As you enter into that most personal place, His chambers, you will come out rejoicing and unable to contain the joy and love experienced there. This excitement will spread like wildfire, and it will ignite revival fire in the church body.

Psalms 45:13-15 is a parallel scripture to this verse:

The king's daughter is all glorious within: her clothing is of wrought gold. She shall be brought unto the king in raiment of

9

needlework: the virgins, her companions that follow her, shall
be brought unto thee. With gladness and rejoicing shall they
be brought: they shall enter into the king's palace.

I am the King's daughter, and the Lord has given me a beautiful garment of gold and fine needlework. I will bring my fellow companions, who are also pure virgins, to come into your presence. There, we will all experience gladness and rejoicing.

We also remember that His love is better than wine. We are filled fresh everyday with His blessed Holy Spirit and our experience with Jesus is vibrant and living everyday. It does not grow stale or ordinary. We stir up our love for Jesus by drawing near to Him and coming into His dwelling place.

My Prayer: Draw me into Your presence and into Your dwelling place. Please help me not to allow Satan to distract my thoughts when I come to You in prayer. Cleanse me and clothe me with Your divine nature. Help me to excite others to run the race with me. We will rejoice and be glad in Your love and favor.

BEAUTY

I am black, but comely, O ye daughters of Jerusalem, as the tents of Kedar, as the curtains of Solomon. Look not upon me, because I am black, because the sun hath looked upon me:
Song of Solomon 1:5, 6a

The Bride addresses the Daughters of Jerusalem. *Jerusalem* means the City of Peace. We long for this city, for it is home. The New Jerusalem is the city of the free from above, and it is called our mother in Galatians 4:26. We come in our spirit to "Mount Zion, and unto the city of the living God, the heavenly Jerusalem, and to an innumerable company of angels, to the general assembly and church of the firstborn, which are written in heaven" (Hebrews 12:22-23a). Ephesians 2:19 says, "Now therefore ye are no more strangers and foreigners, but fellow citizens with the saints, and of the household of God." We become a citizen of the New Jerusalem when we join the family of God.

The Bride speaks of being black, but comely as the tents of Kedar. "Kedar and being black" are both symbols of the fleshly nature that still resides in me. Kedar was the offspring of Ishmael, making Kedar the grandson of Abraham and Hagar. We know that the union between Abraham and Hagar was a fleshly union because Abraham was impatient to wait for God's promise. Hagar is likened to Mount Sinai, the mountain of darkness and blackness, and she gave birth to bondage (Galatians 4:22-24). The descendants of Kedar are a nomadic people who lived in tents in desert places.

In Psalms 120, the pilgrim describes himself as living in the tents of Kedar when he has problems with his fleshly nature and tongue. He cried out to God to deliver him from the old nature, so that he could live in peace.

Deliver my soul, O LORD, from lying lips, and from a deceitful tongue. What shall be given unto thee? or what shall be done unto thee, thou false tongue? Sharp arrows of the mighty, with coals of juniper. Woe is me, that I sojourn in Mesech, that I dwell in the tents of Kedar! My soul hath long dwelt with him that hateth peace.

We, too, were strangers or nomads until Jesus saved us out of the fleshly nature and gave us a new nature. We look daily to our

11

Lord; that He will keep us from returning to the bondage of the flesh and the law. The *old man* will fight to be in control of our lives again, but we are to walk in the Spirit as stated in Galatians 5:16-17: "This I say then, Walk in the Spirit, and ye shall not fulfill the lust of the flesh. For the flesh lusteth against the Spirit, and the Spirit against the flesh: and these are contrary the one to the other: so that ye cannot do the things that ye would." With God's power and grace, we are able to maintain our freedom.

Yes, I am black with sin, and yet I have become lovely through the new birth bestowed on me though Jesus. I still war against the old nature that keeps trying to rise up its ugly head, but I am a new creature in Christ.

Praise the Lord!   He gives me a new song and a new life, and I am a new man in Christ:

> I am the LORD: that is my name: and my glory will I not give to another, neither my praise to graven images. Behold, the *former things are come to pass, and new things* do I declare: before they spring forth I tell you of them.   Sing unto the LORD a new song and his praise from the end of the earth, ye that go down to the sea, and all that is therein; the isles, and the inhabitants thereof. Let the wilderness and the cities thereof lift up their voice, the villages that Kedar doth inhabit: let the inhabitants of the rock sing, let them shout from the top of the mountains. Let them give glory unto the LORD, and declare his praise in the islands.   Isaiah 42:8-12

My Prayer: Yes, Lord, I will praise You, for I no longer live in the wilderness of sin (in the tents of Kedar). I am in the Rock. I am on Mount Zion and Jerusalem is my mother. I was so black when You found me. Now I am beautiful, for You gave me beauty for ashes. Jesus, take control of my body, soul, and spirit. May I walk in newness of life through Your Holy Spirit.

KEEPER OF THE VINEYARD

My mother's children were angry with me; they made me the keeper
of the vineyards; but mine own vineyard have I not kept.
Song of Solomon 1:6b

I was so excited about the leadership position the church had given to me. Now I could really do something great for the Lord. I prayed, laid out plans, and started to execute those plans. It seemed like everything was moving along toward my goal for this group. All of a sudden, I started hearing rumors of dissatisfaction and then outright grumbles concerning my work. I was surprised and very hurt. After all, I thought I was working so hard for the good of everyone involved in this ministry of the church!

I struggled with this so much that I could not sleep, and I had no rest in my spirit. Thus, in my humanness, I wanted to quit. This was when the Lord began to speak to my heart and dealt with my innermost attitudes and motives.

You see, my brothers and sisters in Christ (God's children—my mother's children), had made me responsible for a portion of God's vineyard, but they became angry with me. They resented the changes that I thought were improvements on things they had done another way in years past. As the Lord began to deal with me as to my work in the vineyard, He actually brought me into the examination of my own vineyard (my own life). He showed me that before I could produce a harvest in the vineyard of this world—I must first do some weeding and pruning in my own field.

The first question He asked me was, "Who is your Master?" Was I actually doing this work out of my love for Him, or was I doing it for the praise of men? Whatever I do, I must do it as unto the Lord.

Secondly, the Lord dealt with me on how I had received this criticism. My first reaction was self-pity. After all, I had prayed about it first and felt that I was doing the Lord's will. Was I truly as consecrated to the Lord as I had thought? I found that as I examined my heart, that I had been anxious to see things change to my way. I had not been as considerate of my brothers and sisters feelings as the Lord would have me to be. My second reaction was judgmental toward my fellow Christians, thinking that I alone had the right directions. I remembered that Jesus said I needed to get the big plank out of my own eye before I can see clearly to remove the speck of sawdust out of my brothers eye (Matthew 7:3).

Thirdly, the Lord reminded me that I am not going to be able to please all men—all the time. After I have examined my vineyard and found that all was in order according to His will, I then should proceed with His love and direction. You see, I am ultimately responsible to my Master. I am His servant. Two scriptures the Lord showed me were, Philippians 2:14, "Do all things without murmurings and disputings"; and Philippians 2:16, "Holding forth the word of life; that I may rejoice in the day of Christ, that I have not run in vain, neither laboured in vain." I must keep my eyes on Jesus and grow my vineyard with the fruit of the Spirit, and then He will lead me in the work He has entrusted into my hands.

Lastly, I do not need to worry about my fellow Christian's vineyard. Jesus foretold that Peter was going to be bound in chains during his latter years. Peter questioned the Lord as to what would be in John's future. Jesus admonished Peter in so many words, "John is accountable to me, and it is not your business what I do concerning him." (My paraphrase of John 21:23)

My Prayer: Lord, I find my flesh rebels when I am criticized or come into conflict with my brothers and sisters. Help me to resolve these problems quickly by love and holding no malice when I am wronged. I know I am nothing and my work is nothing if it is not based on Your command and love for my spiritual family. May I take into consideration that my brothers and sisters are also growing in You, even as I am growing. We need each other's prayers and understanding. Father, make us one in love and labor.

WHERE DO YOU FEED YOUR FLOCK?

Tell me, O thou whom my soul loveth, where thou feedest, where thou makest thy flock to rest at noon: for why should I be as one that turneth aside by the flocks of thy companions?
Song of Solomon 1:7

As the sheep of His pasture, we desire to be with Jesus, to be fed by Him, and to enter into His rest. My love for the Lord is so deep that I want to continually be in His presence. The shepherd never leaves the sheep unattended. We hold dear the beautiful word picture that the beloved shepherd, David, gave us in Psalms 23:1-3, "The LORD is my shepherd; I shall not want. He maketh me to lie down in green pastures: he leadeth me beside the still waters. He restoreth my soul."

The Lord God, the Great I Am, desired to lead His chosen people into Canaan (the land of rest), but they refused. Moses had sent ten spies into the land and eight of them came back with a fearful report of giants who lived there. The writer of Hebrews states that the people's hearts were filled with unbelief, and they rebelled against God's plan. Unbelief and fear will prevent us from entering into the rest of the Lord. We must keep our hearts open to the Word of the Lord and follow where He leads so that we do not fall into the same mistake as the Israelites (Hebrews 3).

We need to give our attention to the latter part of this verse. "Why should I be as one that turneth aside by the flocks of thy companions?" Here we are being warned that we should not be deterred from His rest by following another shepherd. Many Christians have fallen for this trick of Satan. They have relied upon a particular preacher or prophet to lead them along—instead of following Jesus. The Lord has given us good teachers, pastors, and evangelists to build us up. On the other hand, we need to remember that they are also subject to temptations. We do not want to follow any man so closely that we also fall into a pit if that man stumbles. The Lord, our Shepherd, is the one who is leading us.

We do not have to fear turning aside and following another shepherd because we have our ear tuned to our Lord. Jesus said, "And when he putteth forth his own sheep, he goeth before them, and the sheep follow him: for they know his voice. And a stranger will they not follow, but will flee from him: for they know not the voice of strangers" (John 10:4-6). It is so blessed to hear my Lord's voice.

15

Sometimes we find ourselves in the heat of trials and it is as if the sun is beating down on us. We struggle just to make it through another day in our own efforts. This is when the Lord leads us into His rest. The sun or trial may continue to be just as hot, but in the middle of this distressful experience, we are able to rest by putting our faith in His promises. As I rest in His all sufficient grace and love, I am at peace in His green pastures. I drink from the wells of His salvation and my soul is restored.

My Prayer: Lord, I want to follow You to the place where You feed the sheep. I do not want to follow man, who may turn aside into unbelief. I need rest and a place of safety during the heat of the noonday sun. Help me to never question Your path, but to follow You in faith. I put my trust in Your Word, for it feeds my soul and I am satisfied. I have my ears tuned to Your voice.

FOLLOW MY FOOTSTEPS

If thou know not, O thou fairest among women, go thy way forth by the footsteps of the flock, and feed thy kids beside the shepherds' tents. Song of Solomon 1:8

In the previous verse, the Bride is asking her Shepherd where He leads the sheep to feed and rest. His answer is to follow the footsteps of the flock. Jesus is the Chief Shepherd of this flock, but He has appointed and called men to be under-shepherds. Jesus instructed Peter to feed His sheep and His lambs (John 21:15-17). Peter exhorts the elders of the church to take their duties as shepherds very seriously (1 Peter 5:1-4).

As a young person, I questioned if I was following the right flock. Was I attending the true church? I decided to explore some other church groups and see for myself if I was following the correct doctrine. I began to see a common thread of doctrine in these other churches that troubled me. They were teaching that many scriptures were not to be taken as literal truth for our modern day and age. They said that such doctrines as healing and miracles were only for Bible times. I was dismayed at this idea because I had seen the supernatural move of God through the Holy Spirit in my own life and in the lives of others. In my confusion, I began to seek the Lord's face and to search the scriptures for myself. I cried out, "O Lord, help me to know You." He showed me through His Word that **ALL** scripture was given to profit the church (2 Timothy 3:16). He does not change with the times for, "Jesus Christ is the same yesterday, today and forever" (Hebrews 13:8).

The Holy Spirit will lead us into all truth if we earnestly seek His leading. I thank God that He has placed in the church shepherds, teachers, pastors, and evangelists who proclaim the pure Word of God. I realize that these leaders of the church are still dwelling in tents (earthly bodies) and they are prone to make mistakes at times; nevertheless, I still esteem them highly for their ministry in the body of Christ.

Our verse for today says that we are to "feed thy kids beside the shepherd's tents." As we follow our Master's footsteps, we will have young ones born into the flock because of our testimony. It is very important that we can bring these new converts into a church family where they can be taught the whole Word of Truth. Jesus is the Way, the Truth, and the Life (John 14:6).

17

Some may say, "Why join a church?", or "I don't need church in order to follow Jesus." It is so easy for us as sheep to go astray. We need each other for strength and guidance. The New Testament Church of Acts plainly gives us the pattern of the church. Paul wrote letters back to the churches he had founded. He gave instructions and guidelines as to the order of the church. The writer of Hebrews says we are not to forsake the assembling of ourselves together even more so as the day of the Lord approaches (Hebrews 10:24-25). We need to be accountable to each other. Jesus is walking among the churches in the book of Revelation. It is His will and purpose for believers to band together in worship and fellowship. We put ourselves in a precarious place when we go off on our own way. Sheep get into all kinds of dangerous—life threatening—places when they stray away from the flock.

My Prayer: Thank you, Lord, for the Church. How I love it! I pray for the pastors and leaders of Your flock. Help them minister to the needs of Your flock and teach them to follow close after You, our Chief Shepherd. Thank You for the Holy Spirit who leads me into all truth. I pledge to follow You all the days of my life.

ALL THE KING'S HORSES

UNDER THE MASTER'S CONTROL

I have compared thee, O my love, to a company of horses in Pharaoh's chariots. Song of Solomon 1:9

King Solomon treasured his horses and chariots. He actually disobeyed God's command because of his desire to build an army of which he could be proud. (Deuteronomy 17:16-17) God wanted the nation of Israel to trust in Him rather than to trust in horses and chariots. (Psalms 20:7) In spite of all Solomon's wisdom, he was very willful in matters of horses and wives. He had not learned how to submit his will to God.

Since Solomon valued his horses so much, he is complimenting the Bride when he compares her to horses. To him the horse was a symbol of strength in battle. He compares his bride to a company or army of horses. The Bride of Christ is a great army going throughout the land conquering Satan and his demons. She is beautiful in strength and power.

As we look on a beautiful horse, we see the muscles rippling under the shining coat and its flowing mane. It is a wonderful sight as it leaps over barriers. Nevertheless, a beautiful horse does not achieve its purpose until it is brought under the master's control. How beautiful is the army of the Lord as He controls us and leads us into battle.

Pharaoh's horses were most likely the best trained horses in the world. Are we, as the church, under the control of our Commander and Chief? I pray that we will yield to the Master's touch and not be rebellious like the Old West bucking bronco.

Will I be part of the last great battle between good and evil? He that is called Faithful and True will be riding upon a white horse and the armies that are in heaven will follow Him. These armies are the raptured church. They will also be riding on white horses, clothed in fine linen, white and clean. What a glorious and victorious army of the Lord! (Revelation 19:11-16)

My Prayer: Control me and make me to be strong in the battles I face. May I be able, through your strength and power, to conquer the rebellion and stubbornness that is in my heart. May I be able to tear down the strongholds in the lives of others. Send Your church throughout the land conquering and winning the battle over evil.

DIAMONDS FOR HER CHEEKS

Thy cheeks are comely with rows of jewels, thy neck with chains of gold. Song of Solomon 1:10

Tears were running down her cheeks again. She thought she had exhausted every tear, but as she recalled the events of the last three days, they had started again. She had recoiled in her spirit as she witnessed the humiliation of her Lord. Roman soldiers had beaten Jesus and mocked him by spitting in His face. They had plucked His beard, and then they had crowned Him with a crown of thorns. How could He forgive them of their hideous sins as He hung upon that cruel cross? In spite of all they had done to Him, He had asked the Father to forgive them for they did not know what they were doing.

Finally, Jesus had commended His spirit to the Father and died. The Roman soldiers pierced His side to make sure He was indeed dead. Blood and water gushed out of His side because He had died of a broken heart. Pilate granted Jesus' followers their request to take His mangled body down and lay it in a borrowed tomb. They had hurriedly wrapped the beloved Rabbi's body, but they had not completed the burial spices since the Sabbath was upon them.

Before the sun rose on Sunday, she was awake and ready to go back to the tomb. She was alarmed to see the stone was not sealing the entrance of the tomb. She timidly looked inside and found it was empty. Where was Jesus body? She ran as fast as she could to the place where Peter and John were staying. They all ran back to the tomb. As Peter and John checked out the tomb, Mary just waited outside in the garden. Puzzled, Peter and John went back home, but Mary stayed at the tomb. She took another look inside the tomb and there were two men in white. They asked her why she was weeping, and she told them that someone had taken her Lord's body away.

Through the tears, she saw a man standing nearby. He also asked her why she was weeping. She thought this man may have seen who was responsible for taking Jesus out of the tomb, so she answered, "Sir, if you have carried him away, tell me where you have put him, and I will get him." Before she could say another word, she heard Him utter her name, "Mary", in that sweet familiar way only Jesus spoke it. "Master!" she cried as she fell at His feet. Her eyes that had been dull with tears suddenly sparkled with joy. The remaining tears on her cheeks looked like glistening diamonds as the rising sun caught their essence. (John 20:11-17)

Jesus looks at our tears and they are like jewels. Tears come when we go through trials, which draw us closer to Him. Tears come when we pray for lost souls: "They that sow in tears shall reap in joy" (Psalm 126:5). Paul said that he served the Lord with great humility and with tears (Acts 20:19).

The chief musician penned that our tears are so precious that God keeps a record of them and stores them in bottles: "Thou tellest my wanderings: put thou my tears into thy bottle: are they not in thy book?" (Psalms 56:8) God is keeping a record of the tears we shed and they are more precious than diamonds to Him. He has transformed us from a useless lump of coal to a valuable diamond fit for the kingdom.

Now we see the Lord through the tears of this life, but we will see Him face to face when the tears are lifted (1 Corinthians 13:12). "God shall wipe away all tears from their eyes; and there shall be no more death, neither sorrow, nor crying, neither shall there be any more pain: for the former things are passed away" (Revelation 21:4)

My Prayer: Help me, Lord, not to complain when the heartaches of life bring tears to my eyes. I know that You are at work to bring out the loveliness in me. You only allow pain and suffering to make me draw closer to you. May I plant tears in prayer that a harvest of souls may be won. Give me a tender heart for all that are in need. I long for that day when tears will no longer be needed, for I will be with You eternally. Nevertheless, until that day, I will be willing to bow my head in tears.

BORDERS ON MY WEDDING GARMENT

We will make thee borders of gold and studs of silver.
Song of Solomon 1:11

Did you notice the use of the plural tense in this verse—"**We** will make thee"? This draws my mind back to the beginning when "God said, Let **us** make man in our image, after our likeness" (Genesis 1:26). Bible scholars have long recognized that the "**us**" in the account of the creation of man refers to God the Father, Son, and Holy Spirit. I can imagine the Son (our Bridegroom) turns to the Father and the Holy Spirit in this passage and says, "**We** are going to make my Bride's garments perfect." "It is not going to be a simple white robe, but we are going to intertwine gold threads and ornaments and studs of silver along the border of the garment."

Isaiah gives us a beautiful word picture of this in chapter 61 and verse 10:

> I will greatly rejoice in the LORD, my soul shall be joyful in my God; for he hath clothed me with the garments of salvation, he hath covered me with the robe of righteousness, as a bridegroom decketh himself with ornaments, and as a bride adorneth herself with her jewels.

The Lord removed my filthy garments of self-righteousness, and he has clothed me with garments of salvation and praise. (Isaiah 64:6; Isaiah 61:3) He has covered my shame with His robe of righteousness. However, the garment is not complete until He adds this border of gold and silver.

The robe of salvation is applied to us as soon as we have given our hearts to the Lord, but to complete our garment takes the work of sanctification and consecration. The high priest was consecrated to be holy and set apart for the Lord. His garment had a unique border of gold bells and pomegranates. This is the detailed work of a master craftsman (Ephesians 2:10).

Our robe becomes more beautiful as Jesus works on it. Times of failing and times of victory weave its beauty throughout the border. Gold is a symbol of God's own **divine** nature. 2 Corinthians 3:18 states, "But we all, with open face beholding as in a glass the glory of the Lord, are changed into the same image from glory to glory, even as by the Spirit of the Lord." Changed into His own image—isn't that what He ordained from the very moment of creation? Adam and Eve disobeyed God's commands and lost the glory. That is where the silver comes in as it represents the **redemptive** power of Jesus Christ. It is not difficult to put on my garment of praise when I think of His love, grace, and power to redeem this lost soul of mine.

Before Jesus redeemed me, I was a good for nothing old pot like that described in Psalms 68:13: "Though ye have lien among the pots [*vessels of dishonor*], yet shall ye be as the wings of a dove covered with silver [*redemption*], and her feathers with yellow gold [*God's own nature*]." (*Italic words added by myself*). I escaped Satan on the wings of the Holy Spirit. The wings of the Holy Spirit bear me up in redemption power to God's throne room. God's own divine nature covers me as a hen's feathers cover the chicks.

The Lord is calling us to be "a glorious church, without spot or wrinkle, or any such thing" (Ephesians 5:27). The call goes out from our Lord strong and clear, "If any man will come after me, let him deny himself, and take up his cross daily, and follow me" (Luke 9:23).

The gold, which is God's divine nature, is produced only in our lives by the purification and refining work of trials in our lives.

Wherein ye greatly rejoice, though now for a season, if need be, ye are in heaviness through manifold temptations: That the trial of your faith, being much more precious than of gold that perisheth, though it be tried with fire, might be found unto praise and honour and glory at the appearing of Jesus Christ.   1 Peter 1:6-7

My Prayer: Thank You for removing that filthy garment of my sin and giving me Your garment of salvation and praise. I cannot help but praise You when I remember where You brought me from to where I am today. The process seems slow at times and the trial of my faith is uncomfortable, but it is worth all the pain to behold Your glory being woven into my life.

SWEET FRAGRANCE FOR MY KING

While the king sitteth at his table, my spikenard sendeth forth the smell thereof. Song of Solomon 1:12

Mary was sitting in the shadows listening to Jesus as He spoke to the men gathered around the table. Her heart seemed to leap for joy as she observed her brother, Lazarus, sitting among the men. Jesus had called Lazarus out of the grave after being buried four days. She listened closely now as she always did whenever Jesus spoke. He was explaining to the disciples that He would be crucified, but they were not to worry, for He would be raised from the dead in three days. (John 12:1-8; Matthew 16:21)

Her heart was overflowing with love as she thought of all the times she had sat at Jesus' feet and marveled at His words of life. She was compelled to show her love for the Master. What could she do to show Jesus how much she loved Him? As she pondered this question, she thought of her most prized possession. It was an alabaster box, which contained spikenard perfume. It was very costly, as it had been imported from the far country of India. She was saving it for just such an occasion.

Mary slipped quietly up to Jesus while He was still speaking. She was trembling like a leaf as she broke the alabaster box and poured out the precious ointment upon His head and feet. As she loosed her hair, she felt a wave of freedom sweep over her soul. She used her hair to wipe the excess oil from Jesus' feet. She was so unworthy and yet so free.

The fragrance of the perfumed oil filled the room. Some of the disciples were outraged at such a waste. They reasoned that she could have sold the oil and given the proceeds to the poor! She could have just opened the box and dabbed a little of the perfume upon Jesus forehead! Why had she wasted the whole pound of spikenard? Jesus rebuked the disciples for their stingy attitude. He explained to His disciples that Mary had anointed His body for burial before He died, rather than wait until He was gone. (John 12:1-8)

As I meditate upon Mary's sacrifice, I ask myself if I love the Lord as much as she did. She gave her most treasured possession. She gave it all, not holding any back. She was not affected by the criticism of the disciples. She even broke the precious container in which it was stored.

To show my love for the Lord, my body is the container that has to be broken before the Lord. Paul says that we are to present our bodies as a living sacrifice, holy and acceptable to God (Romans 12:1). The spikenard was a symbol of death, for it was used for burial. Its fragrance is only released when death occurred. I need to crucify my flesh so that Christ can live in and through me. "I am crucified with Christ: nevertheless I live; yet not I, but Christ liveth in me: and the life which I now live in the flesh I live by the faith of the Son of God, who loved me, and gave himself for me" (Galatians 2:20).

Out of my brokenness comes sweet fellowship with Christ. He in me and I in Him. Out of this fellowship comes the sweet fragrance of my love, service, and praise.

My Prayer: Lord, You are my King. You are always welcomed at my table. May I be willing to be broken before You so that You can remove any dross from my life. Fill me instead with Your holiness and purity. May I be so in love with You that I will not be affected by any criticism from others as I pour out my praise on You. I pray that my praise is a sweet aroma in Your nostrils.

CLOSE TO MY HEART

A bundle of myrrh is my wellbeloved unto me; he shall lie all night betwixt my breasts. Song of Solomon 1:13

Clouds of dust rose from the desert floor as the caravan made its way from the mountains of Gilead to Egypt. The camels were heavily laden with spices of balm and myrrh. This merchandise should sell for an excellent profit on the Egyptian market since it was in demand for the purposes of embalming their dead. The Midianite Traders could see some men signaling them to stop in the distance from their lofty vantage point upon the camel's backs.

As they drew closer, they saw two men clutching onto each side of a young boy. There were tears in the young boy's eyes, but he was not struggling to escape them. One of the men shouted, "We will sell you this lad for twenty pieces of silver. He is very strong and will make a good slave." The deal was quickly made since the going price for a young slave was thirty pieces of silver.

Joseph's brothers rejoiced in the fact that they did not have to put up with the young lad and his fancy dreams any longer. Jacob believed a wild animal had killed Joseph when his sons showed him the coat of many colors that they had dipped in the blood of a goat. Jacob mourned for his son many days and none of the other children could comfort him. (Genesis 37:25-36) Jacob was still mourning Joseph's death many years later, and did not want to allow Joseph's younger brother, Benjamin, to go with his older brothers to Egypt. He allowed it only as a last resort, for the family was in dire need of food. (Genesis 42:36-38)

The life of Joseph portrays a picture of Jesus, the Son of God, who would become the Savior of the world. God the Father gave up His precious Son so that the world could be saved from spiritual starvation. Jesus came to earth and was imprisoned by a human body. He died, but God raised Him from the dead on the third day.

Myrrh was used for the embalming of the dead in Bible times. Nicodemus brought a hundred pounds of a mixture of myrrh and aloes to wrap in the linen cloths around Jesus body (John 19:39).

Coming back to our verse in the Song of Solomon, the original Hebrew and many other translations of the Bible denote that the bundle of myrrh lay between her breast, rather than the lover lying between the breasts. The woman lover (the church) hangs a bundle of the myrrh around her neck and lets it hang between her breasts near to

26

her heart as a constant reminder of her well Beloved. The myrrh gave off a sweet smell. She was at peace all night long with this reminder of His love.

We have heard told how a spouse will keep a garment of a dearly departed one for a long time after that person's death. They find comfort in holding the garment and smelling the scent of the loved one. In like manner, we, as the Church of Christ, hold the death of our Lord close to our hearts. It was the most significant demonstration of His love for us. We should never count His sacrifice as commonplace.

Although we hold His death as precious, we know that He lives and is in our hearts. Ephesians 3:17-21 says Christ dwells in our hearts and we experience His love though faith.

That Christ may dwell in your hearts by faith; that ye, being rooted and grounded in love, May be able to comprehend with all saints what is the breadth, and length, and depth, and height; And to know the love of Christ, which passeth knowledge, that ye might be filled with all the fulness of God. Now unto him that is able to do exceeding abundantly above all that we ask or think, according to the power that worketh in us, Unto him be glory in the church by Christ Jesus throughout all ages, world without end. Amen.

My Prayer: The sweet fragrance of Your death and resurrection gives me reason to cherish You above all. I marvel that You would love me so much that You gave up Your riches in glory to become a lowly human being. That You would lay down Your life for me. In the night seasons, when my life seems the darkest, I find rest in Your love. Dwell in my heart forever.

CRIMSON STREAM

My beloved is unto me as a cluster of camphire in the vineyards of En-gedi. Song of Solomon 1:14

The spy reported to King Saul, "Behold, David is in the wilderness of En-gedi" (1 Samuel 24:1). Saul, who was possessed of an evil spirit and extremely jealous of David took three thousand chosen warriors and pursued David with the intent to kill him. They had searched most of the day when they found a cool, inviting cave. They decided to camp there for the night. What Saul did not know was that David and his small army was hiding in the recesses of the same cave. Saul went to sleep thinking he was perfectly safe with his bodyguards watching over him.

Saul's guards went to sleep during the long night watch. David's men saw this situation as a God send. They whispered to David, "This is the day the LORD spoke of when he said to you, 'I will give your enemy into your hands for you to deal with as you wish'" (1 Samuel 24:4-NIV). David could have taken the easy way out and ended his troubles with Saul that day, but he knew he should not touch the Lord's anointed. Instead of killing Saul, he cut off the bottom of Saul's robe. Even this caused him to have a guilty conscience. David willingly humbled himself before men and God. David knew that God would take care of Saul in His own time and in His own way. David would wait patiently for the Lord to exalt him as king. (1 Samuel 24: 1-19)

The Lord promised to turn the wilderness of En-gedi into a fruitful vineyard. This world is like a wilderness, ruled by an evil king named Satan, or the Devil. He was determined to kill and destroy the rightful heir to the throne, Jesus, the son of David. Just like David, Jesus refused to get ahead of God's plan and time. He was willing to humble Himself before God and man to fulfill the plan of God the Father (Philippians 2:5-11).

The Bride extols her Beloved and likens him to a cluster of camphire in the vineyard of En-gedi. This shrub is also known as henna. It has bunches of small lilac and yellowish white flowers which are very sweet to smell. Sometimes the blossoms were woven for a bridal headpiece. The dry leaves were crushed to make a red dye. Women have used this dye for hair coloring and nail stain in times past.

The crushing of the dry leaves of the camphire plant to make the red dye reminds me of the blood that my Savior spilt on the cross. The crimson stream of blood flows over me, cleansing me from my sin. His sweat in the Garden of Gethsemane was as if drops of blood—so that my mind could be renewed and sanctified. His body was beaten and crushed until He was bleeding all over. By His stripes we are healed. (Isaiah 53:5, 1 Peter 2:24) He has set me free from death and its dominion.

> Forasmuch then as the children are partakers of flesh and blood, he also himself likewise took part of the same; that through death he might destroy him that had the power of death, that is, the devil.   Hebrews 2:14

My wilderness has become a vineyard in which I bear fruit for Him. The flowers from the camphire bush were woven into a beautiful crown for the Bride. My Beloved wore a crown of thorns upon His head that I may wear a crown of glory on my wedding day.

Without the stripes—there would be no healing. Without the blood—there would be no remission of sin. Without the death—there would be no resurrection.

My Prayer: Lord, make me willing to wait patiently for Your plans to be fulfilled in my life. Let me have the same humble mindset as You had when You took on human nature. Cover me with Your precious blood, which brings salvation, healing, and protection from the Evil One.

DOVES' EYES

Behold, thou art fair, my love; behold, thou art fair; thou hast doves' eyes. **Song of Solomon 1:15**

Wonder and amazement gripped the crowd of people who witnessed the baptism of Jesus at the Jordan River. Although John felt that he was unworthy to baptize Jesus, he had done it at Jesus' command. As Jesus came out of the water, a snow-white dove descended from heaven and rested on Him. The dove was an outward sign that the Holy Spirit had come to rest upon Jesus and empower Him for ministry. The beautiful eyes of the dove were fixed upon Jesus. John the Baptist recognized the dove as the sign from God that this man, Jesus, was indeed the Son of God. Thundering out of heaven, God said, "This is my beloved Son, in whom I am well pleased" (Matthew 3:17). There was no doubt that this was the Promised One who had come to baptize them with the Holy Spirit and with fire. (Matthew 3:11-17)

We understand that the dove is a type of the Holy Spirit from this passage of scripture. Jesus looks at His Bride (the church) and declares her a fair and beautiful creation with gentle, innocent, and harmless eyes of a dove. Just as lovers can sit by the hour just gazing in each other's eyes drinking in each other's love, Jesus loves to look into our eyes. Does He see the Holy Spirit within us shining forth with attributes of love, joy, peace, longsuffering, gentleness, and meekness?

Jesus gave these instructions to the disciples as He was sending them out to minister, "Behold, I send you forth as sheep in the midst of wolves: be ye therefore wise as serpents, and harmless as doves" (Matthew 10:16).

I am sent "as a sheep among wolves", but I am not afraid, for my Shepherd is guarding me. I am wise as a serpent out-witting the old serpent, the devil. I am not ignorant of the devil's lies or devises. Nevertheless, I can be as harmless as a dove when faced by adverse men or circumstances because the gentle Holy Spirit is within me and gives me the words of testimony that I need. The Lord fights my battles. I do not fear the fiery darts of the wicked one, for God is my shield and my reward. (Genesis 15:1, Ephesians 6:16)

The wolves may surround me, but Jesus gives me wings of a dove that I might fly straight to Him who is my Rock. "Dwell in the rock, and be like the dove that maketh her nest in the sides of the

30

hole's mouth" (Jeremiah 48:28; Psalms 55:6). The dove makes its nest right by the cave's mouth (the wolves den), for she is wiser than the wolf (Satan). The Church is wiser than her enemy is and swift to accomplish her work.

Jesus is so proud of His Bride. He calls everyone not only once but twice to come see His fair one. It is as if He is saying, "Come and see my fair one; my beautiful church, who has eyes only for me. She is fair because the Holy Spirit rests upon her, and she shall fly like a dove to the ends of the earth proclaiming the gospel. Nothing will stop My Church, not even the gates of hell."

My Prayer: Unworthy as I am, You see me as Your fair one. It is only because You love me so much. You see in me Your work perfected through the Holy Spirit. Holy Spirit, continue to produce Your fruit of a gentle and meek spirit within me. I fix my eyes on You, Lord, the author and finisher of my faith.

GREEN PASTURES

*Behold, thou art fair, my beloved, yea, pleasant: also our bed is green. **Song of Solomon 1:16***

In verse fifteen, the King is extolling the Bride as being fair and beautiful. In this verse we have the Bride exclaiming, "You are the fair one, you are so pleasant (handsome in some translations)." They loved to just look at each other and admire each other as true lovers often do. The chief musician, Maschil of the Sons of Korah, extolled the King in this song.

My heart is overflowing with a good theme;
I recite my composition concerning the King;
My tongue is the pen of a ready writer.

You are fairer than the sons of men;
Grace is poured upon Your lips;
Therefore God has blessed You forever.
Psalms 45:1-2, NKJV

The words just poured forth from the musician's tongue as he praised the King who is fairer than the sons of men. This King is Jesus who is indeed fairer, more appealing to us than any man because He is the divine Son of God. The modern day composer, William S. Hays, writes in the Hymn of the church entitled, THE LILY OF THE VALLEY: "I have found a friend in Jesus, He's ev'rything to me, He's the fairest of ten thousand to my soul."

The Bride goes on to say, "*our* bed is green." It was not *your* bed or *my* bed but *our* bed. In other words, they rested in a common bed that was a very special and private place. It is a green bed. We have seen in earlier scriptures about the green pastures in which Jesus leads us. These pastures are where the sheep find food and rest.

Jesus tried to escape the crowds for a few hours of rest, but the crowd soon found out where He was and followed Him. It was a solitary place where He could pray. The people were so hungry to hear the living words of Jesus, for grace poured from His lips. Jesus sat and taught them many things concerning the kingdom of God. He had compassion on them because He saw them as sheep without a shepherd. Sheep need to be led to green pastures, to be cared for, and protected by the shepherd.

32

It was growing late and the disciples were worried about the people since they had been out in the hot sun all day without any food. The disciples advised Jesus to send the people away to neighboring villages to purchase food, but Jesus replied, "Give ye them to eat." Jesus did not want to send the people to other sources of supply, for He is the Bread of Life. The disciples, looking at it from human limitations, told Jesus that they did not have enough money. Jesus asked, "What do you have?" They could only find one little boy who had five loaves and two fish. Jesus said to bring what they had to Him. He blessed it and started to break the bread. All were astonished to see the miracle as there was more than enough bread and fish for everyone to eat. Five thousand men plus women and children were fed until they were satisfied, and there were twelve baskets left over. (Mark 6:33-44)

Have you found that secret pasture (that green bed) to share with your Lord? It is there that He will feed you and cause you to rest. There is plenty, for He has a great supply: "My God shall supply all your need according to his riches in glory by Christ Jesus" (Philippians 4:19). He supplies my spiritual, emotional, and physical needs. He has all the riches in glory at His disposal.

My Prayer: As I look into Your face, I see the beauty of Your love. As I listen to Your word, I am awed by Your grace. By faith, I rest in Your care and protection. I'm hungry and I thirst for more of You. Help me to find that secret place of communion each day.

BUILDING UP THE TEMPLE

The beams of our house are cedar, and our rafters of fir.
Song of Solomon 1:17

King David was still in the spirit of highest praise after bringing the Ark of the Covenant into Jerusalem, when he said to Nathan, the prophet, "See now, I dwell in an house of cedar, but the ark of God dwelleth within curtains" (2 Samuel 7:2). The Lord was very pleased with David's desire to build a temple, but God had used David to slay many of the enemies of Israel. Consequently, he had shed much blood. As a reward for David's devoted love and service, the Lord ordained that David's son would build the house of God. (2 Samuel 7:1-15, 1 Chronicles 22:6-10)

King David accepted the Lord's word, but he still pursued his dream by gathering all kinds of building materials needed to build the temple. David had the plans prepared that the Lord had revealed to him by the Holy Spirit (1 Chronicles 28:11, 12). He gave the blueprints to his son Solomon along with precious metals that would go into the construction. He had made arrangements with King Hiram of Tyre for lumber of cedar, fir, and cypress.

Solomon began the building of the temple after his father had died. Huge stones were cut at the query and brought to the temple site. There was no hammering or cutting on the actual grounds of the temple in reverence to God (1 Kings 6:7). The foundation was stone, overlaid with fir, and then overlaid with gold. The walls were stone, overlaid with cedar, and then the cedar was overlaid with gold. It took seven years and thousands of workmen to complete the temple and its furnishings. It was a magnificent sight to see set upon Mount Zion. The gold sparkled brilliantly, but remember hidden beneath the gold was fir and cedar wood.

Some 400 years after Solomon's temple was built, King Nebuchadnezzar of Babylon destroyed it. God had allowed this destruction because Israel had fallen into sin and did not honor His name. (2 Kings 25:9-17) During Jesus ministry, the temple that King Herod had built was standing on the temple mount. It was not as rich or ornate as Solomon's temple. The disciples pointed out to Jesus the beauty of the temple and its buildings. Jesus made a statement that later turned out to be His death warrant, "Destroy this temple, and I will raise it again in three days" (John 2:19 NIV). The Jews indignantly replied that it had taken 46 years to build the temple. How did

Jesus expect to raise it up in 3 days? They did not understand that Jesus was speaking of His body that would be dead for 3 days and then rise again to life. Jesus likened His body to the temple made of stone, wood, and gold. He was both God and man—the gold being a type of His divine nature and the wood a type of his flesh or human nature. (John 2:19-21, Luke 21:5, 6)

The Bride is saying the beams of our house are cedar, and our rafters are of fir—*Our* house denoting a house shared by Christ and the Church. The modern day temple prepared for the dwelling place of the presence of God is our bodies. Paul explains, "What? Know ye not that your body is the temple of the Holy Ghost which is in you, which ye have of God, and ye are not your own?" (1 Corinthians 6:19) We have been joined together flesh of his flesh and bone of his bone: "For we are members of his body, of his flesh, and of his bones. For this cause shall a man leave his father and mother, and shall be joined unto his wife, and they two shall be one flesh. This is a great mystery: but I speak concerning Christ and the church" (Ephesians 5:30-32).

The cedar beams (a type of Jesus flesh) supports the Church. The rafters of fir are my covering because He was made flesh. He is able to relate to my feelings and struggles because He took the form of flesh. Hebrews 4:14-15 says it this way:

Seeing then that we have a great high priest, that is passed into the heavens, Jesus the Son of God, let us hold fast our profession. For we have not an high priest which cannot be touched with the feeling of our infirmities; but was in all points tempted like as we are, yet without sin.

My Prayer: I come into the throne room and bow before Your throne of grace. So many times, I have cried out to You when I was upset with my fleshly faults. I become impatient with other members of Your body when they display the carnal nature. You have always comforted me in these times because I know You faced similar tests when You clothed Yourself with human flesh. Please cover my flesh with Your divine nature.

CHAPTER 2

ROSE OF SHARON

I am the rose of Sharon, and the lily of the valleys.
Song of Solomon 2:1

It is questionable as to which party is speaking at this time, whether it is the bride or the groom. "The majority of Christian fathers assigned this verse to the King (Christ). Hebrew commentators generally assign it to the bride." [1] I believe that we can take it both ways, due to the fact that we are a reflection of our Savior. He is the Rose of Sharon, and the church mirrors His likeness as a rose of Sharon.

The plains of Sharon were very fertile when the tribe of Gad inherited the land (1 Chronicles 5:16). The lush pastures were covered with wild flowers that Solomon identified as the rose of Sharon. The roses sent forth a refreshing, sweet fragrance on the evening breezes after a long, hot day.

Judgment came to this lush plain, with its wild roses, due to Israel's sin. The prophet Isaiah foretold of this judgment: "The earth mourneth and languisheth:...Sharon is like a wilderness; and Bashan and Carmel shake off their fruits" (Isaiah 33:9). Sin often results in barren and wilderness times.

Only two chapters after this prediction, Isaiah tells of a time of restoration:

> The wilderness and the solitary place shall be glad for them; and the desert shall rejoice, and blossom as the rose. It shall blossom abundantly, and rejoice even with joy and singing: the glory of Lebanon shall be given unto it, the excellency of Carmel and Sharon, they shall see the glory of the LORD, and the excellency of our God. Strengthen ye the weak hands, and confirm the feeble knees.   Isaiah 35:1-3

There is always the promise of glorious restoration when God's people repent. Jesus became sin for me so that I might have restoration as also foretold by Isaiah:

> Yet it pleased the LORD to bruise him; he hath put him to grief: when thou shalt make his soul an offering for sin, he shall see his seed, he shall prolong his days, and the pleasure of the LORD shall prosper in his hand. He shall see of the travail

of his soul, and shall be satisfied: by his knowledge shall my righteous servant justify many; for he shall bear their iniquities.

Isaiah 53:10-11

There are times when we all go through wilderness experiences, sometimes due to our sin and other times just due to living in this sinful world. It is during these times that we call out to Jesus, and He turns our wilderness into green pastures and our dryness into lush and fragrant fields. He was bruised so that the sweet fragrance of His love could fill our lives. We may also experience some bruising of body and soul during these trying times so that the sweet fragrance of Jesus will be reflected in our lives.

This verse in the Song of Solomon goes on to say, "I am the lily of the valleys." The lily exceeds the value of the sweet rose of Sharon. Jesus said that King Solomon in all his glory could not be compared to the loveliness of the lily that grows in the field. Jesus was explaining that we do not need to fret or be anxious for our daily needs because the Father, who watches over the lilies, cares and watches over us (Matthew 6:28-34).

Yes, there are many valleys of trial and trouble—valleys of sickness, heartache, disappointment, broken friendships, and even death. Nevertheless, "Yea, though I walk through the valley of the shadow of death, I will fear no evil: for thou art with me" (Psalms 23:4).

Jesus is my Lily in the valleys of my life—for in the valley, I feel His presence close to me. His fragrance fills the air that I breathe.

My Prayer: In the wilderness and in the multiple valleys, You restore my soul. I am confident that You are with me through each and every trial, for I sense Your presence. You are the sweet refreshing air that I breathe. You are my strength when my hands are weak and when my knees are feeble. All of these blessings were purchased for me when You were broken and bruised. You truly are my sweet Rose of Sharon and the Lily of my valleys.

[1] Barnes' Notes, Electronic Database. Copyright (c) 1997 by Biblesoft

BEWARE OF THE THORNS

As the lily among thorns, so is my love among the daughters.
Song of Solomon 2:2

Sweat poured from Adam's brow as he tried to plow a patch of earth with a crude instrument he had fashioned from a stick. He remembered the lush and pleasant Garden of Eden, where no thorns, thistles, or weeds grew. Now, the earth was so hard and unyielding since sin and the curse had taken control. Adam battled thorns and weeds continually. The thorns would choke out the good vegetation if he neglected to pull them out. God had said the earth would be cursed with thorns and thistles due to Adam's disobedience; thus, thorns are a symbol of sin and the curse in the Bible (Genesis 3:18).

The King says that his Bride is like a lily among thorns. The lily represents purity, worth, and beauty. We saw in the previous verse (Song of Solomon 2:1) that Jesus is our Lily in the valleys. He now turns and says to the Bride "you are a lily also, but you are planted among the thorns." We are "born again not with corruptible seed, but of incorruptible seed, by the word of God" (1 Peter 1:23).

This leads me to the parable Jesus taught concerning the *Sower and the Seed.* The good seed is the Word of God that is planted in various types of soil, and it is affected by various conditions. Jesus taught in Matthew 13:22, "He also that received seed among the thorns is he that heareth the word; and the care of this world, and the deceitfulness of riches, choke the word, and he becometh unfruitful." This is such a serious warning that we have to be careful not to let the thorns of cares, the worries of life, and the desire for riches to grow up and choke out the Word of God that has been planted in our hearts.

It is so easy to get caught up in some activities that do not seem wrong in themselves. The *born again* person may start out with all the good intentions of providing for his family, and then Satan plants the thorns of worldly desires all around him. Before he realizes what is happening, his spiritual life is choked out. This poor soul becomes physically tired and probably neglects the study of God's Word and his prayer life. He lacks the desire to seek after the kingdom of God and the treasures that he should be laying up in heaven. (Matthew 6:19-21)

The second part of this verse, "so is my love among the daughters", was difficult for me to understand because I could not see how the *daughters* were comparable to the *thorns.* I believe that the *daughters* throughout the Song of Solomon represent my fellow Christians. How could a fellow Christian be entangled with the thorns of the world and still be part of the church? These daughters were surrounding the lily (the true righteous Bride). There are two thoughts, which I believe the Lord gave me that answer this question.

The first is also found in a parable of Jesus that comes right after the parable of the *Sower and the Seed*. It is the parable of the *Tares (or Weeds)* found in Matthew 13:24-30. Jesus told the disciples that a farmer planted good seed [*God's word*] in his field, but by night, his enemy (*Satan*) planted bad seeds in the field. When the seed sprouted, it all looked the same, but as it matured to the stage of producing heads of grain the workers discerned that there was good wheat and weeds growing up together. The workers asked the Lord of the harvest if they should tear out the weeds. The Lord said, "No", because by pulling up the weeds, they might destroy some of the good crop; thus, He said to let them grow up together until harvest time. Then the reapers would save the good grain and burn up the weeds. The good grain represents the faithful believer; whereas, the weeds represent the one who looks like a believer, talks like a believer, but their hearts are not true to Jesus. They grow up side by side, but only the Lord, who sees the heart, can distinguish the true from the false. The Lord looks at the field and sees his Bride—His beautiful lily, standing tall, yet she is surrounded by weeds and thorns.

The second thought is found in Hebrews chapter six where the church is being called to go on to perfection. There is a danger of going back into the world after once tasting the good Word of God and even experiencing the Holy Spirit (verses 4-6). The extreme danger is when a person rejects, rebels, and turns completely over to unbelief, in which case it would be impossible to restore such a one. [1]

Our desire is for our hearts to be *good ground* where the Word can take root and grow up to maturity. The Lord provides the seed and the means to grow a fruitful crop.

> Land that drinks in the rain often falling on it and that produces a crop useful to those for whom it is farmed receives the blessing of God. But land that produces thorns and thistles is worthless and is in danger of being cursed. In the end it will be burned.
> Hebrews 7:6, NIV

Good ground represents the heart that is drinking up the rain (a type of the Holy Spirit). It will produce a good crop—it will bear good fruit. Good hearts receive the blessings of God both here and in eternity. However, the heart that allows thorns and thistles to grow is the one who allows the cares of this life and the deceitfulness of riches to overtake their desire for the things of God.

My Prayer: Oh Lord, keep me true, pure, and holy—pursuing Your righteousness. As I read and meditate on Your Word daily, let me see any weed or thorn that is creeping into my life. I set my affections on things eternal. Although, I know there are those who pose as fellow believers who have allowed the world to take over their hearts—help me not to judge, for You are the judge. Help me to pray and uplift them and tenderly woo them back to You.

(1) A note of caution: if you think you may have gone this far away from God, it is probably not true because you would not be seeking God by reading this book based on His Word. This apostasy comes about by deliberately and continually sinning and rejecting God's Word.

SIT UNDER THE APPLE TREE

As the apple tree among the trees of the wood, so is my beloved among the sons. I sat down under his shadow with great delight, and his fruit was sweet to my taste. Song of Solomon 2:3

The Bride says that her King (Jesus) is like an apple tree among the trees of the wood. Wood represents Jesus taking on the form of human flesh. The apple tree is choice for fruit compared to the other trees of the wood. Even so, Jesus is best and most desired among the sons of men. He is even better than all the angels of heaven: "Being made so much better than the angels, as he hath by inheritance obtained a more excellent name than they" (Hebrews 1:4). God has exalted Jesus above all other powers and kings of this world:

> Wherefore God also hath highly exalted him, and given him a name which is above every name: That at the name of Jesus every knee should bow, of things in heaven, and things in earth, and things under the earth;   And that every tongue should confess that Jesus Christ is Lord, to the glory of God the Father.   Philippians 2:9-12

He is so superior, the angels of heaven bow to Him; all the men who have ever walked this earth both great and small will bow to Him; every demon of hell trembles at His presence.

Jesus came to earth in human flesh for the purpose of showing us the true character of God. To behold Jesus, is to behold the Father.

> God, who at sundry times and in divers manners spake in time past unto the fathers by the prophets, Hath in these last days spoken unto us by his Son, whom he hath appointed heir of all things, by whom also he made the worlds; Who being the brightness of his glory, and the express image of his person, and upholding all things by the word of his power, when he had by himself purged our sins, sat down on the right hand of the Majesty on high.   Hebrews 1:1-3

Jesus took on human flesh to provide the sinless sacrifice necessary to purge us of our sins. Now He has taken His rightful place on the right hand of our majestic God.

It is the believer's delight to sit under the shadow of Jesus—our apple tree. When we are under His shadow, it speaks of His blessing and protection for the Church:

> O LORD, thou art my God; I will exalt thee, I will praise thy name; for thou hast done wonderful things; thy counsels of old are faithfulness and truth.....For thou hast been a strength to the poor, a strength to the needy in his distress, a refuge from the storm, *a shadow from the heat*, when the blast of the terrible ones is as a storm against the wall.   Isaiah 25:1, 4

We praise our Lord, for He is the refuge from the storm and a cool shadow from the heat. Under the shadow of the apple tree, we find refuge, strength, and rest from the battles of life. There is nothing more refreshing on a hot day than to find a good shade tree.

This apple tree not only serves the purpose of shade but also for a nutritious treat. There is the old proverb that says, "an apple a day keeps the doctor away." The apple contains vitamins and minerals to keep the body strong; antioxidants to strengthen the immune system; carbohydrates for energy. When we take in the Lord by feeding on His Word, our spiritual soul is fed, and we build up our immune system against the temptations that come our way.

The apple was a special treat in Bible times. So many times we discover a precious promise in God's Word; it is a sweet and refreshing apple to our souls. Could we start a new adage, "a promise a day, keeps the enemy away"? The Psalmist puts it this way: "How sweet are thy words unto my taste! Yea, sweeter than honey to my mouth!" (Psalms 119:103) In another Psalm he says, "O taste and see that the LORD is good: blessed is the man that trusteth in him" (Psalms 34:8).

My Prayer: Jesus, I put You in the highest place in my heart and life, for You are higher than any other. I put my trust in the shadow of Your protection. I love to just sit in a quiet, cool place and meditate on Your words, for they are life and health to my soul. When I am feeling weak, I reach out and take one of Your precious promises, and my strength is renewed. I delight myself in You, Oh my Lord!

BANNER OF LOVE

He brought me to the banqueting house, and his banner over me
was love. *Song of Solomon 2:4*

We spoke of partaking of the apples of promise from God's
Word in the previous verse, but we do not need to be satisfied with
only these delicate morsels. He has prepared a banquet feast for us!
He has **brought** me into His house and caused me to sit at the King's
table and feast on heaven's best. We cannot come into the King's
presence without His invitation. He has said, "Come, follow me"
(Luke 18:22).

The story in 2 Samuel, chapter nine, illustrates this thought in
a special way. King David wanted to show kindness to anyone that
was still alive in Jonathan's family. As the word spread, they found a
servant from the house of Jonathan's father, Saul, named Ziba. Ziba
revealed that there was a son of Jonathan's still living, and he was in
hiding in the house of Machir. The son's name was Mephibosheth.

He was hiding because it was the custom for the conquering
king to kill the descendants of the outgoing king. As soon as it was
reported that Saul and Jonathan had been killed in battle, Mephibosheth's nurse had hurriedly taken him into hiding. In her rush, she
had dropped him and from that time on, he was lame. Some years
later, Mephibosheth came trembling before King David as he thought
David would want to do away with him. To his surprise, David ex-
tended love to Mephibosheth and insisted that he come and live in the
palace and eat at the king's table everyday of his life.

Can you see the picture? David can be seen as a type of God
the Father who loves Jesus the Son. Because we have received Jesus
we have become sons of God (John 1:12). We are then privileged to
sit at King Jesus' table everyday, for He has brought me into His banqueting house. Although we come lame and unworthy, He loves us
and has mercy on us. Not only do we sit at His table and feast on His
Word, but also we are under His banner.

The banner was a flag used to proclaim the victorious kingdom during the battles of Old Testament times. It is similar to the
modern tradition of a conquering nation raising its national flag as a
declaration of victory. We declare our victory to the world as Paul
writes: "Now thanks be unto God, which always causeth us to triumph
in Christ" (2 Corinthians 2:14).

45

If we fear and honor the Lord, with all truth, we are under His banner: "Thou hast given a banner to them that fear thee, that it may be displayed because of the truth" (Psalms 60:4). The Lord fulfills the petitions of those who dwell under His banner: "We will rejoice in thy salvation, and in the name of our God we will set up our banners: the LORD fulfil all thy petitions" (Psalms 20:5).

A banquet is a time of rejoicing. We rejoice in our salvation. But, most of all, we rejoice because His banner over us is LOVE! As God's people looked toward the tabernacle, they could see the twelve tribes' banners as an emblem of their father's house waving in the air (Numbers 2:2). As we seek Jesus in His sanctuary, we see His loving kindness that is better than life itself. Praise flows from our lips as we look back to the crippled life we once lived and how Jesus has changed our lives to blessing—living under the banner of His love.

> So I have looked for You in the sanctuary,
> To see Your power and Your glory.
> Because Your lovingkindness is better than life,
> My lips shall praise You.
> Thus I will bless You while I live;
> I will lift up my hands in Your name.
> My soul shall be satisfied as with marrow and fatness,
> And my mouth shall praise You with joyful lips.
> Psalms 63:2-6, NKJV

My Prayer: Thy loving-kindness is indeed better than life! I thank You for Your Word as it fills me with Your salvation, truth, peace, and love. Thank You for bringing me into Your house. It was not because I earned it by my works or worthiness, but because of Your mercy. I declare my allegiance to Your kingdom by dwelling under Your banner of love.

LOVESICK

Stay me with flagons, comfort me with apples: for I am sick of love.
Song of Solomon 2:5

New King James Version translates this verse like this:
Sustain me with cakes of raisins,
Refresh me with apples,
For I am lovesick.

The New King James denotes that this is the Shulamite speaking to the daughters of Jerusalem. In my way of thinking, the Shulamite is the soon-to-be Bride of Christ or the Church, and the daughters of Jerusalem are her fellow believers or other Christians that affect her walk with Christ.

The, soon-to-be, Bride is crying out to her fellow companions that she is actually feeling sick because she is so in love with Jesus. If you have ever been in love, you can probably remember that feeling down in the pit of your stomach when you longed to see or talk to your lover. We long for the presence of the Lord even as David did:

My soul longs, yes, even faints
For the courts of the LORD;
My heart and my flesh cry out for the living God.
Psalms 84:2, NKJV

Our Bridegroom has been away for approximately two thousand years. He left with these tender words: "Let not your heart be troubled: ye believe in God, believe also in me. In my Father's house are many mansions: if it were not so, I would have told you. I go to prepare a place for you. And if I go and prepare a place for you, I will come again, and receive you unto myself; that where I am, there ye may be also" (John 14:1-3).

He continues in this same teaching to tell us that He is not leaving us alone, but He is sending a Comforter, Counselor, and Helper who is the Holy Spirit. Jesus' words to the disciples were:

And I will pray the Father, and he shall give you another
Comforter, that he may abide with you for ever.....

But the Comforter, which is the Holy Ghost, whom the
Father will send in my name, he shall teach you all things,
and bring all things to your remembrance, whatsoever I
have said unto you.   John 14:16 & 26

The Holy Spirit's work is to bring all the words of Jesus back into remembrance. Not only to bring them to remembrance, but to teach us
and give us understanding of those words. The Bride understands that
she is sustained by the rich words of her lover; just as we, in the
church, are sustained and comforted by the Word of God and the guidance of the Holy Spirit.

We have already said that the apples represent the rich promises that comfort us. They are as Solomon says, "A word fitly spoken
is like apples of gold in pictures of silver" (Proverbs 25:11). Gold
represents the divine word spoken at just the right time for our specific
need. It is encased in pictures of silver that stands for the redemption
and grace of our Lord. What a delight to our souls when
Jesus gives us a revelation word for a specific need.

The flagons or raisin cakes were rich in natural sugars and
were often eaten to assist someone that was feeling faint (1 Samuel
30:10-13). They were also given as gifts. When David brought the
Ark of God into Jerusalem, he blessed all the people in the name of
the Lord and gave them gifts of bread, flesh, and cakes of raisins
(2 Samuel 6:17-19).

Jesus sustains us with His words and with His gift of the Holy
Spirit. Our hearts yearn for Him, and we feel that we cannot live another day without seeing His face. We spill out our burdens to believers of like precious faith, and they remind us of the promises, gifts,
and His marvelous grace. Paul clarified the coming of the Lord to the
Thessalonians: "Wherefore comfort one another with these words"
(1 Thessalonians 4:18). We are to comfort one another with the words
of hope seeing that our redemption draws near for Jesus is coming
back for His church (Luke 21:28).

My Prayer: Oh Lord, how I long for You. I could not make it without
Your words of comfort and Your gifts of the Holy Spirit. Thank you
for fellow believers who encourage me. Help me to take every opportunity to be an encouragement to the body of Christ.

EMBRACE OF LOVE

His left hand is under my head, and his right hand doth embrace
me. Song of Solomon 2:6

The Bride is still speaking to her companions as she shares
how close the Bridegroom holds her. She feels secure and loved
while she is in His tender embrace. Nothing can come between them
in these precious times, just as nothing can separate us from the love
of Christ:

Who shall separate us from the love of Christ? shall tribulation, or distress, or persecution, or famine, or nakedness, or
peril, or sword?

Nay, in all these things we are more than conquerors through
him that loved us. For I am persuaded, that neither death, nor
life, nor angels, nor principalities, nor powers, nor things present, nor things to come, Nor height, nor depth, nor any other
creature, shall be able to separate us from the love of God,
which is in Christ Jesus our Lord.   Romans 8:35; 37-39

I rest in His love with my head cradled in His left hand. This
left hand is assuring me that He will cover my mind with His love.
"For God hath not given us the spirit of fear; but of power, and of
love, and of a sound mind" (2 Timothy 1:7). I set my mind on the
Lord, my God, because He has commanded: "Love the Lord your
God with all your heart and with all your soul and with all your mind"
(Matthew 22:37, NIV). I love Jesus with everything that is within me,
for His love is all I need.

His right hand is embracing me, holding me gently close to
His heart. The right hand speaks to us of His saving might: "He will
hear him from his holy heaven with the saving strength of his right
hand" (Psalms 20:6). Although there is strength in His hand, His embrace is gentle: "Thou hast also given me the shield of thy salvation:
and thy right hand hath holden me up, and thy gentleness hath made
me great" (Psalms 18:35). Isaiah tells of the Lord's strength and gentleness in this way:

49

Behold, the Lord GOD shall come with a strong hand,
And His arm shall rule for Him;
Behold, His reward is with Him,
And His work before Him.
He will feed His flock like a shepherd;
He will gather the lambs with His arm,
And carry them in His bosom,
And gently lead those who are with young.
Isaiah 40:10-12, NKJV

Therefore, we see that His left hand guards our minds from the internal conflict and temptation of our enemies, while His strong right hand shelters us from the storms and outside circumstances that come against us.

My Prayer: I marvel in Your strong and yet gentle protection. You are there to meet my every need. You shield me from every direction that the enemy would try to hurt me.   Help me to learn how to, by faith, relax in Your embrace, knowing that You love me so much—You would not let anything overcome me.

WAITING IN SILENCE

I charge you, O ye daughters of Jerusalem, by the roes, and by the hinds of the field, that ye stir not up, nor awake my love, till he please. Song of Solomon 2:7

As we have established in previous verses, the daughters of Jerusalem are the children of promise and the children of the free. Paul states that Jerusalem is the mother of us all. Thus, the daughters of Jerusalem are the blood-bought ones who trust in the words of the Lord. They are members of the universal—living Church of Jesus Christ. (Galatians 4:21-31)

Each believer is at differing levels of maturity in Christ. Our Bride in the Song of Solomon has drawn very close to her King, and she has shared a deeper relationship in Him than the general assembly of the daughters. Just as Paul, the experienced apostle, charged the novice pastor, Timothy; even so, our Bride charges the daughters of Jerusalem (1 Timothy 1:18, 19). The Bride is more mature because she understands the heart of her Beloved; therefore, she earnestly pleads with them not to stir up or awaken her Master until He pleases.

The charge is by the roes and hinds of the field. I do not think we can take this firm statement made by the Bride as an oath, but rather, she is trying to get their undivided attention to her instructions. Why does she bring attention to the roes and hinds of the field? The roe usually refers to the male fallow deer species, and the hind refers to the female of the red deer species. [1] They both were admired for their agility and grace, their ability to sense danger quickly, and their swiftness. [2] The deer could be easily stirred up or quickly awakened out of sleep. By using the roe and the hind in her charge, she is portraying the idea of her Beloved being a light sleeper who could be aroused at the least bit of stirring.

We know that God never slumbers or sleeps (Psalms 121:4). In spite of that, we feel like He is asleep, at times, when He does not answer our prayers right away. Sometimes our prayer resounds like that of David:

> My God, My God, why have You forsaken Me?
> Why are You so far from helping Me,
> And from the words of My groaning?
> O My God, I cry in the daytime, but You do not hear;
> And in the night season, and am not silent.

But You are holy,
Enthroned in the praises of Israel.
Our fathers trusted in You;
They trusted, and You delivered them.
They cried to You, and were delivered;
They trusted in You, and were not ashamed
Psalms 22:1-5, NKJV

Jesus even repeated the first words of this prayer from the cross, as he felt separated from His Father. In verse 3-6, the Bride has been praising, and as it were, **enthroning**, her love in the sight of the daughters of Jerusalem. She has told them how she sits under His shade and delights in the apples and raisins (His words of hope and promise); how He had brought her into His banqueting house and prepared a feast for her; how His banner over her is love; how He embraces her with His left hand under her head (guarding her mind), and His right hand of strength (guarding from outside enemies). Jesus is enthroned, rests, and dwells in the praise of His Church. The Bride has created this restful atmosphere with her praise.

Can you picture how she does not want to create a stir of unrest, as she is just happy being in her Lord's presence? There is a correct time for everything. There is "a time to keep silence, and a time to speak" (Ecclesiastes 3:7). There is a time to cry out our petitions to the Lord, and there is a time to wait in silence. Let us be aware that the Lord is Sovereign, and He will take care of our needs in His time and in His divine way: "The LORD is in his holy temple: let all the earth keep silence before him" (Habakkuk 2:20). "Wait on the LORD: be of good courage, and he shall strengthen thine heart: wait, I say, on the LORD" (Psalms 27:14, NKJV).

My Prayer: "Teach me Your ways, O LORD, and I will walk in Your truth; give me an undivided heart, that I may fear Your name. I will praise You, O Lord my God, with all my heart; I will glorify Your name forever" (Psalms 86:11-12, NIV).

[1], [2] From Nelson's New Illustrated Bible Dictionary; Ronald F. Youngblood, General Editor; copyright 1995, 1986 by Thomas Nelson Publishers

VICTORY UPON THE MOUNTAIN TOPS

The voice of my beloved! behold, he cometh leaping upon the mountains, skipping upon the hills. Song of Solomon 2:8

Silence is broken by the voice of the Beloved King! Praise God, there is always a break in the heavens and the voice of the Lord comes through loud and clear. It may seem that the Lord has withdrawn, but we know that He is always there. Can you hear the shout of victory?

The voice of the LORD is over the waters;
the God of glory thunders,
the LORD thunders over the mighty waters.
The voice of the LORD is powerful;
the voice of the LORD is majestic.
The voice of the LORD breaks the cedars;
the LORD breaks in pieces the cedars of Lebanon.
He makes Lebanon skip like a calf,
Sirion like a young wild ox.
The voice of the LORD strikes
with flashes of lightning.
The voice of the LORD shakes the desert;
the LORD shakes the Desert of Kadesh.
The voice of the LORD twists the oaks
and strips the forests bare.
And in his temple all cry, "Glory!"
Psalms 29:3-9, NIV

He is victorious over every mountain or problem that we encounter. He is even concerned with the small hills of our everyday difficulties. With Jesus holding our hand, we too can skip with joy upon our hills and leap over the mountains.

He showed us how to be victorious on the mount of temptation as he wrestled with Satan. By the Word of God, He resisted Satan's three temptations. We also have the sword of the Spirit, which is the Word of God, as a mighty weapon to resist Satan's temptations. (Luke 4:1-14; Ephesians 6:17)

Unresolved hurt and unforgiveness will mount up in our lives and cause bitterness to overwhelm our souls. Jesus showed us how to overcome this mountain when He forgave the Roman soldiers and the Jewish religious leaders who were putting Him to death (Luke 23:34).

He showed us how to overcome sin as He hung on the cross on the hill called Calvary. He said, "If any man will come after me, let him deny himself, and take up his cross daily, and follow me. For whosoever will save his life shall lose it: but whosoever will lose his life for my sake, the same shall save it" (Luke 9:23-24).

He defeated death, hell, and the grave as He came leaping and skipping out of the tomb. Paul exclaims, "O death, where is thy sting? O grave, where is thy victory? The sting of death is sin; and the strength of sin is the law. But thanks be to God, which giveth us the victory through our Lord Jesus Christ" (1 Corinthians 15:55-57).

The victories of our Lord Jesus Christ are not finished yet. It was on the Mount of Olives where he fought with His own will and that of Satan. He cried out to the Father, "Not my will, but thine, be done" (Luke 22:42). It was from this mountain that He ascended up into heaven, His earthly work complete (Acts 1:9-12). We look forward to the day when Jesus will return to the Mount of Olives as King of kings and Lord of lords. As His feet stand on the Mount of Olives, it will split in half, and a valley will be created for the final battle with Satan. The saints (the church) will be with Him as He returns in all of His glory. (Zechariah 14:3, 4; Revelation 19:11-16)

Jesus will then reign from Mount Zion as foretold by Isaiah the prophet in Isaiah 2:2-3:

> And it shall come to pass in the last days, that the mountain of the LORD's house shall be established in the top of the mountains, and shall be exalted above the hills; and all nations shall flow unto it. And many people shall go and say, Come ye, and let us go up to the mountain of the LORD, to the house of the God of Jacob; and he will teach us of his ways, and we will walk in his paths: for out of Zion shall go forth the law, and the word of the LORD from Jerusalem.

When the Lord leaps upon the mountains, they come down. He is the Lord of Hosts. "Lift ye up a banner upon the high mountain", (Isaiah 13:2a)......"the Lord of hosts mustereth the host of the battle. They come from a far country, from the end of heaven, even the LORD, and the weapons of his indignation, to destroy the whole land" (Isaiah 13:4b-5).

54

This great God of the mountains has given you and me the authority and power over the mountains that come in our path. Whether they are temptations, habits, unforgiveness, discouragement, or sickness, He gave this word:

"Have faith in God,".... "I tell you the truth, if anyone says to this mountain, 'Go, throw yourself into the sea,' and does not doubt in his heart but believes that what he says will happen, it will be done for him. Therefore I tell you, whatever you ask for in prayer, believe that you have received it, and it will be yours."   Mark 11:22-24, NIV

The voice of the LORD has spoken!

My Prayer: Thank You Lord, for You have overcome every mountain. You are victorious, and in You, I am victorious. You are in control of all my mountains and hills and nothing is impossible for You. You never intended that Your church would be weak, but that it would storm the very gates of hell. What a glorious day when You reign from Mount Zion and the whole earth will be full of Your glory.

INSIDE, OUTSIDE, UPSIDE, DOWN

My beloved is like a roe or a young hart: behold, he standeth behind our wall, he looketh forth at the windows, shewing himself through the lattice. **Song of Solomon 2:9**

The Bride is beholding her Beloved as a roe or young hart. The deer, again, is quick and fleeting—ready to run or leap at anytime. Yet at this moment, her Beloved is standing just behind a wall. She calls it *our* wall. Why is there a wall between them? I believe this wall is our mortal bodies. Jesus dwells within our mortal bodies, and He looks out the windows onto the world that He wants to save. He uses this body of flesh to shine forth His glory to the world, so that the world might be saved. Paul compares our body to an earthen vessel in which we hold the light and glory of the Lord:

> For God, who commanded the light to shine out of darkness, hath shined in our hearts, to give the light of the knowledge of the glory of God in the face of Jesus Christ. But we have this treasure in earthen vessels, that the excellency of the power may be of God, and not of us.   2 Corinthians 4:6-7

The power and glory that shines forth from our mortal bodies is of God. The glory is in the face of Jesus Christ looking out the windows (our eyes). (See Luke 11:34) The world recognizes that there is something different about the child of God. The difference is Christ within us.

> Even the mystery which hath been hid from ages and from generations, but now is made manifest to his saints: To whom God would make known what is the riches of the glory of this mystery among the Gentiles; *which is Christ in you, the hope of glory*.   Colossians 1:26-27

Christ is inside of me, yet because of His omnipresence, He is also in heaven looking down at me. I am here in the world being His eyes looking upon the lost. He is standing, watching with loving eyes, as I struggle to do His will, and He is always making intercession for me (Hebrews 7:25). Jesus is waiting for the day when I set aside this mortal body and there is no longer a wall between us. Face to face, I shall behold Him as He is (1 Corinthians 13:12).

56

Paul goes on in 2 Corinthians, chapter five, to tell us that his body is like an earthly house of the tabernacle. We are going to receive a new house that is eternal:

> For we know that if our earthly house of this tabernacle were dissolved, we have a building of God, a house not made with hands, eternal in the heavens. For in this we groan, earnestly desiring to be clothed upon with our house which is from heaven.   2 Corinthians 5:1-3

John, the Revelator, saw the New Jerusalem coming down from heaven in the last day. The angel told him that this was the Bride, the Lamb's wife. The city has great and beautiful walls of Jasper. "The Lord God Almighty and the Lamb are the temple of it" (Revelation 21:9-11, 22). Remember, Jesus said He was going away to prepare a place for us and that His Father had many mansions (John 14:2). I believe we are sending up some of the building materials for the walls of our new house. These materials represent the works that we do as unto the Lord. Are we sending up gold, silver, and precious stones? (1 Corinthians 3:12, 13)

I can envision the Lord standing, waiting, and helping me finish the walls of my glorious home. When all is ready, He will come like a roe and a young hart to catch me away to Himself. There will then be no walls between us.

My Prayer: Oh Lord, thank You for dwelling in this mortal body of mine. Thank You for making me a part of Your body—the Church. Now this body of mine becomes *our wall*. It seems as though I am a prisoner in my body, but soon it will be changed to be like Your glorified body. Until You release me from this vile body and set me free, please keep looking forth from my eyes. Help me to see others as You see them with love and compassion. May Your glory shine through me so that I will attract many lost souls into Your kingdom.

RISE UP

My beloved spake, and said unto me, Rise up, my love, my fair one, and come away. Song of Solomon 2:10

The Lord Jesus, our Beloved, speaks to us today through His Word and through His Holy Spirit. He commands us to rise up! He is calling us **His love** and **His fair one**. Through the eyes of His love, we are already the completed work of the purified—glorious Bride. "Being confident of this very thing, that he which hath begun a good work in you will perform it until the day of Jesus Christ" (Philippians 1:6).

This command indicates that the Bride has the ability to hear and move at His instructions. We are enabled by the Holy Spirit to rise up and be a separated, holy people, even while we walk in this sinful world. His command is, "Come out from among them, and be ye separate, saith the Lord, and touch not the unclean thing; and I will receive you" (2 Corinthians 6:16, 17). We are to come out of this world's system and sinfulness to be a holy people.

His voice within us tugs at our soul: "I will come again and receive you unto myself" (John 14:3). How our hearts yearn for the day when He will break through the clouds; we will hear the trump of God and the shout of the Lord, "come away with me"; and we will rise up to meet Jesus in the air (1 Thessalonians 4:16, 17). Goodbye world, goodbye!

John, the beloved disciple, experienced "being caught up" when he was in the Spirit on the Lord's Day. He tells of his experience:

> After this I looked, and, behold, a door was opened in heaven: and the first voice which I heard was as it were of a trumpet talking with me; which said, Come up hither, and I will shew thee things which must be hereafter. And immediately I was in the spirit: and, behold, a throne was set in heaven, and one sat on the throne.　　　　　　　　　　Revelation 4:1-2

First, John saw the open door. Second, he heard the voice of the trumpet saying to "come up hither." Then he was immediately transported, in the Spirit, into the throne room of heaven. It all happened in a moment—in the twinkling of an eye—just as it will happen to us when Jesus calls us up higher. John was transported in the Spirit, but we will receive a new, immortal body when our time comes. We will be changed in a twinkling of the eye (1 Corinthians 15:51-51). We will have a new body that will be like the glorified body of our Lord (1 John 3:2). The dead in Christ will be resurrected first, and then the Christians who are living at that time will be caught up to meet the Lord in the air (1 Thessalonians 4:16, 17).

Although we are longing for that wonderful day when Jesus comes to take us home, we are blessed while still on earth. Paul tells us that we are blessed with all spiritual blessings and lifted up to heavenly places in Christ (Ephesians 1:3). Even now, He calls us to cast our cares on Him and come up into heavenly places. He provides a sanctuary, a safe place, a blessed place for those who would draw near. We must take the time to lay aside the world's cares and come away with Him each day.

My Prayer: Jesus, how my heart yearns to hear You call me to "come up here." Nevertheless, until then, I seek Your blessed heavenly places which I find when I draw near to You. I love to hear Your voice as I read Your Word and as the Holy Spirit directs me day by day. My cry is that You will keep me close and do not let me fall. May You find me faithful when You come in all of Your glory.

THE GREAT WINTER

For, lo, the winter is past, the rain is over and gone;
Song of Solomon 2:11

The whole earth groans and travails in pain together until the day when it is restored to its former state, as it was in the time of the Garden of Eden. Now we are in a winter season, cold, and barren of life. Darkness and death covers the planet (Romans 8:22). Despite the fact that the Bride still remains in the earth, she is given the power of the Holy Spirit to withstand the trials and tribulations that have been caused by sin and the curse. When Jesus takes the Bride away, the Holy Spirit, who is her comforter, will go with her. The church will cease to be troubled with the winter and rain of this life. This will be the end of the dispensation of grace (2 Thessalonians 2:7, 8).

The earth and the people left behind when the Bride is caught away will experience the darkest time on earth. It will be "A day of darkness and of gloominess, a day of clouds and of thick darkness" (Joel 2:2a). It will be a great and terrible time of tribulation for the earth and all its inhabitants.

During the Great Tribulation, the Lord will once again call His chosen people from the house of David. "In that day there shall be a fountain opened to the house of David and to the inhabitants of Jerusalem for sin and for uncleanness" (Zechariah 13:1). Many in Israel will be saved at the end time, for the Lord shall rise up against the enemy. "And the LORD shall utter his voice before his army: for his camp is very great: for he is strong that executeth his word: for the day of the LORD is great and very terrible; and who can abide it?" (Joel 2:11) There will be spiritual deliverance as well as military deliverance.

Military deliverance

In that day shall the LORD defend the inhabitants of Jerusalem; and he that is feeble among them at that day shall be as David; and the house of David shall be as God, as the angel of the LORD before them. And it shall come to pass in that day, that I will seek to destroy all the nations that come against Jerusalem.   Zachariah 12:8, 9

60

Spiritual deliverance

And I will pour upon the house of David, and upon the inhabitants of Jerusalem, the spirit of grace and of supplications: and they shall look upon me whom they have pierced, and they shall mourn for him, as one mourneth for his only son, and shall be in bitterness for him, as one that is in bitterness for his firstborn.   Zechariah 10:9, 10

Israel will be visited with the Spirit of supplication and repentance because of the grace of God. Just before springtime, the latter rain will fall upon them. They will realize that Jesus, the One with nail pierced hands, is the promised Messiah, and they will weep and repent. The tears will fall like rain and spiritual new birth will spring up. The earth will be renewed out of this rain of repentance and it will usher in the reign of Jesus Christ and a thousand years of peace.

The LORD will surely comfort Zion
and will look with compassion on all her ruins;
he will make her deserts like Eden,
her wastelands like the garden of the LORD.
Joy and gladness will be found in her,
thanksgiving and the sound of singing.
Isaiah 51:3, NIV

My Prayer: Lord, help me to be filled with Your Holy Spirit when You come in the clouds to take away Your Bride. I pray that I will be counted worthy to escape the Great Tribulation when God's wrath will be poured out upon sinful men. Thank You for Your comfort during the winter seasons of my life. What a wonderful day it will be when winter is past and the rains are gone.

NEW LIFE COMES IN THE SPRING

The flowers appear on the earth; the time of the singing of birds is come, and the voice of the turtle is heard in our land;
Song of Solomon 2:12

It is so exciting to see the first shoots of green grass and flowers peeking out of the earth after a long, cold winter. The birds migrate back from the warmer climates, and their singing is a welcomed relief from the sounds of cold, blistering wind. Even the gentle turtledove's coo is heard. Scripture often compares our short life span to that of the flowers that appear and are soon cut off (1 Peter 1:24; Psalms 103:15). The child of God has the hope of eternal life though Jesus Christ our Lord. Jesus was the first fruits of the resurrection and we, His children, will be raised in like manner. Just like Jesus, we will have a glorified, immortal body (1 Corinthians 15:23; 42-44). This is our hope and we are to comfort one another with this promise.

> For I know that my redeemer liveth, and that he shall stand at the latter day upon the earth: And though after my skin worms destroy this body, yet in my flesh shall I see God: Whom I shall see for myself, and mine eyes shall behold, and not another.   Job 19:25-27a

The voice of the turtledove reminds us of peace. We are admonished to pray for the peace of Jerusalem. This land is a land of turmoil, strife, and war. Satan has caused so much blood to flow on this portion of the earth which the Lord has claimed as His own (1 Kings 14:21). After the winter of tribulation upon this earth, the Prince of Peace, Jesus our Lord, will come and avenge Jerusalem of its enemies. As Zechariah prophesied, Jesus shall come to the Mount of Olives, and when His feet touch the mount, it will break in two, forming a great valley. He claims it for Himself and for His Bride. It is our land! Though we die, we shall appear on the earth again, in our immortal bodies, to rule and reign with Jesus (Revelation 20:6). The turtledove of peace will once again be heard in the land.

Of the increase of his government and peace there shall be no end, upon the throne of David, and upon his kingdom, to order it, and to establish it with judgment and with justice from henceforth even for ever. The zeal of the LORD of hosts will perform this.   Isaiah 9:7

   We face personal winters of sickness, grief, and loss during our time upon this earth. If we are to have the peace of the Lord in our lives, we must see these heartaches with the perspective of eternity. Winter only lasts for a season. I was admiring the lilacs that grow near my daughter's house in Iowa. I wondered why we do not grow lilacs in Hawaii. Then I read in a magazine that lilacs must have at least one frost during the winter in order to bloom in the spring. Isn't this true of our spiritual life? The beauty and fragrance of spring is only possible when we have gone through the cold of winter trials.

My Prayer: Lord, grant my desire to one day stand with You on the Mount of Olives. I want to see that final war when Satan is defeated. I want to see the New Jerusalem come down from heaven above. By faith in Your precious blood, I shall stand in You complete. Help me not to complain when I experience winter times in my life, for I know that spring and joy will follow. Seeing You will erase all the heartaches of winter. All praise and glory to my Beloved Savior!

SUMMER IS NIGH

The fig tree putteth forth her green figs, and the vines with the ten-
der grape give a good smell. Arise, my love, my fair one, and come
away. Song of Solomon 2:13

Israel is likened to the fig tree and the vine in scripture:
"When I found Israel, it was like finding grapes in the desert; when I
saw your fathers, it was like seeing the early fruit on the fig tree"
(Hosea 9:10, NIV). (Also, see Jeremiah 24 and Joel 1:6, 7) Jesus explained to His disciples that one of the signs of the last days would be
the budding of the fig tree. He said in Matthew 24:32-34:

> Now learn a parable of the fig tree; When his branch is yet
> tender, and putteth forth leaves, ye know that summer is nigh:
> So likewise ye, when ye shall see all these things, know that it
> is near, even at the doors. Verily I say unto you, this genera-
> tion shall not pass, till all these things be fulfilled.

Israel became a nation and proclaimed its independence on
May 11, 1948. [1]   In Luke chapter twenty-one, the disciples asked
Jesus when the end of days would come. He said to watch for the fig
tree (Israel), for when it started to bud—summer was near and the
kingdom of God was at hand (verses 29-31). Then they would see the
Son of man coming in the clouds with power and great glory (verse
27). I believe this *coming* is referring to the glorious return of Christ,
when He comes for the believing Israelites and those who have been
martyred during the Tribulation period.   We want to be ready for the
time Jesus comes for His Bride before the Great Tribulation. He tells
us how we are to be ready for that day:

> And take heed to yourselves, lest at any time your hearts be
> overcharged with surfeiting, and drunkenness, and cares of this
> life, and so that day come upon you unawares. For as a snare
> shall it come on all them that dwell on the face of the whole
> earth. Watch ye therefore, and pray always, that ye may be
> *accounted worthy to escape* all these things that shall come to
> pass, and to stand before the Son of man.
>
> Luke 21:34-36

Watch and pray and don't get caught up in this world's pleasures, ambitions, and distractions of life. This is the only way we can b counted worthy to escape the horrible things that are coming whe God's judgment is poured out.

Jesus also told a parable that speaks to us as to how importan it is for His followers to bear fruit. This parable is found in Luke 13:6 9. The owner of a vineyard had a fig tree planted in it. He looked fo fruit three years, and it did not bear any fruit. He instructed the keepe of the vineyard to cut it down. The keeper begged the owner to give him one more year to prune it, water it, and fertilize it. The owne consented to give the tree one more year to bear fruit. This is paralle to Jesus' words in John chapter 15. He said that the branch that doe not bear fruit should be pruned. If the branch continued to be fruitless. it would be cut off. Jesus gives us the remedy for unfruitfulness:

> Abide in me, and I in you. As the branch cannot bear fruit of itself, except it abide in the vine; no more can ye, except ye abide in me. I am the vine, ye are the branches: He that abideth in me, and I in him, the same bringeth forth much fruit: for without me ye can do nothing.   John 15:4-5

Daily communion with our Lord—taking in His Word and living in His presence is the key to bearing fruit. The Lord is patient and long-suffering with us, but He expects us to bear fruit for Him. As we watch and pray, we must be busy doing His work and gathering in the harvest of souls, for summer is near.

My Prayer: Lord, I thank You for showing me signs of Your coming. They are everywhere. As I see the nation of Israel growing stronger, I cannot help but wonder how soon You will come for Your church. I pray for more workers to be sent into the last days of harvest. May I be watching, praying, and working when you come.

---

[1]   From Wikipedia, the free encyclopedia

THE SECRET PLACE

*O my dove, that art in the clefts of the rock, in the secret places of
the stairs, let me see thy countenance, let me hear thy voice; for
sweet is thy voice, and thy countenance is comely.*
Song of Solomon 2:14

Just as a dove is a type of the Holy Spirit, likewise, the Bride
is like the dove because the Holy Spirit dwells in her. There is a great
abiding joy in knowing that I carry the blessed Holy Spirit within my
body. The Holy Spirit, whose purpose is to exalt and magnify the
Lord Jesus, rises up within me to praise and magnify my Lord. (John
14:17; 15:26; 16:14, 15)

The Rock speaks to me of a solid and sure foundation. When
the circumstances of my life seem to turn my world upside down, I go
to my Lord—the Rock. I would like to bring your attention to
Jeremiah 48:28: "O ye that dwell in Moab, leave the cities, and dwell
in the *rock*, and be like the *dove* that maketh her nest in the sides of
the hole's mouth." Moab was a very proud and wicked nation, thus a
type of sin and the world. God says to come out of the cities of Moab,
or the world, and be as a dove that makes her nest in the clefts of the
rock. Jesus prayed to the Father to keep his disciples from the evil that
is in the world, even while they were sent into the world to proclaim
the gospel to the world (John 17:15-18).

The only way for the Christian to survive the onslaught of evil
is to build his life upon the Rock and to take refuge in the clefts of the
Rock. When we build upon Jesus, the Rock, we are able to stand in
times of storm. Sometimes the wind and rain are beating on us so
hard; we need to take refuge in the cleft of the Rock until the storm
passes by. (Luke 6:47-49; 1 Corinthians 3:11)

When the children of Israel were wandering in the wilderness, God provided water in a miraculous way. God told Moses to
strike a large rock and water would flow out of it providing plenty of
water for everyone. Paul explains this rock in 1 Corinthians 10:4:
"And *they* did all drink the same spiritual drink: for they drank of that
spiritual Rock that followed them: and that Rock was Christ." Surely,
this spiritual drink is the Holy Spirit, for Jesus cried out in a loud
voice on the last day of the feast of Tabernacles:

If any man thirst, let him come unto me, and drink. He that
believeth on me, as the scripture hath said, out of his belly

66

shall flow rivers of living water. (But this spake he of the Spirit, which they that believe on him should receive: for the Holy Ghost was not yet given; because that Jesus was not yet glorified.) John 7:37-39

This rock and source of water followed the children of Israel through out their travels, but they did lightly esteem the rock (Deuteronomy 32:15). Let us not fall into the same apostasy. We should cherish Christ, our Rock, and the water of the Holy Spirit above all else.

Not only is the dove hidden in the clefts of the rock, but also in the secret places of the stairs. "For in the time of trouble he shall hide me in his pavilion: in the secret of his tabernacle shall he hide me; he shall set me up upon a rock" (Psalms 27:5). The tabernacle was where the presence of God dwelt upon the mercy seat, and the bread of His presence was renewed everyday (Exodus 25:22; 30). Jesus longs for us to come into the secret place of His presence. He longs to commune with us and bring us into a deeper understanding of His love. Our voice is sweet to Him as we praise Him through the power of the Holy Spirit. Satan would try everything in his power to distract us from finding that secret place. We must push past all the hindering forces and come into the presence of the Lover of our souls. "For in His presence, there is fulness of joy" (Psalms 16:11).

There is a secret stairway into the Lord's presence, and the angels of God are ascending and descending upon it to guide our prayers to God and to bring down the answers. (Genesis 28:12; Daniel 10:10-13)

My Prayer: Lord Jesus, I know how much You love to hear my worship and praises. Help me to realize how important my prayer life is to You. I hide myself in the safety of Your Rock. I long to dwell in the secret place of Your presence. I am determined to not allow Satan to hinder me. Each day I will press into the presence of the Lord through the power of the Holy Spirit.

THE LITTLE FOXES

Take us the foxes, the little foxes, that spoil the vines: for our vines have tender grapes. **Song of Solomon 2:15**

The New International Version states the verse this way: "Catch for us the foxes, the little foxes that ruin the vineyards, our vineyards that are in bloom." Foxes are very fond of young tender grapes. It is best to catch and destroy the foxes while the vineyards are still in bloom—just before the tender grapes are on the vine.

This scripture is a warning to catch and destroy anything, no matter how small it is, before it is capable of destroying our fruit. Our fruit is love, joy, peace, longsuffering, gentleness, goodness, faith, meekness and self-control (Galatians 5:22, 23). These attributes make the Bride attractive.

We used to sing a song in Sunday school that said, "the devil is a sly old fox, if I could catch him, I'd put him in a box." We had a lot of fun making the motions to this little song. The truth be told, Satan is like the sly fox. He comes in to our lives (our vineyard) like a thief while we are spiritually asleep or too busy to be aware of what is going on and steals our love, joy, or faith (John 10:10). It is not the big sins such as murder, robbery or even adultery that usually trip us up. It is the small foxes that give us so much trouble. Some examples of how Satan spoils our fruit are:

1. He steals our love and joy with anger, jealousy, covetousness, unforgiveness, and gossip.
2. He steals our peace with worry and quarrels.
3. He steals our longsuffering and gentleness with impatience and irritability.
4. He steals our faith with doubt.
5. He steals our meekness with pride and arrogance.
6. He steals our self-control with self-indulgence.

How are we to protect ourselves from the little foxes? We should be meditating on the Word of God day and night; thirsting after His loving kindness and tender mercies; looking for His power to protect us; and being present when the doors of His sanctuary (our church) are open (Psalms 63:1-11). We must abide in Christ and keep His commandments, as we can do nothing on our own. (John 15:5-11)

O God, You are my God; Early will I seek You;
My soul thirsts for You; My flesh longs for You
In a dry and thirsty land
Where there is no water.
So I have looked for You in the sanctuary,
To see Your power and Your glory.
Because Your lovingkindness is better than life,
My lips shall praise You.
Thus I will bless You while I live;
I will lift up my hands in Your name.
My soul shall be satisfied as with marrow and fatness,
And my mouth shall praise You with joyful lips.
When I remember You on my bed,
I meditate on You in the night watches.
Because You have been my help,
Therefore in the shadow of Your wings I will rejoice.
My soul follows close behind You;
Your right hand upholds me.
But those who seek my life, to destroy it,
Shall go into the lower parts of the earth.
They shall fall by the sword;
They shall be a portion for jackals. [*foxes*]
But the king shall rejoice in God;
Everyone who swears by Him shall glory;
But the mouth of those who speak lies shall be stopped.

Psalms 63, NKJV

My Prayer: Thank You, Lord, for Your Holy Spirit who ever stands on guard over my life to protect my tender fruit. Help me to recognize and catch the little foxes of jealousy, backbiting, malice, or anything Satan tries to bring into my spirit. May I always have a loving, humble, and contrite spirit. "Search me, O God, and know my heart: try me, and know my thoughts: And see if there be any wicked way in me, and lead me in the way everlasting" (Psalms 139:23-24).

FEEDING MY BELOVED

My beloved is mine, and I am his: he feedeth among the lilies.
Song of Solomon 2:16

Jesus last prayer expressed His great desire that we be in perfect union with Him just as He and the Father are in perfect unity. "The glory which You gave Me I have given them, that they may be one just as We are one: I in them, and You in Me; that they may be made perfect in one, and that the world may know that You have sent Me, and have loved them as You have loved Me" (John 17:22-23, NKJV).

Paul told of how Jesus sanctifies and cleanses the members of His church by His Word. He says that we are members of His body, of His flesh, and of His bones. Man and wife become one when they are joined in marriage; therefore, the man loves his wife as if she were part of his own body. He makes sure that her physical and emotional needs are supplied. He assures her with his words that she is loved, that she is beautiful, and that she is the dearest person on earth to him. When we become one with Jesus, He nourishes us and cherishes us. "My beloved is mine and I am His." This knowledge of oneness boggles my mind, and yet I know it is true. (Ephesians 5:26-30)

He nourishes us by feeding us His Word, and He, in turn, feeds among us. It says in our verse, "he feedeth among the lilies." He is the Lily of the valley, and we are the lilies that He feeds among.

Let us consider the lilies of the field as Jesus instructed us to do in Luke 12:27. Consider how they grow. The lily is grown from a dry, scaly bulb. The bulb lays dormant all winter long and appears to be dead. Then spring comes, and that dead bulb sends up shoots of new life, straight and tall. Finally a beautiful flower is born.

We, as Christ's lilies, are similar as we are a dried up—dead soul—until Jesus shines His sunlight upon us and pours out the spring rain of the Holy Spirit. Then we come to life as a beautiful child of God. The lily does not toil or spin; it does not accomplish the transformation by anything it does. We do not earn our salvation. for we are saved by grace and it is the gift of God. Nevertheless, we are changed into the image of "The Lily of the Valley' as we too, identify with Christ and crucify our fleshly desires.

Put to death, therefore, whatever belongs to your earthly nature: sexual immorality, impurity, lust, evil desires and greed, which is idolatry. .... You used to walk in these ways, in the life you once lived. But now you must rid yourselves of all such things as these: anger, rage, malice, slander, and filthy language from your lips. Do not lie to each other, *since you have taken off your old self with its practices and have put on the new self, which is being renewed in knowledge in the image of its Creator.* Colossians 3:5, 7-10, NIV

Paul said that his goal in life was to enter into the fellowship of Christ suffering and of His death and resurrection. "That I may know him, and the power of his resurrection, and the fellowship of his sufferings, being made conformable unto his death" (Philippians 3:10).

To recap this thought, we are lilies of the field because we are partakers of Christ death. We die to the old man and his earthly ways, and then we are resurrected in newness of life. Therefore, we take on the image of Christ and become one with Him.

Jesus engaged in a deep conversation with the Samaritan woman he met by the well. He led her to believe on Him as the Messiah – the Promised One. All this time His disciples were in town trying to buy some food. When they returned to Jesus and offered Him food, He said He was not hungry, for "I have meat to eat that ye know not of" (John 4:32). The disciples questioned this and Jesus went on to explain: "My meat is to do the will of him that sent me, and to finish his work" (John 4:34). In the next verses in that chapter, He tells the disciples to gather in the harvest. We are to actively witness and gather in the harvest of souls. This is Christ's will for the Church. To do His will is to feed Him until He is satisfied.

My Prayer: Father, make us one. I desire to be in complete union with You, for Your love is better than life. Help me to put to death the things in my life that are not pleasing to You. Cause me to see the lost souls that are ready to harvest. May I put Your will and purpose above my desires. I surely know that to do Your will is most pleasing to You.

NOTHING BETWEEN MY SOUL AND THE BELOVED

Until the day break, and the shadows flee away, turn, my beloved,
and be thou like a roe or a young hart upon the mountains of
Bether. Song of Solomon 2:17

When Jesus comes, the splendor of His light shines and the shadows flee away. Peter says: "We have also a more sure word of prophecy; whereunto ye do well that ye take heed, as unto a light that shineth in a dark place, until the day dawn, and the day star arise in your hearts" (2 Peter 1:19). We can trust the written Word of God even more than we can trust Peter's eyewitness report. If we allow ourselves to believe in this Word, Jesus, the Day Star, will arise in our hearts and bring the dawn.

Our blessed hope is when Jesus will come again for His Bride. This will be the dawn of our glorious homecoming. Until that day, we must keep working on this earth where we only see through the glass darkly (1 Corinthians 13:12). We call upon the Lord to turn to us and be like the swift, sure-footed deer. Do you remember in verse eight, of chapter two, how we said that Jesus is like the deer that skips upon the mountains—He being victorious over all our mountainous trials and temptations?

In the verse we are currently studying, there is a specific range of mountains named, **Bether. Bether** means division, separation, or mountains intersected with deep valleys. [1] The Bride calls out to the Beloved to turn back to her, for she does not want to be separated from Him. The only thing that can separate us from the Beloved is our sin. The Bride who is truly awaiting her Beloved to return is continually choosing to separate herself from the world. We are called to be consecrated, holy, and pure when Christ returns. Peter tells the church, "Ye are a chosen generation, a royal priesthood, an holy nation, a peculiar people; that ye should shew forth the praises of him who hath called you out of darkness into his marvellous light" (1 Peter 2:9). He has called us out of darkness into His light so that we might show the world His praises. We praise Him with our lives as we live in a holy manner before men.

We cannot love the world and love the Lord at the same time (1 John 2:15). We should not be double minded wanting to be like the world and still wanting to serve the Lord: "A double minded man is unstable in all his ways" (James 1:8). Our minds must be completely

72

set upon our love of the Master: "Thou shalt love the Lord thy God with all thy heart, and with all thy soul, and with all thy mind" (Matthew 22:37).

My Prayer: I feel the warmth of Your light shining within my heart. You have opened my eyes so that I can understand Your love for me. Please shine Your light of conviction on any area of my life that needs to be cleansed. I do not want anything to come between You and me. I am looking forward to that Day when You will break through the clouds and the shadows of this life will flee away forever.

[1] From Fausset's Bible Dictionary, Electronic Database Copyright (c) 1998 by Biblesoft

CHAPTER 3

THERE IS NO REST

By night on my bed I sought him whom my soul loveth: I sought him, but I found him not. **Song of Solomon 3:1**

The Bride enters into a night season—perhaps it is a time of trial, or some hurtful situation, or a temptation that has overcome her. In the darkness, we find her troubled. She is not resting on *our* bed as noted in chapter one, verse sixteen. She is tossing and turning on *my* bed. This leads me to believe that she is trying to rely on her own strength instead of resting in the Lord.

Peter tried to go through a very dark time in his life using his own strength. Jesus was telling his disciples at the Last Supper that they would be offended, stumble, or fall away that very night. Peter confidently declared, "Even if *all* fall away, I will not" (Mark 14:29, NIV). Peter told the Lord that he would be willing to die for Him. Jesus replied, "Simon, Simon, behold, Satan hath desired to have you, that he may sift you as wheat: But I have prayed for thee, that thy faith fail not: and when thou art converted, strengthen thy brethren" (Luke 22:31-32). Jesus went on to tell Peter that he would disown Jesus three times, that very night, before the rooster crowed two times (Mark 14:30). This prophecy did come to pass, and Peter went out from the presence of the Lord and wept bitterly.

Early in our Christian walk, we know that we are weak and we must rely on Jesus. After we have been walking with Jesus for a while, we may become self-confident. We know how to talk the talk and go through the motions as if we are close to the Beloved; however, in reality we have neglected our prayer life, our study of God's Word, and our communion with Him. Paul says, "Wherefore let him that thinketh he standeth take heed lest he fall" (1 Corinthians 10:12). Many saints have stumbled and fallen into temptation during the night seasons.

It may seem like He does not hear us when we turn back and seek Him. We may complain like the Shulamite maiden did, "I sought him, but I found him not." This may be a test to see if we are sincere in our repentance. The lesson learned is that we cannot live the Christian life in our own strength.

David felt like the Lord was angry with him. He cried out to the Lord with weeping. During a time of prosperity, he had declared self-confidently that he would not be moved. He thought the Lord had hidden His face or removed His blessing. We are thankful that God does not stay angry with us a long time, and He brings joy in the morning.

> Sing praise to the LORD, You saints of His,
> And give thanks at the remembrance of His holy name.
> For His anger is but for a moment,
> His favor is for life;
> Weeping may endure for a night,
> But joy comes in the morning.
>
> Now in my prosperity I said,
> "I shall never be moved."
> LORD, by Your favor You have made my mountain stand strong;
> You hid Your face, and I was troubled.
>
> I cried out to You, O LORD;
> And to the LORD I made supplication: ...
> Hear, O LORD, and have mercy on me;
> LORD, be my helper!"
>
> You have turned for me my mourning into dancing;
> You have put off my sackcloth and clothed me with gladness,
> To the end that my glory may sing praise to You and not be silent.
> O LORD my God, I will give thanks to You forever.
>   Psalms 30:4-8, 10-12, NKJV

We leave our Bride still searching for her Beloved in this verse. She is troubled and confused—read on to see what happens.

My Prayer: Lord, help me not to be satisfied with past blessings that I have experienced. Satan loves to make me think that I am strong, and that I do not need to rely on You for everything. This is when I have to be alert to Satan's devices. My help comes from You alone. When I go through the night seasons, help me to hold on to You with all my might.

SEARCHING IN ALL THE WRONG PLACES

I will rise now, and go about the city in the streets, and in the broad ways I will seek him whom my soul loveth: I sought him, but I found him not. **Song of Solomon 3:2**

Realizing that the sweet communion she had enjoyed was broken, she decides to rise up, go out, and search for her love. The only problem is that she moves in the wrong direction. She begins her search in the city, the street, and the broad way.

Cities are known for their sinfulness. Cain was the first man to build a city. He had miserably failed the Lord. He was stubborn and did not want to submit to God's plan—he became the first murderer (Genesis 4:1-17). Our Bride goes into a sinful place, with all kinds of different philosophies, to find her love.

We cannot expect to find the presence of the Lord by returning to the beggarly elements of the world. Paul reproved the Galatians for trying to go back to their old system of worship: "But now, after that ye have known God, or rather are known of God, how turn ye again to the weak and beggarly elements, whereunto ye desire again to be in bondage?" (Galatians 4:9) We will not find peace of mind when we go back to our old ways or sinful friends.

Jesus said, "Broad is the way, that leadeth to destruction, and many there be which go in there at" (Matthew 7:13). It does not take any effort to drift down the broad way. The end of that way is eternal damnation. We do not want to be sidetracked from the straight and narrow way that leads to everlasting life. It is possible to become cold in our spirit and become wayward—not putting the love of the Lord as our highest priority.

Many who are troubled and searching will try to find help through worldly means such as doctors, psychiatrists, relatives, or even friends. These fine people may direct us in the right way if they base their diagnosis on Christian values, but ultimately, only Jesus will satisfy the soul. The Lord will not be found when we seek Him in the wrong places. The love of our spouse, family, and friends is a wonderful thing, but our greatest love is Jesus. We must not lean upon our own understanding or the wisdom of this world.

Solomon, in all of his wisdom wrote, "Trust in the LORD with all thine heart; and lean not unto thine own understanding. In all thy ways acknowledge him, and he shall direct thy paths" (Proverbs 3:5-6). When it feels like we have lost our way and lost the Lord, we need to come back to the basics, and put our trust in the Lord who will direct our paths.

My Prayer: Lord, help me to stay true to You and not to put my trust in the world's system. Help me not to take the lazy, broad way. Satan whispers, "You're too tired to pray", or "You're too tired to go to God's house." When I listen to his bidding, I start looking for love in all the wrong places. I will only find love and peace as I seek You in prayer, in Your Word, and in Your house.

FALSE WATCHMEN

The watchmen that go about the city found me: to whom I said, Saw ye him whom my soul loveth? Song of Solomon 3:3

The watchmen of the city (place of sinfulness) find the Bride as she is seeking for her Beloved. These watchmen are not concerned about her spiritual condition. They just want to get rid of her. They are self-centered, and their minds are on this world. A watchman is supposed to warn the city of danger, but remember, this city is a sinful place that is located on the broad way. Later on in this book, we will find the same watchmen brutally attack her.

Reading Isaiah 21:11, 12, we find a clue concerning the false watchmen [*italics words are my own*]:

> He [*referring to God*] calleth to me out of Seir [*the country of Edom or the world*], Watchman, what of the night? [*are you concerned about the darkness of the world?*] Watchman, what of the night? The watchman said, the morning cometh, and also the night [*in other words, all things continue*]: if ye will inquire, then inquire." [*The Bride's inquiry was 'have ye seen the one my soul loveth?'*]

The watchmen portrayed here do not care about the sin that is around them. Their attitude is "what will be, will be." So what if the morning is coming. Day follows night, night follows day, just as they always have in the past. It reminds me of the scripture in 2 Peter 3:9.10:

> The Lord is not slack concerning his promise, as some men count slackness; but is longsuffering to us-ward, not willing that any should perish, but that all should come to repentance. But the day of the Lord will come as a thief in the night.

The day of the Lord—the day He comes for His Bride—will come when the watchmen of this world are nonchalantly going about business as usual.

They are similar to the watchmen referred to in Isaiah 56:10-12 who were blind, drunken, and lacked understanding. They sought their own gain. Peter's description of the false prophet is very similar to this scripture in that he says the false prophets are like brute beast;

80

they speak evil of things they don't understand; they seek pleasure even during the day time hours; they are feasting; they commit adultery; they have forsaken the right way; they are greedy (2 Peter 2:1-3, 12-22). We must beware of the false prophets of this world who do not have our welfare in mind. They will only lead us down the road to destruction. They are watchmen of the night and are blind leaders of the blind. They will never be able to answer our question as to the whereabouts of our true love. Jesus will only be found as we turn back to the true way.

Let us follow our Bride in the next verse and see how she will find her love!

My Prayer: Lord, please help me to distinguish Your voice from the voice of a false shepherd. I thank You that You have clearly listed the marks of the false watchman or prophet in Your Word. Open my eyes of understanding that I will not be blind to Satan's lies. Oh Jesus, I cling to You. I never want to let You go.

FIRST LOVE

It was but a little that I passed from them, but I found him whom my soul loveth: I held him, and would not let him go, until I had brought him into my mother's house, and into the chamber of her that conceived me. **Song of Solomon 3:4**

When the Bride leaves the city, the broad way, and the false watchmen, she quickly finds her lover. Jesus is not far off or difficult to find when we seek Him with all of our hearts in the correct places.

Mary and Joseph thought they had lost Jesus when He was a lad of twelve years old. They frantically looked for Him among the relatives and friends. They sought for Him along the roadside and in the camps of other pilgrims. They finally backtracked all their steps and found Him in the temple. He was not lost—He had purposely stayed at the temple because He was about His Father's business. (Luke 2:41-52)

Jesus will be found in the same place today. He is in the Father's house, making intercession for us (Romans 8:34). He is as near as the whisper of His name. It is not Jesus who is lost, but we, His wayward children.

When the Bride found the One her soul loved, she clung to Him and would not let Him go. Looking back to chapter two and verse six, He is holding her, but now she is holding on to Him. When we have been disobedient, we have to return. We are the ones who have to prove our love to the Lord.

We spoke of Peter's denial that terrible night of Jesus' trial. Jesus asked Peter to proclaim his love for the Lord three times, just as Peter had denied the Lord three times. Jesus asked, "lovest thou me?" Peter answered, "Lord you know that I love you." Peter was offended the third time Jesus asked the question. Although the Lord knows all things, He still wants to hear us say the words. Even more than just hearing us say the words of love, He wants to see our love by our actions. He told Peter to feed His lambs and His sheep. Peter went on to be an under-shepherd of Jesus Christ, winning souls and nurturing those who would accept the message. (John 21:15-17; 1 Peter 5:1-4)

Please observe where the Bride takes her Love as she holds onto Him tightly. She takes Him to her mother's house and into the very chamber where she was conceived. As we stated earlier, our mother is the New Jerusalem— the city of the living God. It is the true church, an innumerable company of angels, and the general assembly of the people whose names are written in heaven. (Hebrews 12:22, 23; Galatians 4:26) We are to return to our first love, to the place where we were conceived, where we were born into the kingdom of God. As in the rebuke given to the church of Ephesus, we must return to our first love, repent, and do the first works again (Revelation 2:4-5).

Do you remember how in love with Jesus you were when you first came to know Him? Do you remember how you felt when He released you from the bondage of sin and habits? Do you remember how you hungered for His Word? Do you remember how you could not wait for the doors of the church to open so you could once again fellowship with mature Christians who would encourage and pray with you? Do you remember how the time just seemed to fly by while you were in His presence? Return to that first love. Do those first works again.

My Prayer: I am so glad I found You, even though—it was I who was lost. Help me to stay so totally in love with You that I will not let You go. Thank You, Father, for Your Holy Spirit who keeps me from falling—but if I fall—I have an advocate, Jesus Christ, my Lord.

DO NOT STIR UP

I charge you, O ye daughters of Jerusalem, by the roes, and by the hinds of the field, that ye stir not up, nor awake my love, till he please. **Song of Solomon 3:5**

This is the second time the Bride issues this charge to the daughters of Jerusalem. The first time is found in chapter two, verse seven. The setting is a little different this time, as the Bride has just brought her Beloved into the chambers of her mother's house. He is resting there after their awesome reunion. She does not want anything to disturb His rest.

The Bride gives this solemn order "by the roes, and by the hinds of the field." The roes and hinds of the field could be referring to the warrior angels. The scriptures refer to the mighty warriors of David as swift roes upon the mountains. More men joined David everyday until his army became like the "hosts of God" (1 Chronicles 12:8-22). The army or hosts of God would most likely refer to the hosts of heavenly angels. The angels of heaven are called "the hosts of God" in Genesis 32:2, Joshua 5:14, and Psalms 148:2. Jesus said we are to pray, "Thy will be done in earth, as it is in heaven" (Matthew 6:10). The angel hosts perform the Father's will without hesitation; therefore, the Church prays that we will perform His will in the same manner.

Her admonition is not to stir up or awake. In other words, "Don't cause trouble." As the body of Christ, we are to be at peace and rest with each other. When we stir up strife and contention, it is as if we are biting ourselves. Paul states in Galatians 5:15, "But if ye bite and devour one another, take heed that ye be not consumed one of another." I like the way the Living Bible interprets this verse: "But if instead of showing love among yourselves you are always critical and catty, watch out! Beware of ruining each other." We can cause so much trouble within the body by refusing to love each other and tearing each other apart. Remember we are all part of the same body. When you are critical or cause trouble for another member of the body, you are being critical of yourself. Jesus said, "Judge not, that ye be not judged" (Matthew 7:1). When we are critical and disruptive, we are actually setting ourselves up as superior to others.

At the end time, the Lord of the harvest will send His mighty angels (the host of heaven) to harvest the field. They will be in charge of separating the wheat (the children of the kingdom) from the tares

84

(children of Satan). We, as the Church, are not to stir up ourselves to make it our business to separate those who are false, lest we take out some of the good wheat. (Matthew 13:37-40)

What an important lesson! I need to listen and learn. It is not my place to judge. I will let the Lord be the judge, for He alone knows the heart of man. It is my place to love and forgive. I, myself, could become a castaway because of a judgmental spirit (1 Corinthians 9:27). Although there may be other ways to interpret this passage, these are the thoughts the Holy Spirit gave me while I studied it at this time. We understand that "no scripture is of private interpretation" (2 Peter 1:20).

My Prayer: Lord, thank You for Your many truths. Please help me not to set myself up as judge. I trust in You to take care of Your Church. May I never be the one to cause trouble in the body of Christ. Just help me, Lord, to be faithful in the work You have called me to do.

WHO'S COMING UP THE ROAD?

Who is this that cometh out of the wilderness like pillars of smoke, perfumed with myrrh and frankincense, with all powders of the merchant? Song of Solomon 3:6

Who is this? First, this mysterious person is coming out of the wilderness. Second, there are pillars of smoke masking the arrival. Third, there is the strong perfumed scent of myrrh, frankincense, and other spices that the merchants sell.

Who is he that is coming out of the wilderness? John the Baptist fulfilled the Old Testament prophecy concerning one who would prepare the world for Jesus' first coming (John 1:27).

> The voice of him that crieth in the wilderness, Prepare ye the way of the LORD, make straight in the desert a highway for our God. Every valley shall be exalted, and every mountain and hill shall be made low: and the crooked shall be made straight, and the rough places plain: And the glory of the LORD shall be revealed, and all flesh shall see it together: for the mouth of the LORD hath spoken it.   Isaiah 40:3-5

When Jesus made His entrance at the River of Jordan where John the Baptist was preaching, John proclaimed to the crowd, "Behold the Lamb of God" (John 1:29, 36). Immediately after being baptized by John, Jesus was led by the Holy Spirit into the wilderness. He was being prepared for His ministry by a time of prayer, fasting, and testing. Having overcome the Devil's temptations, Jesus came out of the wilderness in the power and anointing of the Holy Spirit (Luke 4:14). As Isaiah prophesied, the glory of the Lord was revealed to all flesh as ***Jesus came out of the wilderness*** and began His earthly ministry.

Who is he that comes out of the wilderness sending up pillars of smoke? There are many references to smoke when the glory of the Lord is revealed to men. Isaiah records that he saw the Lord high and lifted up in the temple. "And the posts of the door moved at the voice of him that cried, and the house was filled with smoke" (Isaiah 6:1-4). Sinai was covered with smoke as God spoke to Moses (Exodus 20:18). The incense used in the tabernacle smoked when it was put into the fire (Leviticus 16:13). One of the great signs of the last day is found in Joel 2:30: "And I will shew wonders in the heavens and in the earth, blood, and fire, and *pillars of smoke*." Therefore, we can see that smoke speaks to us of the presence of the Lord—His power and glory. Smoke is produced when myrrh and frankincense are ignited with fire.

The wise men brought gold, frankincense, and myrrh as gifts for the baby Jesus. Many scholars have believed, throughout the centuries, that these gifts represent facets of Jesus' ministry and mission. The gold represents his deity as King of kings; frankincense was burned in the sanctuary and represents Him as our High Priest; myrrh was used for embalming and represents His atoning death. These are the very spices that the women used to wrap Jesus' body in after the crucifixion. Not only did Jesus come out of the wilderness victorious, but He came forth from the grave victorious!

At the end of our verse, we see the short phrase, "with all powders of the merchant." Jesus left heaven and came into our world to purchase His Bride. The price was not silver or gold, but His precious blood (1 Peter 1:18, 19). Jesus is the merchant who sold everything He had for the pearl of great price (*the church*) in Matthew 13:45.

Because Jesus has come up out of the wilderness—we also have the power to overcome Satan's temptations and the various trials that would cause us to stumble. Because Jesus bought us with the price of His precious blood—we are cleansed and made holy, and we belong to the King of kings. Because Jesus is our High Priest—we are allowed to come into the most holy place with our incense of prayer and praise.

We wait with great expectation as our King comes up out of the wilderness surrounded with great pillars of smoke and power. We long for His presence in our daily lives here and now, but we also look forward to the day when we will live eternally in the presence of our Almighty God.

Prayer: Thank You, Lord, for the victory You won for me by Your life and death. I know You were tempted in all points, just as I am tempted, yet You came through with no sin by the power of the Holy Spirit. Your sweet Holy Spirit guides me through the wilderness. I long to be surrounded by Your presence daily.

ANGELS WATCH OVER ME

Behold his bed, which is Solomon's; threescore valiant men are about it, of the valiant of Israel. They all hold swords, being expert in war: every man hath his sword upon his thigh because of fear in the night. Song of Solomon 3:7-8

As the mystery person is revealed, we behold that it is Solomon. The scripture calls us to look upon him as he reclines on a portable couch. He is at ease and resting. We understand from these verses that we are speaking of King Jesus who is greater than Solomon.

Jesus won the battle over Satan, his archenemy, when He cried out, "it is finished", from the cross (John 19:30). When Jesus died on the cross, He fulfilled the Messianic prophecy found in Genesis 3:15. Satan bruised the heel of Jesus, but Jesus dealt a deadly wound to Satan's head. Jesus has allowed Satan a little more time to use his devices to sway humanity to his evil ways. However, Satan has no power over the blood-bought child of God. His days are numbered (Revelation 20:10).

Jesus is now at rest, seated at the Father's right hand surrounded by the angelic hosts. Paul prays that the Ephesians would understand the great power that is the believer's inheritance, as the result of Jesus' sacrifice.

And what is the exceeding greatness of his power to usward who believe, according to the working of his mighty power, which he wrought in Christ, when he raised him from the dead, and *set him at his own right hand* in the heavenly places, far *above all principality, and power, and might, and dominion*, and every name that is named, not only in this world, but also in that which is to come: And *hath put all things under his feet*, and gave him to be the head over all things to the church, which is his body, the fulness of him that filleth all in all. Ephesians 1:19-23

Please note that Jesus is sitting down. He is far above any other power of this earth (Satan). All enemies are under His feet.

Jesus is the captain of the Lord of hosts. This host is the army of God whose soldiers are the angels of heaven. (Genesis 32:2; Joshua 5:14; Psalms 148:2) Just as the expert bodyguards protected Solomon's bed of rest, a great and mighty angelic force surrounds our King. They are poised and ready to fight any scrimmage that Satan might instigate. Satan knows that he would surely lose such a battle, so he turns his attacks toward the Body of Christ that is still on this earth.

Angels surrounded Jesus when He walked among humanity. The angels announced His birth to the shepherds outside of Bethlehem (Luke 2:8-15). Angels ministered to Jesus after His forty day fast, and His victory over Satan's temptations (Matthew 4:11). Jesus told Peter to put his sword away because if He needed any defense, He could pray and the Father would send twelve legions (thousands) of angels to come to His aid (Matthew 26:53).

The Scripture states in Hebrews 1:13,14 that the angels are sent to be ministering spirits to do service for those who have inherited salvation (that is you and me). "The angel of the LORD encamps all around those who fear Him, and delivers them" (Psalms 34:7, NKJV).

Remember the account of Elisha's worried servant as the Syrian army surrounded the city? The young servant thought they would never be able to survive such an attack. Elisha told his servant, "Do not fear, for those who are with us are more than those who are with them." Elisha prayed and asked the Lord to open the servant's eyes. Lo and behold, the Lord's army of angels had surrounded them with a protective shield of horses and chariots of fire. (2 Kings 6:13-18)

We can be assured that the God of the Old Testament is still the God and protector of the New Testament believer. Beloved, "greater is he that is in you, than he that is in the world" (1 John 4:4). I am sure that if our physical eyes were opened to the spirit world, we would see the angels around us. They are protecting us and hindering the work of Satan.

My Prayer: Jesus, it thrills my soul to know that You are sitting at the Father's right hand. By faith, I accept the ministering spirits that You send to me. I have no fear of the kingdom of darkness because I walk in the light of Your power and glory.

JUST A HUMBLE PIECE OF WOOD

King Solomon made himself a chariot of the wood of Lebanon.
Song of Solomon 3:9

King Solomon, again a type of Christ, has made himself a chariot (or carriage) of cedar wood. The chariot represents a means of transportation. Jesus was transported from the side of His Father into this world by the means of a human body. "And the Word was made flesh, and dwelt among us, (and we beheld his glory, the glory as of the only begotten of the Father,) full of grace and truth" (John 1:14).

Wood is a temporary substance, as it is easily destroyed. God came in a body of flesh that could be put to death in order to be offered up as a sacrifice for our sins. "Wherefore when he cometh into the world, he saith, Sacrifice and offering thou wouldest not, but *a body hast thou prepared me*" (Hebrews 10:5). A lowly virgin girl of Nazareth birthed Jesus.

The wood that made up the family tree of David had all but been completely cut off. Out of the decaying tree stump, a tender branch came forth. Observe this prophecy spoken by Isaiah.

There shall come forth a Rod from the stem of Jesse,
And a Branch shall grow out of his roots.
The Spirit of the LORD shall rest upon Him,
The Spirit of wisdom and understanding,
The Spirit of counsel and might,
The Spirit of knowledge and of the fear of the LORD.
Isaiah 11:1-2, NKJV

Out of such humble circumstances, came Jesus Christ—the Branch. The sevenfold Spirit of God rested upon Him. The spirit of anointing, wisdom, understanding, counsel, might, knowledge, and the fear of the Lord. [1] The Rod stood for the authority of the King.

The Holy Spirit is a witness to the death of God's own Son, for he raised Jesus from the dead. Jesus came out of the grave with a glorious body that was incorruptible and would never see death again. We have such a blessed hope because of Jesus' death and resurrection. "But if the Spirit of him that raised up Jesus from the dead dwell in you, he that raised up Christ from the dead shall also quicken your mortal bodies by his Spirit that dwelleth in you" (Romans 8:11-12).

90

It is out of our humbleness that Jesus is glorified. I should not despise humble beginnings. As long as I am walking in the Spirit of God and have His anointing—no work is too small. Jesus called fishermen, tax collectors, and sinners to continue His work on earth. Out of these humble and uneducated men, He has built a church which the gates of hell cannot prevail against (Matthew 16:18). This life is fleeting and only what is done for Christ will stand the test.

My Prayer: Thank You, Father God, for sending Your only begotten Son into this world. I am so glad that Jesus was willing to take upon Himself humble flesh, so He could become the spotless sacrifice for my sin. Thank You for taking my judgment and for justifying me by rising from the dead. Oh, that I would be filled with the same Spirit that raised You from the dead. I desire to be able to speak and work under the anointing of Your Holy Spirit.

---

[1] *"the fear of the Lord" does not mean that Jesus was afraid of God. It means that He respected His Father with reverence and obedience. Isaiah 11:3 goes on to say that He would have a quick understanding of the fear of the Lord. We see that even when Jesus was a boy of 12 years old, His understanding of the scriptures and God surprised the religious teachers in the temple. (Luke 2:46-48)*

SURROUNDED BY LOVE

He made the pillars thereof of silver, the bottom thereof of gold, the covering of it of purple, the midst thereof being paved with love, for the daughters of Jerusalem. Song of Solomon 3:10

This verse is a continuation of the description of Solomon's chariot. We have seen that it is a picture of Jesus as our King. The wood signifies His taking on flesh and bone and being made of a woman. This verse gives us more detail about the divine nature that Christ embodied. He was Emmanuel—God with us (Matthew 1:23). Let us look at the other details of this fine means of transportation that Solomon built for himself, and see how they apply to our King.

Keep in mind that Solomon was very wealthy, and this was probably the most eloquent mode of transportation of his time. He is not just taking an afternoon spin—he is in his wedding procession. The chariot was beautiful for the eye to behold, and it was only used for the king and his bride. As we look at each detail of construction, we see a remarkable parallel to the pattern of the tabernacle. This is not surprising because the pattern of the tabernacle, given to Moses, was also a picture of Jesus.

The pillars, which supported the overhead covering, were made of silver. Silver speaks to us of redemption and purity. During the Old Testament order, there were times when redemption was necessary, and the price was usually paid in silver. (Exodus 13:2, 3; Numbers 18:16; Leviticus 25:47-55) Silver is also an emblem of His purity: "The words of the LORD are pure words: as silver tried in a furnace of earth, purified seven times" (Psalms 12:6).

Jesus came in the human body that God had prepared for Him for the purpose of being the pure and perfect sacrifice. This sacrifice was made in order to redeem mankind from their sins. "For you know that it was not with perishable things such as silver or gold that you were redeemed from the empty way of life handed down to you from your forefathers, but with the precious blood of Christ, a lamb without blemish or defect" (1 Peter 1:17-19, NIV).

The bottom of the bed or seat is made of gold. Gold always reminds us of the purest and most costly of metals. It stands for the one and only true God. God instructed Moses to build the Ark of the Covenant. The body of the Ark was built of acacia wood, which was then overlaid with gold. The atonement cover, or the mercy seat, was to be made of one piece of pure gold. The Ark was adorned with two cherubim who were facing each other. Their wings were outstretched over the cover and touching each other. It was on this mercy seat that the Lord's presence and glory came down, and God accepted the atonement for sin (Exodus 25:8-22). This is again a picture of our Lord Jesus as He came in the flesh (wood) and was all man; nevertheless, He was all divine (gold). The divine Son of God is able to forgive sin.

The covering or curtains of Solomon's chariot were made of purple fabric, and the pillars of silver supported them. It was the custom for kings to wear purple as it was a very rich and expensive fabric (Judges 8:26). The Roman soldiers put a purple robe on Jesus while mocking Him as "King of the Jews" (Mark 15:17-20). It is actually a reddish purple that speaks to us of the blood of Christ.

The veil of the tabernacle divided the Holy Place from the Most Holy Place. It was also supported by pillars of silver (Exodus 26:31-34). This veil was really a heavy tapestry made of fine linen and woven in blue, *purple*, and scarlet yarn. The veil was literally torn in two from the top to the bottom when Jesus finished His work on the cross (Matthew 27:51). The author of Hebrews writes that the significance of this veil is that it stood for the flesh of our Lord Jesus Christ: "Having therefore, brethren, boldness to enter into the holiest by the *blood of Jesus*, by a new and living way, which he hath consecrated for us, *through the veil, that is to say, his flesh*" (Hebrews 10:19-20). The blood of Jesus is our covering, which gives us access into the Most Holy Place where the glory of the Lord dwells. We come into this awesome place only because Jesus' flesh was torn for us.

The greatest message of this passage in the Song of Solomon is that the interior is inlaid or paved with LOVE!

In this was manifested the love of God toward us, because that God sent his only begotten Son into the world, that we might live through him. Herein is love, not that we loved God, but that he loved us, and sent his Son to be the propitiation for our sins.   1 John 4:9-10

Satan has no power to stop this chariot of God, for it is God who is protecting the Bride of Christ. There are angels around her to protect, fight, and minister to her. She is surrounded by God's love. God has delivered her out of bondage, redeemed her with the blood of Christ, and is taking her to the kingdom of His Son. "He has delivered us from the power of darkness and *conveyed* us into the kingdom of the Son of His love, in whom we have redemption through His blood, the forgiveness of sins" (Colossians 1:13-15, NKJV). All of this was done because He loves us so much.

The church is transported in this beautiful carriage of grace and love. She goes forth spreading the message of love throughout the world. We, the daughters of the New Jerusalem, have a new song of praise. "Thou art worthy to take the book, and to open the seals thereof: for thou wast slain, and hast redeemed us to God by thy blood out of every kindred, and tongue, and people, and nation; and hast made us unto our God kings and priests: and we shall reign on the earth" (Revelation 5:9-10).

My Prayer: Lord, You have redeemed me, and I trust You to take me all the way to glory. You are carrying me through this old world, which is truly a wilderness. I do not fear the night, and I do not fear Satan because I am surrounded by Your love. Help me to spread this message of love far and wide to every corner of this earth.

A CROWN OF JOY

Go forth, O ye daughters of Zion, and behold King Solomon with the crown wherewith his mother crowned him in the day of his espousals, and in the day of the gladness of his heart.
Song of Solomon 3:11

"Go forth, O ye daughters of Zion." We have established in prior verses that the daughters of Jerusalem refer to the members of the Church in general. Zion is a hill within the city of Jerusalem. It was a fortress and stronghold of the Jebusites when King David conquered it (1 Chronicles 11:4, 5). Later on in history, people recognized the district of Zion to include the Temple Mount and often times used the name Zion interchangeably with Jerusalem as the name of the city. [1]

We, as the daughters of Zion, are told in this verse to *go forth*, so we can look upon the crown with which His *mother crowned Him*. Although Solomon, no doubt, had a magnificent crown of gold and jewels, our Savior wore a crown of thorns. His *mother*, Mary, portraying the human side of Jesus, gave Him His fleshly body. His Father, the Creator of all, gave to Him of His Spirit and His divine nature.

Christ has espoused Himself to all who will believe in His vicarious death. The day of His engagement to the Church was the day of His crucifixion. Although there was sadness on that day, His heart was full of gladness because He had paid the price for His glorious Bride. He became my substitute by taking my sins and my pain, thereby, making it possible for me to partake of His divine nature (2 Peter 1:4).

Even the thief hanging on the cross next to Jesus believed that Jesus was the King as he pleaded, "Lord, remember me when thou comest into thy kingdom." Jesus answered this request of faith with words of assurance and hope, "Today shalt thou be with me in paradise" (Luke 23:42, 43). I am sure Jesus experienced joy in that moment even though His body was racked with pain. Jesus says, "There is joy in the presence of the angels of God over one sinner that repenteth" (Luke 15:10).

God has replaced His Son's crown of suffering with a crown of glory and honor:

But we see Jesus, who was made a little lower than the angels for the suffering of death, *crowned with glory and honour*; that he by the grace of God should taste death for every man. For it became him, for whom are all things, and by whom are all things, in bringing many sons unto glory, to make the captain of their salvation perfect through sufferings.

Hebrews 2:9-11

The Lord will reign from Mount Zion. It is situated in Jerusalem and called the mountain of His holiness. "Beautiful for situation, the joy of the whole earth, is mount Zion, on the sides of the north, the city of the great King" (Psalms 48:2). We, as the redeemed of the Lord, will return to Zion with great joy: "Therefore the redeemed of the LORD shall return, and come with singing unto Zion; and everlasting joy shall be upon their head: they shall obtain gladness and joy; and sorrow and mourning shall flee away" (Isaiah 51:11). This scripture reminds me of the description of the New Jerusalem in Revelation:

And I John saw the holy city, *New Jerusalem*, coming down from God out of heaven, prepared as a bride adorned for her husband. And I heard a great voice out of heaven saying, Behold, the tabernacle of God is with men, and he will dwell with them, and they shall be his people, and God himself shall be with them, and be their God. And God shall wipe away all tears from their eyes; and there shall be no more death, neither sorrow, nor crying, neither shall there be any more pain: for the former things are passed away.   Revelation 21:2-5

What a glorious day that will be when Jesus is crowned King, and we will be in His presence. There will be no more tears or sadness, for all will be joy and gladness.

My Prayer: Help me, Lord, to ever behold You and to contemplate on how much You suffered for me. Thank You for using a mere woman (Mary) in order to become a man of flesh and blood. I rejoice because I am espoused to You. I await the joy of our marriage and the grand supper You will prepare for Your Bride.

[1] Nelson's New Illustrated Bible Dictionary, General Editor, Ronald F Youngblood, Nelson Publishing, Copyright 1995

CHAPTER 4

HERE COMES THE BRIDE

EYES AND HAIR

Behold, thou art fair, my love; behold, thou art fair; thou hast doves' eyes within thy locks: thy hair is as a flock of goats, that appear from mount Gilead. Song of Solomon 4:1

Jesus, our King and Bridegroom, begins His description of the Bride—His Church—His espoused one—His very own body for whom He has died. "Behold", or in other words, "take a close look at yourself, how beautiful you are to me." The Bride is the fair one because she reflects the fairness and beauty of Jesus. "But we all, with unveiled face, beholding as in a mirror the glory of the Lord, ***are being transformed into the same image*** from glory to glory, just as by the Spirit of the Lord" (2 Corinthians 3:17, 18, NKJV). There are seven features of beauty listed in the fourth chapter of the Song of Solomon. Seven is significant as it is the number of perfection. The Spirit of the Lord is perfecting the Bride. The seven features are eyes, hair, teeth, lips and speech, temples, neck, and breasts.

Many of us come to the Lord with a lot of negative thoughts about ourselves. We feel very unworthy and inferior. Nevertheless, when Jesus pours out His mercy and love upon us, we become beautiful. Even in our natural love affairs, there is a change in appearance many times. It seems that the person who is loved just sparkles. There is a saying that, "all brides are beautiful." How beautiful we feel when we realize that "Jesus loves me!"

The first thing a lover notices is the eyes. Jesus looks into the eyes of His Bride and compares them with dove's eyes. Dove's eyes speak of gentleness, and they are eyes that are filled with the Holy Spirit. The Bride's eyes are fixed on only one thing—Jesus, her lover.

Her hair is like a flock of goats that appear on Mount Gilead. The goats in this area of the East have hair that resembles fine silk thread. When looking at the hillside from a distance, it would appear to be long, black, wavy hair. [1] The hair reveals the consecration and submission of the Bride.

God made provision for a man or woman who desired to make a special promise to the Lord for a specific lapse of time and/or a specific purpose. He or she would abstain from wine; allow their hair to grow and not cut it; they were not to come near a dead body.

(Numbers 6:1-9) This special sign of separation and consecration was called a Nazarite vow.

Samson was called to be dedicated as a Nazarite from birth. When Delilah cut off Samson's hair, it was a sign of broken dedication to the Lord—he lost his God given strength. (Judges 13:5; Judges 16:17, 18) As the Bride of Christ, we too are called to be a holy, consecrated, and a peculiar people (1 Peter 2:9). That does not mean that we all have to grow long hair, as prescribed in the Law, but there is a consecration of the heart and mind. It takes a zealous person who is sold out to Jesus—heart, soul, and mind—to be set apart from the world (Titus 2:14).

Daniel was just such a person. Daniel and his companions found themselves captives in a foreign land. They were singled out because they were intelligent, handsome, and descendants of Judah's royal family. It went against all their beliefs when they were served food and drink from King Nebuchadnezzar's table. They took a stand and did not deny their consecration to the Lord. Daniel asked the eunuch in charge to feed them only vegetables and water for ten days. "At the end of ten days their *countenances appeared fairer* and fatter in flesh than all the children which did eat the portion of the king's meat" (Daniel 1:15).

When we love the Lord with all our hearts and commit ourselves totally to Him, the Lord is pleased, and He views us as the fairest of them all. We may look strange to other people, but that does not matter. What matters is how I look to my Lord. Does He see loving, gentle eyes that only look to Him? Does He see flowing hair that shows my separation from the world, my dedication to Him, and my love for Him alone? Does He see Himself reflected in my countenance, my actions, and my words?

My Prayer: Oh Lord, I bask in Your love and mercy. I know You will not let me fall as I keep my eyes fixed on You. Help me to live in total surrender and dedication to You.

---

[1] From Jamieson, Fausset, and Brown Commentary, Electronic Database. Copyright (c) 1997 by Biblesoft

PERFECT SET OF TEETH

Thy teeth are like a flock of sheep that are even shorn, which came up from the washing; whereof every one bear twins, and none is barren among them. Song of Solomon 4:2

The third feature of the Bride, which the Bridegroom adores, is her teeth. He compares them to, "a flock of sheep just shorn, coming up from the washing. Each has its twin; not one of them is alone" (Song of Solomon 4:2, NIV). Picture the Bride smiling and laughing, thereby, showing her lovely set of white teeth. There is great joy in knowing Jesus. Jesus said, "These things have I spoken unto you, that my joy might remain in you, and that your joy might be full" (John 15:11). What are the words Jesus has spoken which bestow on us this everlasting—full of joy—life? They are the words of love from our Father. Our joy is complete when we abide in His love and keep His commandments (John 15:7-10).

The teeth are not just for good looks, but they are necessary for chewing and assimilating food into the body. Food gives the person energy to perform their everyday work and play. The Word of God will feed our inner life in Christ. By feeding on His words, we are assimilating His essence of life into our spirit. Jesus said, "Moses gave you not that bread from heaven; but my Father giveth you the true bread from heaven" (John 6:32). In this same chapter, verse fifty-one, He said, "I am the living bread which came down from heaven: if any man eat of this bread, he shall live for ever: and the bread that I will give is my flesh, which I will give for the life of the world." We eat of this living bread as we study the Word of God, for Jesus is the Word. It becomes a part of our being and our mental processes as we chew on it and meditate on it, and as we allow the Holy Spirit to guide us.

It is the Holy Spirit's quickening (bringing it to life) that enables us to hear, understand, and apply the Word. "It is the spirit that quickeneth; the flesh profiteth nothing: the words that I speak unto you, they are spirit, and they are life" (John 6:63). As the Bride feeds upon the words of Jesus and digests those words, she is made clean as a sheep that has just been shorn and washed.

The priests were not to wear wool because it is a type of sinfulness. They were to appear before the Lord in clean, white linen. (Ezekiel 44:17) The new life in Christ is a cleansed life. The Word of God sanctifies us: "as Christ also loved the church, and gave himself

100

for it; *that he might sanctify and cleanse it with the washing of water by the word*" (Ephesians 5:25-26). This daily sanctification is not just a rinse and go: it is a deep down cleansing of every fiber of our being. As it says in Hebrews 4:12, the Word of God probes down into the thoughts and intents of the heart.

Christ loved the church and gave Himself for it. Jesus took my place. "He was oppressed, and he was afflicted, yet he opened not his mouth: he is brought as a lamb to the slaughter, and as a sheep before her shearers is dumb, so he openeth not his mouth" (Isaiah 53:7). Jesus suffered as a sheep before the shearers. They removed the wool, which was my sin, from Him.

Going on in our description of the Bride's teeth, "every one of her teeth bears twins." Applying this to the Word of God, every scripture must be carefully compared to other scripture. Hereby, the Bride finds the pure truth. We cannot isolate a scripture to prove some doctrine that seems right to our way of thinking. There is a mate (or a twin) for every scripture. "Seek ye out of the book of the LORD, and read: no one of these shall fail, *none shall want her mate*: for my mouth it hath commanded, and his spirit it hath gathered them" (Isaiah 34:16).

The Bride is not missing any teeth: "none is barren of her teeth." We must assimilate the whole Word of God. We cannot tear it apart and only choose verses that suit us. "*All scripture* is given by inspiration of God, and is profitable for doctrine, for reproof, for correction, for instruction in righteousness: that the man of God may be perfect, thoroughly furnished unto all good works" (2 Timothy 3:16-17).

Her teeth are like a *flock* of sheep. We must be careful not to become a loner in our study of the Word. We need each other in the body, sharing the Word of God, admonishing and teaching one another. Jesus, our head, has given us the gift of teachers to keep us in the straight and narrow path of the Word and to prepare each of us for ministry. "And he gave some, apostles; and some, prophets; and some, evangelists; and some, pastors and teachers; for the perfecting of the saints, for the work of the ministry, for the edifying of the body of Christ" (Ephesians 4:11-12).

My Prayer: Thank You, Jesus, for a beautiful set of teeth. Help me to eat and meditate upon Your precious Word. May I digest it, so that I can be a doer of the Word and not just a casual hearer. Your Word is my light and my salvation. I rejoice in every word that proceeds from Your mouth!

SCARLET THREAD OF SALVATION

Thy lips are like a thread of scarlet, and thy speech is comely: thy
temples are like a piece of a pomegranate within thy locks.
Song of Solomon 4:3

Now we come to the King's description of the Bride's lips.
Her lips and speech are lovely or inviting. He says the lips are like a
thread of scarlet. I immediately think of Rahab when I hear of a scarlet
thread. She had hidden the two Hebrew spies from Jericho's
officials. She had faith that God would be with the Hebrew children,
and she asked that she and her household would be saved when they
invaded the land. The spies told her that God would honor her faith if
she would hang a scarlet cord out of her window. When the walls of
Jericho came tumbling down, Rahab and her family were the only citizens to be saved. Therefore, we understand that the scarlet thread
represents the salvation of her household. (Joshua 2:1-15; 6:25)

Rahab believed in God and His power, and she became a
woman who was used to participate in the promised bloodline. Rahab
gave birth to Boaz. Boaz married Ruth, and Ruth became the great-
grandmother of King David. (Matthew 1:5, 6) Both Rahab and Ruth
were Gentile women brought into the lineage of Christ. Some may
argue that this was Joseph's side of the family, and since he was not
really the natural father, it does not apply to Christ. However, Jesus
was Joseph's son by adoption. This is a wonderful example of how
the Gentile believer has been brought into the family of God.

For ye have not received the spirit of bondage again to fear; but
ye have received the Spirit of adoption, whereby we cry, Abba,
Father. The Spirit itself beareth witness with our spirit, that we
are the children of God.   Romans 8:15-16

With my lips and words, I cry out, "Abba, Father", for I have been
adopted into the blessed family of God.

The fruit of my lips are precious to my King when I praise
Him and express my love for Him (Hebrews 13:15). Oh, that I may
exalt the name of Jesus everywhere I go. I pray that my words would
be instrumental in bringing my entire household to the saving knowledge of Jesus Christ (Acts 16:31).

Let us go on to the description of the Bride's temples. The
temples represent her mind. It is like a piece of a pomegranate—

103

meaning that it is fruitful. The locks of her hair, which confirms her consecration, covers her mind. The scripture says in the fifteenth chapter of John that we bear fruit when we abide in Jesus and His words abide in us (John 15: 5-7). We know that the words of Jesus must take root in our minds before they become a part of our everyday life. By meditating upon His Word, we are transformed from the way of this world's thinking, and our minds are renewed by the Spirit (Romans 12:2).

The temple is a vulnerable part of the head if it is wounded. This is why we need to guard it so carefully. Ephesians 6:17 says that we need to arm ourselves by putting on the helmet of salvation. Knowing that I have salvation gives me peace that passes all understanding, gives me joy beyond measure, and assures me that I have everlasting life.

My Prayer: Oh Lord, so saturate my heart and mind with Your Word that words of salvation will flow like a river out of my mouth. Bless my family and loved ones through my words. I pray for the salvation of my household. Help me to keep all thoughts out of my mind that are not pleasing to You. Help me to have a renewed mind each day. May I have an open mind and a teachable spirit as I study Your Word.

HER REGAL NECK

Thy neck is like the tower of David builded for an armoury,
whereon there hang a thousand bucklers, all shields of mighty men.
Song of Solomon 4:4

The Lord continues His picturesque description. Her neck is like the tower of David. A tower, in Bible days, was built as a lookout for any trouble upon the surrounding areas. This tower is like a military outlook or fortress, which was also used as an armory. An armory is the military storage facility for weapons, including the shields (also called bucklers). Let us examine how this tower applies to the Bride of Christ.

First, the neck speaks to us of her will, determination, and attitude. When a person is intent on doing something, the attitude shows in the neck's body language. For example: the runner's neck is outstretched and is straining to reach his goal; an angry person's veins will protrude in the neck area; a stubborn or rebellious person's neck will stiffen; an embarrassed person's neck will turn red; a proud person holds his head high so that his nose points upward; a lover's neck will soften and bend in order to lay his head on the other person's shoulder.

The Bible warns us not be become stiff-necked. *Stiff-necked* is a figure of speech denoting a stubborn, rebellious, and unbelieving attitude. King Hezekiah issued a decree for all the people to observe the Passover, thereby, reviving true religion in Israel. He beseeched the backslidden nation, "Now do not be stiff-necked, as your fathers were, but yield yourselves to the LORD" (2 Chronicles 30:8). The Bride of Christ should not be stubborn or set in her ways. She should be ready to yield her will to her loving Lord, so that He can use her for His glory.

As the Bride holds her head upon a stately tower of a neck, it is not stiff—but regal. She is serving as a watchtower for the King (tower of David). She keeps a watchful eye out for any attack of the enemy. Her will is strong to protect herself and the other citizens of the kingdom of God (Luke 17:20, 21). "Be *sober, be vigilant*; because your adversary the devil, as a roaring lion, walketh about, seeking whom he may devour: *Whom resist stedfast in the faith....*" (1 Peter 5:8-9a).

Not only is the Church vigilant and watching for an attack, but the Church resists the enemy with steadfast faith. The Bride has

105

shields of mighty men hanging in rows around her neck. Ephesians 6:16 says that it is the shield of faith that quenches the darts of the enemy. The mighty army of God has thousands of shields of faith within easy reach at any sign of spiritual war. We are never outnumbered even though it may seem like the enemy has more soldiers in his army. God's promise is, "One man of you shall chase a thousand, for the LORD your God is He who fights for you, as He has promised you" (Joshua 23:10-11, NKJV). We have faith because our Lord is our strong tower and shield.

> For thou hast been a shelter for me, and a strong tower from the enemy.
> Psalms 61:3, KJV

> The LORD is my rock and my fortress and my deliverer;
> My God, my strength, in whom I will trust;
> My shield and the horn of my salvation, my stronghold.
> Psalms 18:2 NKJV

Another way to think of these shields is that they may be trophies from past battles. Perhaps they have been taken away from the enemy soldiers as they were defeated. This interpretation would surely suit our Bride. As the Church goes forth into battle, she comes back with many testimonies of faith. Faith is our victory!

Thus, we see that as the Bride of Christ, we are to always be watchful for Satan's attacks. We are not fearful because Jesus has promised to fight for us. By faith in His promises, we go forth with our heads held high on determined, stately—yes, regal necks.

My Prayer: Lord, I do not fear the enemy who would like to attack me on every side, for You are my shield, my fortress, and my strong tower. Help me not to be spiritually sleepy, but may I be always watching and praying. I delight in sharing the testimonies of how You have brought me through trials and temptations. Surely, "I can do all things through Christ who strengthens me" (Philippians 4:13-14, NKJV).

MEET THE TWINS

FAITH AND LOVE

Thy two breasts are like two young roes that are twins, which feed among the lilies. Song of Solomon 4:5

The seventh feature of the Bride is her breasts. The number seven is the number of perfection or completeness. We, as the Bride of Christ, are complete—not wanting any good thing. (Ephesians 4:13; Colossians 4:12)

You will notice the emphasis on the number two in this verse. There are **two** breasts that are compared to **two** young roes, and the young roes are **twins**. The number two is the number of agreement; also, it is the number of witnesses needed to affirm the truth. The Law required more than one witness to establish true testimony:

One witness shall not rise up against a man for any iniquity, or for any sin, in any sin that he sinneth: at the mouth of two witnesses, or at the mouth of three witnesses, shall the matter be established.   Deuteronomy 19:15

It is also written in your law, that the testimony of two men is true.   John 8:17

There is power when two persons agree. They can work, walk, and witness together. When they pray together, they can expect heaven to intervene on their behalf.

Can two walk together, except they be agreed?   Amos 3:3

And he called unto him the twelve, and began to send them forth by *two and two*; and gave them power over unclean spirits.   Mark 6:7

Again I say unto you, That *if two of you shall agree* on earth as touching any thing that they shall ask, it shall be done for them of my Father which is in heaven.   Matthew 18:19

Although all of these subjects involving the number two are very important, and they could lead us into further study, I am going to concentrate on another set of twins in the Word. This set of twins make up the breastplate of the believer. They are faith and love. Paul tells us to put on "the breastplate of faith and love" (1 Thessalonians 5:8). Faith and love need to come into agreement if they are to be effective. They work hand in hand. If they become lopsided in the Christian's life, there will be problems. In Paul's famous writing, which we call the "Love Chapter", he says, "Though I have all faith, so that I could remove mountains, but have not love, I am nothing" (1 Corinthians 13:2, NKJV). It is by our faith that we are able to perform good works, but our good works are for nothing if we are not motivated by love. Paul commended the church at Thessalonica for their unceasing work of faith and labor of love (1 Thessalonians 1:3). He told the Galatians, "The only thing that counts is faith expressing itself through love" (Galatians 5:6, NIV).

We cannot function as an overcoming believer if we have fear in our lives because it will suppress the faith that is necessary for our daily walk and growth. If we have perfect love, it will conquer fear: "There is no fear in love; but perfect love casteth out fear: because fear hath torment. He that feareth is not made perfect in love" (1 John 4:18). Love is a gift from God, for He is Love: "For God hath not given us the spirit of fear; but of power, and of love, and of a sound mind" (2 Timothy 1:7). Many saints have gone into extremely dangerous places without fear because the love of God compelled them to reach the lost. Love overcomes fear.

The breasts of a woman are one facet of her beauty, but the practical purpose of her breasts is to feed her babies. Many young converts die for lack of love and compassion. We must nourish the babes in the Lord by having faith to pray for them, and by our love and compassion to care for them. (1 Peter 3:8; 1 Peter 2:2; Hebrews 5:13) We are responsible to feed the newborn babes the milk of the Word (1 Corinthians 3:2). They must be fed the milk of the fundamentals of faith and be taught how to love God and others.

Her breasts are like young roes, ready and alert to the dangers of sin—swift-footed or quick to flee from temptation. She holds her children close to herself to protect them from Satan, as he would love to capture one of the babies. She is teaching and feeding her young among the lilies. The lilies represent our Lord who was crucified and has risen from the dead. Oh, that we may know Christ; that we may be crucified with Him and be raised in newness of life! (Galatians 2:20) True motherhood demands the giving of oneself for the sake of the children. If we truly desire to disciple new believers, we will need to give of ourselves. If need be, crucify our flesh. We will have faith in the new convert and in the God who is perfecting them in love.

My Prayer: Lord, help me to keep my breastplate of faith and love working in total agreement in my life. May I have faith that removes mountains. May I have love that will embrace the lost and set them free. Please show me how to nurture and disciple the babes in Christ which You would bring into my life. I pray that I will be an example to them of how to work in faith and labor in love.

LONGING FOR DAY BREAK

Until the day break, and the shadows flee away, I will get me to the
mountain of myrrh, and to the hill of frankincense.
Song of Solomon 4:6

This scripture seems like a repeat of chapter two, verse seventeen, but there are some differences I would like to point out. It is the Bride who is praying to her Beloved in chapter two as she awaits the day break. Her request is to "turn, my beloved, and be thou like a roe or a young hart upon the mountains of Bether." She is longing for the return of her lover. I believe the verse we are looking at now, in chapter four, is the Bridegroom speaking. He is speaking in the scriptures before and after this one as He has just given us the description of the Bride, and He continues His dialogue in verses seven through the end of the chapter. This being the case, the Bridegroom is longing for the same day that the Bride longed for—when *the day breaks and the shadows flee away.*

There are a couple "day breaks" for us to contemplate. The first is when Jesus came to this earth as a human being to bring the light of salvation to men, and the second is when He shall come again in all of His glory. Jesus brought light into the world on His first visit: "Through the tender mercy of our God, with which the *Dayspring from on high has visited us; To give light to those who sit in darkness and the shadow of death,* To guide our feet into the way of peace" (Luke 1:78, 79, NKJV). The Light of the World visited us, and the church now lives in that light.

He says that until the day breaks the second time, "I will go to the mountain of myrrh and to the hill of incense" (Song of Solomon 4:6, NIV). Jesus' mission and driving force in His earthly life was to give His life as a sacrifice for our atonement. As we have discovered before, myrrh represents His death, burial, and resurrection. In the prophecy of Isaiah concerning Jesus' death, it says that Jesus "set His face like a flint" (Isaiah 50:6-7). There was nothing in heaven or earth that could deter Him from laying down His life for us.

After Jesus' blood was shed on the Mountain of Calvary, He went into the heavenly tabernacle and presented His sacrifice to the Father. (Hebrews chapters 8 and 9) Sweet incense arises in that tabernacle not made with hands as He makes intercession before the Father for us. (Hebrews 7:25) He is high and lifted upon our praises (incense). Therefore, Jesus is sitting upon the hill of frankincense—He is at rest at the right hand of His Father.

However, the Bride still looks forward to the day when all shall be fulfilled, and the shadows of this life, sorrow, and death will never cross her path again. Although we have the peace of God, even in the shadow of death, it is nothing compared to the things He has prepared for us. Christ will dispel all darkness from our hearts. He longs to be with us in the eternal light just as much as we long to be with Him. Jesus says:

> "Behold, I am coming soon! My reward is with me, and I will give to everyone according to what he has done. I am the Alpha and the Omega, the First and the Last, the Beginning and the End."...

> "Blessed are those who wash their robes, that they may have the right to the tree of life and may go through the gates into the city"...

> "I, Jesus, have sent my angel to give you this testimony for the churches. I am the Root and the Offspring of David, and the **bright Morning Star**."   Portions of Revelation 22:13-16

My Prayer: Sometimes my path seems so dark, but I know that I always walk in the light of Your presence. You have promised that You would never leave me nor forsake me. I walk in the light of Your Word. The afflictions that I experience are so small compared to the glory You have prepared for me. Until the day breaks, I will love You and serve You with all of my heart.

WITHOUT SPOT

Thou art all fair, my love; there is no spot in thee.
Song of Solomon 4:7

My daughter, Ginger, relates this almost disastrous wedding story. "My daughter, Sharon, and I had decided that I would sew her wedding dress. Since we were on a strict budget, we had only purchased enough fabric and lace to complete a simple, very lovely, wedding dress. I had worked for weeks on the bodice of the dress— hand sewing on rose patterned lace and pearls. The skirt of the dress was made of fine white satin with the only decoration of rose lace that was glued all along the bottom. This proved to be a very tedious detail, but it was worth all the effort as it was just beautiful. At last, my work of love was finished and Sharon looked like a princess in it. I put it on the ironing board to give the completed dress one last pressing. As I hung it up, to my dismay, there were tiny brown spots on the back of the perfectly white skirt. My ironing board legs were a little rusty, and some of the rust had rubbed off onto the dress. I had only a few scraps of rose lace left, but the Lord helped me to use it to cut out and appliqué little roses over the soiled areas."

Jesus would never fix His Bride's wedding dress in such a way, for she will be without spot. He will not cover up our soils of sin—He will completely cleanse them.

> Christ also *loved the church*, and gave himself for it; that he might sanctify and cleanse it with the washing of water by the word, that he might present it to himself a glorious church, *not having spot*, or wrinkle, or any such thing; but that it should be *holy and without blemish.* Ephesians 5:25-27

Love is the key. Oh, how He loves you and me! He loved us and gave Himself for us that we might stand fair and lovely in His eyes. We are not imitators of Christ, but we are actually partakers of His flesh and His bones: "For we are members of his body, of his flesh, and of his bones" (Ephesians 5:30). The Bride is a vision of loveliness, for the Lord sees her as perfect and spotless, created in His image (Colossians 3:10). The new man that Christ has created in us is not living according to the former conduct of lust and sinfulness, but he is created in true righteousness and holiness (Ephesians 4:22-24).

We are perfecting holiness as we walk day-by-day—growing and maturing in Christ: "And the very God of peace sanctify you wholly; and I pray God your whole spirit and soul and body be preserved *blameless* unto the coming of our Lord Jesus Christ" (1 Thessalonians 5:23). Ultimate perfection will be ours at the coming of our Lord. We are still subject to the onslaught of Satan, and we may fall, but we are not knocked out. We run to Jesus as soon as we find any spot of sin upon our garment of righteousness: "If we confess our sins, he is faithful and just to forgive us our sins, and to *cleanse us* from all unrighteousness" (1 John 1:9). Jesus will forgive our sins and restore us.

Christ, the Bridegroom, looks upon us and sees that we are fair— no spots. We are perfect **in** Him and **by** Him.

My Prayer: Oh Lord, search me and try me—see if there are any blemishes or spots. Do not let me try to cover up the impurities of my thoughts and actions. May I come to You daily with all my imperfections and allow You to cleanse me by Your blood and wash me with the water of Your Word.

I want to believe that You do not see me as sinful, but that you see me as holy and without spot, for Your precious blood has been applied to my heart. Thank You, Lord, for You do not see me with all my flaws, but You see me as perfect in You.

WHERE HE LEADS, I WILL FOLLOW

Come with me from Lebanon, my spouse, with me from Lebanon:
look from the top of Amana, from the top of Shenir and Hermon,
from the lions' dens, from the mountains of the leopards.
Song of Solomon 4:8

The Lord is drawing His Bride away from the mountains of Lebanon and Anti-Lebanon. The mountains of Lebanon are divided into two mountain ranges; the western range is close to the Mediterranean Coast, and it is called Lebanon proper. The eastern range (toward the sun rising) is called Anti-Lebanon (Joshua 13:5). These two mountain ranges run parallel to each other with the northern tip of the Jordan valley in between them.[1] Amana, Shenir, and Hermon are peaks within the Anti-Lebanon Range. Shenir is probably a peak on Mount Hermon as the Amorites named Mount Hermon, Shenir (Deuteronomy 3:9). Lebanon was promised to Israel, but Joshua did not conquer this land. Therefore, it became the northern border of the land, and it proved to be troublesome to Israel. (Deuteronomy 1:7; Joshua 13:2-6) "The five rulers of the Philistines, all the Canaanites, the Sidonians, and the Hivites living in the Lebanon mountains from Mount Baal Hermon to Lebo Hamath. They were left to **test the Israelites** to see whether they would obey the Lord's commands, which he had given their forefathers through Moses" (Judges 3:3-4, NIV). It was a land of constant conflict (1 Chronicles 5:18-23).

The Lord leads the Bride into warfare against the enemy. We are always moving forward, gaining more territory from Satan—taking it by force if need be (Matthew 11:12). "For we wrestle not against flesh and blood, but against principalities, against powers, against the rulers of the darkness of this world, against spiritual wickedness in high places" (Ephesians 6:12). What type of battles do we have to fight in high places? We get some clues from the meanings of the names of the mountains in this passage.

The first mountaintop is **Amana** whose meaning is "truth and integrity." [2] Truth is a vital piece of our Christian armor: "Stand firm then, with the belt of truth buckled around your waist" (Ephesians 6:14, NIV). The truth is very important in our battle with Satan, as he is the father of lies. He also questions the truth of God's Word, thereby, causing the Christian to doubt. He used this tactic of warfare way back at the first temptation in the Garden of Eden. He asked Eve, "Did God **really say**, 'You must not eat from any tree in the garden'?"

114

(Genesis 3:1, NIV). Then he had the audacity to refute God's words with, "You will not surely die" (Genesis 3:4, NIV). We must stand firm and fight for every word of truth the Lord has given to us. Paul said, "But though we, or an angel from heaven, preach any other gospel unto you than that which we have preached unto you, let him be accursed" (Galatians 1:8). Therefore, let us confirm everything by the pure Word of our Lord and Savior, Jesus Christ. He is by our side in this battle, and His Holy Spirit will witness with our spirit if the truth is being spoken (Romans 9:1). We go forth into this world with the witness of truth, for the truth sets men free (John 8:32).

The second battle is at Mount *Shenir*, meaning a, "lantern or a light that sleeps." [2] The kingdom of God will not advance if we as the, "light of the world", are sleeping (Matthew 5:14-16). Sleeping means that we are complacent and not aware of the battle that rages around us. One of the most disturbing events in Christ's life was in the Garden of Gethsemane.

> "Simon, are you sleeping? Could you not watch one hour? Watch and pray, lest you enter into temptation. The spirit indeed is willing, but the flesh is weak." Mark 14:37-38, NKJV

Yes, we battle against our flesh that is weak. We need to be careful not to fall asleep. We must be watching and praying if we are to resist the temptations of our enemy.

The third, and last, mountain peak mentioned in this verse is Hermon. The meaning of *Hermon* is, "devoted to destruction." [2] Jesus tells us that the Devil, our adversary, is out to destroy us: "The thief cometh not, but for to steal, and to kill, and to *destroy*" (John 10:10). Satan may be devoted to destroying us, but Jesus will not allow it. Satan was out to destroy Peter. Jesus told Peter that Satan had desired to sift him like wheat, but Jesus had prayed that his faith would not fail (Luke 22:31, 32).

Upon the high places are many dangers. There are lions and leopards. We know that Satan walks about like a roaring lion. The Bridegroom calls His Bride to come down from the mountains. It is not wise to go into a sin-infested place where the devourer is waiting. Lot and his family found that out when they were caught in Sodom. The valley of Jordan looked pleasant, just like sin looks pleasant, but the pleasures of sin only last for the moment.

If we should come face to face with Satan, the lion, while doing battle for our King, we do not need to be afraid: "Thou shalt tread upon the lion and adder: the young lion and the dragon shalt thou trample under feet. Because he hath set his love upon me, therefore will I deliver him: I will set him on high, because he hath known my name" (Psalms 91:13-14).

When Jesus speaks, "*Come with me*", I must follow wherever He leads. He may lead me into some difficult places of service, but I will stand firm, holding onto truth, watching and praying, and being courageous. Satan may try to destroy me, and I may seem weak, but I am delivered out of the mouth of the lion.

My Prayer: Lord, help me to be courageous, standing firm in the faith. Give me the understanding I need to test all ideas and thoughts against the Word of Truth. I want to follow You wherever You lead me. It may be on foreign soil where dangers lurk, but I will not fear. It may be to my neighbor that scoffs at my beliefs, but You will give me the words to say. It may be to my family who will point out my past failures, but I will declare that You have made me a new creation.

[1] From Easton's Bible Dictionary, PC Study Bible formatted electronic database Copyright © 2003, 2006 Biblesoft, Inc. All rights reserved.
[2] From Hitchcock's Bible Names Dictionary, PC Study Bible formatted electronic database Copyright © 2003, 2006 Biblesoft, Inc. All rights reserved.

CAPTURED BY LOVE

Thou hast ravished my heart, my sister, my spouse; thou hast ravished my heart with one of thine eyes, with one chain of thy neck.
Song of Solomon 4:9

There are unspoken gestures, which speak volumes of love. I (Ginger) will never forget a wink and a sheepish grin from across the room as my future husband played his guitar. I knew at that moment that I wanted to be with him for the rest of my life. This is the kind of scene described in our verse. Perhaps sitting side by side, the young girl looks out the side of her eye into the face of her lover, raising her head slightly, so that he catches just a glimpse of her necklace. His heart swells up in his chest, and he wants to take her in his arms and embrace her. His heart is captured forever. This is how Jesus is describing His love for us. We have stolen or captured His heart for all eternity. What a beautiful picture of His love. It is not time for that full embrace now, but one day, we will be gathered into His loving arms.

This truth really stirred my heart when my Father (Vivian's husband and Ginger's dad) passed away. He had been terribly sick for three years with an enlarged heart. Nights were torture because his legs and back hurt so bad that he could not sleep. Every night as I lay down to sleep, I would pray that the Lord would help my dad get through another night of pain. Dad went to heaven the afternoon of January 6, 1993. That night as I lay down, tears flowed as I could see in my mind's eye— Dad in the loving arms of Jesus. Daddy used to laugh in the pulpit as he would say, "I've never been a Bride, but I fix'n to be one." The love of Jesus is so great that we will never be able to comprehend it while we are still held captive to this earth. He anticipates our coming marriage even more than we can imagine.

We see a new name for the Bride in this verse, which is "my sister." Jesus takes the position not only of our spouse but as our elder brother. One day, while Jesus was teaching, a great crowd of people was about Him in the house. Word filtered through the crowd that His mother and brothers were outside and had requested to speak to Him. He looked around at the attentive faces in the crowd and said, "Here are my mother and my brothers! Whoever does God's will is my brother and sister and mother" (Mark 3:34, 35, NIV). He has included me as part of His family. I always admired girls who had an older brother as there is a bond between them. The older brother always looks out for his sister and will not let any harm come to her.

Our relationship to Jesus as *sister* could only be accomplished because Jesus took on the flesh of mankind. The writer of Hebrews says it this way:

> So now Jesus and the ones he makes holy have the same Father. That is why Jesus is not ashamed to call them his brothers and sisters. For he said to God,
> "I will proclaim your name to my brothers and sisters.
> I will praise you among your assembled people."
> Hebrews 2:11-12, NLT

There is a type of our relationship as spouse and sister seen in the Old Testament with the relationship between Abraham and Sarah. Sarah was Abraham's wife, yet she was his sister because they had the same father. We have the same father as Jesus—God the Father. (Genesis 20:12-13)

The King says that I ravish His heart. I have seized and carried away His heart to His great delight and joy—with just one eye, for my eyes are fixed on Jesus, the author and finisher of my faith. I am wearing the chain of His divine love around my neck. He has given me His love, so that I, in turn, can love Him. His divine love has captured my heart and my will. "This is the Lord's doing; it is marvellous in our eyes" (Psalms 118:23).

My Prayer: Dear Lord, I do love You with all of my heart, soul, and mind. You are my all in all. Thank You for loving me with Your all surpassing love. Thank You for bringing me into this wonderful relationship of spouse and sister.

David and Vivian Thompson

On their 50th Anniversary

SACRIFICES OF LOVE

How fair is thy love, my sister, my spouse! how much better is thy love than wine! and the smell of thine ointments than all spices!
Song of Solomon 4:10

The Lord and I are one flesh (Ephesians 5:31, 32). His nature is my nature. I am married to Him who is raised from the dead, that I should bring forth fruit unto God (Romans 7:4).

We are His love, His sister, and His spouse. We are a new creation by the blood of Jesus. We are able, with the help of the Lord, to live the crucified life. This is how our love is poured out, and our lives become a sweet savor to Him. The sacrifices of the Old Testament ascended to God as a sweet savour in His nostrils. There were drink offerings of fine flour, oil, and wine poured out in addition to the lambs that were slain (Exodus 29:40).

Paul was chosen by the Lord to be one of the first missionaries. Jesus told Ananias to not be afraid of Paul, but Ananias was to go to Paul and pray for the healing of his eyes because: "he is a chosen vessel unto me, to bear my name before the Gentiles, and kings, and the children of Israel: For I will shew him how great things he must suffer for my name's sake" (Acts 9:15-16). Paul's life was a living sacrifice from that day on. He gave up his reputation as a Pharisee of Pharisees; he was willing to face all kinds of persecution; he went without warm clothes and food at times; he was wrongfully imprisoned. He willingly did this all for Christ and for the sake of the gospel. Paul followed the example of his Lord in love, which caused him to become a sweet savour even as Christ: "walk in love, as Christ also hath loved us, and hath given himself for us an offering and a sacrifice to God for a sweetsmelling savour" (Ephesians 5:2-3).

Paul commended the Church of Philippi for ministering to his needs. They had sent him some necessities of life. He did not ask for this, but he was very grateful for their gifts as it showed that they were indeed bearing fruit. He said, "The things which were sent from you, an odour of a sweet smell, a sacrifice acceptable, wellpleasing to God" (Philippians 4:18). We may not be called to go on the mission field, but each of us is called to sacrificial giving for the furtherance of the kingdom of God. This is a sweet smell unto the Lord and well pleasing in His sight. All gifts are to be given out of the love we have for our Lord.

Jesus declares that our love is better than wine. The Bride had made a similar statement concerning His love for her in chapter one, verses two and three. Wine represents the crucified life she is living, for she is crushed even as grapes are crushed to obtain the wine. Her ointments and spices are better than any fragrance He had ever smelled, for her **poured out** life is the fruit of the Spirit flowing forth to Him and to the whole world. How He rejoices over His Bride and her dedicated love.

I can relate to this crucified life as my husband, David, and I have been called by our Beloved Savior to leave everything to follow Him to various places of ministry. Probably the hardest time for me to let go and surrender all to Him was the time He called us to go to the Marshall Islands in 1969. We had always known in our hearts that God had called us to missionary work, but we questioned the timing since we had just become proud grandparents. Part of me wanted to answer the call and serve the Lord with all my love, and the other part wanted to stay close to my grandchildren and family. As I wrestled with this conflict, the Lord led me to this scripture:

> Verily I say unto you, There is no man that hath left house, or brethren, or sisters, or father, or mother, or wife, or children, or lands, for my sake, and the gospel's, but he shall receive an hundredfold now in this time, houses, and brethren, and sisters, and mothers, and children, and lands, with persecutions; and in the world to come eternal life.   Mark 10:29-30

With the assurance from the Lord that I would receive a hundredfold if, I would take up my cross and follow Him, I gladly left my family behind. The Lord was so gracious and gave us the opportunity to prepare young people for the ministry in a combination Bible school/ high school on the atoll of Majuro.

My Prayer: Help me to give of myself and of everything that belongs to me. All I have belongs to You. I desire to give freely out of the abundant love and blessings You have bestowed upon me. May my life be as a sweet odor— saturated with love for You.

Pictures of the grandchildren we left behind

Picture taken in front of the Haleiwa Assembly of God
David and Vivian Thompson were the Pastors there just before going
to the Marshall Islands

SWEET WORDS- SWEET SMELL

Thy lips, O my spouse, drop as the honeycomb: honey and milk are under thy tongue; and the smell of thy garments is like the smell of Lebanon. Song of Solomon 4:11

In verse three of this fourth chapter, the King states that His Bride's lips were like a scarlet thread. We discovered that this represented her and her whole family's salvation due to her faith. Now He addresses her as His spouse, with lips that drop honey in a honeycomb.

Drop by drop, honey is made as the bees gather the nectar of flowers and store it in the honeycomb for future use. Honey is sweeter than sugar, and it is purer. Liquid honey does not spoil. Honey was used in ancient times to give an energy boost. When Jonathan ate of it after being very weary from battle, his eyes were enlightened (1 Samuel 14:27). The statutes of the Lord are pure and are said to be even sweeter than honey.

> The statutes of the Lord are right, rejoicing the heart: the commandment of the Lord is *pure*, *enlightening* the eyes.
> The fear of the Lord is clean, enduring for ever: the judgments of the Lord are true and righteous altogether.
> More to be desired are they than gold, yea, than much fine gold: *sweeter also than honey and the honeycomb*.
> Psalms 19:8-11

The Bride has honey and milk under her tongue. We have already seen how the milk of the Word of God is fed to newborn babes, in Christ, helping them to grow in the faith. The words of the Bride are also like honey. Honey words are sticky and sweet. The stickiness helps them to linger longer, thus, being enjoyed for a longer period of time. The Bride must have the encouraging, strengthening Word of God stored under her tongue, so that she is ready to share it at anytime the need arises.

The tongue is a little member of our body, but it has the power of life or death; blessing or cursing; bitter or sweet. (Proverbs 18:21; James 3:6-11) The tongue that speaks pleasant, uplifting, and encouraging words is very sweet to the ears of all who hear it: "Pleasant words are as an honeycomb, sweet to the soul, and health to the bones" (Proverbs 16:24).

Don't you just love to be in the company of the person who always has that word of faith and encouragement for you? It lifts up your spirit just as honey "enlightens the eye." It gives you the strength and determination to press on and overcome any obstacle that would block your Christian walk. I have had dear brothers and sisters come my way from time to time that just seem to have the right word to say at the right time. "A man hath joy by the answer of his mouth: and a word spoken in due season, how good is it!" (Proverbs 15:23) The Word of the Lord is on the Bride's lips and more is stored under her tongue to bring forth nourishment, encouragement, and direction to others within the body of Christ.

Not only does the Bride have the edifying word ready, she also smells good. We used to go camping in the forests of California when I was a child. I could not get enough of the smell of the trees and the fresh air. Lebanon is known for its cedar trees, which are some of the most fragrant of all trees. The sweet, kind, encouraging saint has the scent of heaven upon her (or him). People are drawn to her because she emanates with the presence of Jesus; consequently, she is given the opportunity to witness to them, to lead them in prayer, and to draw them closer to her Sweet Jesus.

My Prayer: Oh Lord, put a guard on my lips. Help me not to be too swift to speak words that I will later regret. Help me to speak in sweet, kind tones. May the scent of Your sweet presence emanate from me, drawing others to walk closer to You. I so desire to encourage my brothers and sisters in the Lord.

GARDEN OF LOVE

A garden inclosed is my sister, my spouse; a spring shut up, a fountain sealed. Song of Solomon 4:12

I have a friend that purchased an older house. I was in despair when I first saw it, as it had not been maintained in years and the yard was dried up and ugly. If it were my place, I would have probably torn it down and started all over again; however, my friend had a dream and saw the potential of how it could look after it was repaired and after she had planted her garden around it. She started her work on the garden right away because it was to be her sanctuary and her place to fellowship with her Lord. Each time I visited her, she would show me a new plant that she tenderly planted and cared for. Before long, the home looked like a delightful cottage, and we enjoyed hours under the tree in the front yard. Being a florist by trade, she planted flowers that could be shared. She has blessed our church with masterpiece bouquets week after week.

God had planted the Garden of Eden as His first meeting place with man. It was so pleasant to walk and talk with Adam and Eve in the cool of the evening. Adam and Eve must have been like little children joyfully showing God the plants and flowers they had discovered during the day. God had planted trees that were pleasant to see as well as to eat. (Genesis 2:16) Disobedience broke the fellowship, and God had to send His prized creation out of the Garden.

Jesus has restored that fellowship. He takes our dried up, weed infested, life and makes it a lovely garden where He can come and fellowship with us. He promises restoration: "And the Lord shall guide thee continually, and satisfy thy soul in drought, and make fat thy bones: and thou shalt be like a watered garden, and like a spring of water, whose waters fail not" (Isaiah 58:11).

Let us look at the garden our Lord compares to His Bride. First, the Gardener plans the garden. He does not just let it grow up with wild plants. He has a design in mind. "For I know the plans I have for you," declares the Lord, "plans to prosper you and not to harm you, plans to give you hope and a future" (Jeremiah 29:11, NIV).

The garden is enclosed. The garden had a wall built around it, or, as custom was in that day, a thorny hedge was planted around it. Satan complained to God because God had put a hedge around Job (Job 1:10). As long as that hedge of protection was intact, Satan could

125

not harm Job. Jesus puts a hedge around His church, and He is in control of Satan's attacks upon His people.

Again, He calls the Bride, *my sister, my spouse*. He must love this term of endearment, as this is the fourth time He uses it. His royal blood applied to my heart flows through my veins making me a blood relative. I have such a wonderful position in God's family and all the privileges that come with being in that position. I am God's child and a sister to His Son, but like Sarah's example—I am also His spouse. [1]

Finally, we see in the garden a spring and a fountain. Water is a necessity for a garden to flourish and grow. Jesus promised the believer springs of living water (John 7:37-39). He is speaking of the promise of the Holy Spirit. The Holy Spirit is the living water that flows from our spirit to water the fruit that He is producing in our lives. I wondered why the spring and the fountain in this verse are shut up or sealed. I think it is because of the exclusive relationship He desires to have with me as His spouse.

My life is sealed unto Him. He alone is my lover—my affections are set upon no other. I am a spring shut up with living water inside my being. He has sealed me with the Holy Spirit: "That we should be to the praise of his glory, who first trusted in Christ. In whom ye also trusted, after that ye heard the word of truth, the gospel of your salvation: in whom also after that ye believed, *ye were sealed with that holy Spirit of promise*, which is the earnest of our inheritance until the redemption of the purchased possession, unto the praise of his glory" (Ephesians 1:12-14). The seal protects the precious water from any contamination of sin, even as the Holy Spirit keeps me pure and separated from the world. This *sealed up* spring is dedicated only to my lover; it is similar to the exclusive marriage illustration found in Proverbs 5:15-19. The Spirit of God wells up within my soul, and it pours out as praise to Abba Father (Galatians 4:6). This is just a foretaste of the inheritance awaiting God's children.

My Prayer: Lord, keep me pure and clean. Let the Holy Spirit water my garden heart and refresh me so that I, in turn, can refresh others. Keep me and protect me from the present evil world. Help me not to give place to Satan, so that He will not be able to break through the hedge of protection. Come, fellowship with me in my Garden of Love.

(1)   Refer back to Song of Solomon 4:9, Sarah was Abraham's wife but also his sister because they had the same father.

FRUIT OF JOY

Thy plants are an orchard of pomegranates, with pleasant fruits;
Song of Solomon 4:13a

The Hebrew children were tired of the wilderness journey, and they began to list the delicious foods they had enjoyed in Egypt. They complained to Moses: "Wherefore have ye made us to come up out of Egypt, to bring us in unto this evil place? it is no place of seed, or of figs, or of vines, or of *pomegranates*; neither is there any water to drink" (Numbers 20:5). Can you imagine how excited they would have been if they had happened along on an orchard of pomegranates, broke them open and sucked the sweet, sour juice out the red fruit? That did not happen right then and there, for the Lord was trying to teach them some endurance and patience before they arrived in the land of milk and honey. The good report came back with the spies as they had surveyed the Land of Canaan (the Promised Land) that there were large bunches of grapes, figs, and pomegranates. (Numbers 13:23) The fruit of the Promised Land was a symbol of prosperity and joy. When the Israelites did not have this fruit, it was a symbol of lack and sorrow. Joel lamented many years later in Israel's history: "The vine is dried up, and the fig tree languisheth; the pomegranate tree, the palm tree also, and the apple tree, even all the trees of the field, are withered: because *joy is withered away from the sons of men*" (Joel 1:12).

Jeremiah is known as the weeping prophet, for his message was very sad, and he endured all kinds of mistreatment. The Lord gave him the prophecy of Judah's future captivity and the fall of Jerusalem into the hands of the Babylonians. It was probably the lowest point in Israel's history, as he observed these prophecies being fulfilled in his own lifetime. God never leaves His people without hope even though they have backslidden into terrible sin. In the middle of all the dire prophecies, God says that He will bring the captivity back to Jerusalem, and He would cleanse them from all their iniquities and pardon them. Observe the joy that is restored to Jerusalem in the following verses:

> Then it shall be to Me a name of joy, a praise, and an honor
> before all nations of the earth, who shall hear all the good that
> I do to them; they shall fear and tremble for all the goodness
> and all the prosperity that I provide for it.' "Thus says the

127

Lord: *'Again there shall be heard in this place…., the voice of joy and the voice of gladness, the voice of the bridegroom and the voice of the bride,* the voice of those who will say:

"Praise the Lord of hosts,
For the Lord is good,
For His mercy endures forever" —

And of those *who will bring the sacrifice of praise* into the house of the Lord. For I will cause the captives of the land to return as at the first,' says the Lord. Jeremiah 33:9-11, NKJV

Yes, on that victorious day when Christ restores Jerusalem, there will be utter joy. The voice of the bridegroom and the bride will be heard; the voice of joy and gladness; the voice of those who bring the sacrifice of praise. The word joy (rejoice) in the original Hebrew text is, "simchah", meaning to feast before God. [1] Could this prophecy of Jeremiah include the feast Jesus is preparing for His Bride?

We have been exploring the fruit of love in various verses of the Song of Solomon. Out of love springs joy. Our Bride is bearing the fruit of the Spirit, and she is filled with joy (Galatians 5:22). She is bearing *much fruit* as she has a whole orchard of pomegranates and other pleasant fruits.

Christian joy does not only display itself in the times of plenty because it is not based on material things. It is based on our love for Jesus and others. "If ye keep my commandments, ye shall *abide in my love*; even as I have kept my Father's commandments, and abide in his love. These things have I spoken unto you, *that my joy might remain in you, and that your joy might be full.* This is my commandment, that *ye love one another,* as I have loved you" (John 15:10-13). The Holy Spirit cultivates the fruit of joy in our garden through hardship because He knows that hardship will also produce patience, endurance, and longsuffering.

May we be fruitful in every good work that the Lord leads us to do—always loving and joyful in the work of the Lord.

That ye might walk worthy of the Lord unto all pleasing, being fruitful in every good work, and increasing in the knowledge of God; Strengthened with all might, according to his glorious power, unto all patience and longsuffering with joyfulness; Giving thanks unto the Father, which hath made us meet to be partakers of the inheritance of the saints in light.

Colossians 1:10-13

My Prayer: Dear Lord, let me be a garden full of fruit for Your enjoyment and pleasure. Let love rule my heart, for all spiritual fruit stems from love. Help me to be joyful during the hard places in my life and realize that each trial is for my good.

[1] Vine's Expository Dictionary of Biblical Words, Copyright © 1985, Thomas Nelson Publishers.

THE SPICE OF LIFE

Thy plants are... camphire, with spikenard, Spikenard and saffron;
calamus and cinnamon, with all trees of frankincense; myrrh and
aloes, with all the chief spices: Song of Solomon 4:13b-14

None of the spices listed here are native to Israel. They were imported and very expensive. The Queen of Sheba brought many spices as a gift when she came to visit the renowned King Solomon (1 Kings 10:1-3). The gift of spices to a king demonstrated the respect and honor due to him. King Hezekiah carried on this tradition and showed off his treasury (which included a rich store of spices) to a visiting king of Babylon (2 Kings 20:12-14). The wise men of the New Testament brought gifts of gold, frankincense, and myrrh to the newborn King of the Jews, Jesus.

Although these spices were not grown in the land of King Solomon, he states that his spouse, who is also his sister, grows them in her garden. Of course, we know that this passage is poetic and spiritual in meaning; thus, he is not talking about an actual garden. He is speaking of her gracious attributes.

We have examined some of these spices in previous verses. We found that camphire is usually called henna, and it is used for dye to beautify a woman's hair, nails, and hands. The dry leaves had to be crushed to obtain the red dye—which we likened to Jesus' body being bruised to purchase our healing. The Bride, too, must suffer at times so that she will be more effective in her ministry to others.

> Praise be to the God and Father of our Lord Jesus Christ, the Father of compassion and the God of all comfort, who comforts us in all our troubles, so that we can comfort those in any trouble with the comfort we ourselves have received from God. For just as the sufferings of Christ flow over into our lives, so also through Christ our comfort overflows.
>
> 2 Corinthians 1:3-6, NIV

We observed Mary anointing the feet of Jesus with spikenard and wiping His feet with the hair of her head. This was a very extravagant act of worship because spikenard was very expensive. Jesus told the disciples to let her alone as she was anointing Him for burial even before He was crucified. Therefore, spikenard speaks to us of extravagant worship in remembrance of Jesus' sacrifice for us (John 12:3-7).

Frankincense is a resin that gives off a fragrant odor or perfume when it is burnt. It was used in the tabernacle as incense, and it was also combined with the meat offerings (Exodus 30:34; Leviticus 2:1). It is an emblem of our prayers ascending to the Father and the Son. David prayed: "Let my prayer be set forth before thee as incense; and the lifting up of my hands as the evening sacrifice" (Psalms 141:2). John saw this vision of heaven: "And another angel came and stood at the altar, having a golden censer; and there was given unto him much incense, that he should offer it *with the prayers of all saints* upon the golden altar which was before the throne" (Revelation 8:3). Our prayers are not in vain, for each one is stored up in heaven—they are the incense used in the heavenly temple.

Saffron is used for spicing up food. It is yellow in color, and it is very useful when traveling. Just a little pinch gives a good flavor to stew or rice dishes. Jesus said that we are the salt of the earth, but if we had lost our saltiness or tastefulness, we are good for nothing (Matthew 5:13). Taste and color are very inviting to the senses. The Church needs to look inviting, and it needs to be satisfying to the spiritual pallet of the hungry. Our cry to the world should be, "O taste and see that the Lord is good: blessed is the man that trusteth in him" (Psalms 34:8). Let us prepare a table before the unsaved that will draw them into the body of Christ.

We have discussed myrrh and aloes in some detail in other scriptures pointing out that they were used for Christ burial, and that they represent the crucified life of the believer.

The Bride's garden not only grows the fruit of the Spirit, but she has spices that represent other fine attributes: she is compassionate to the suffering; she is an extravagant worshiper; she is a prayer warrior; she is the witness to the world—calling "come and taste of the Lord"; she is walking in the sacrificial lifestyle.

My Prayer: Lord, the further I go in this study, the more I realize that I can do nothing without You. None of these attributes comes naturally to my human nature. Only as You rule my life, will I bring forth from the King's storehouse precious, fragrant spices.

HOLY ANOINTING OIL

Spikenard and saffron; calamus and cinnamon, with all trees of frankincense; myrrh and aloes, with all the chief spices:
Song of Solomon 4:14 (continued)

Did you think I missed a few spices in the previous verse? I thought it best to separate three special spices because when they are combined, according to God's formula, they make up the holy anointing oil.

Take thou also unto *thee principal spices*, of pure *myrrh* five hundred shekels, and of sweet *cinnamon* half so much, even two hundred and fifty shekels, and of sweet *calamus* two hundred and fifty shekels, and of *cassia* five hundred shekels, after the shekel of the sanctuary, and of *oil olive* an hin: And thou shalt make it an oil of holy ointment, an ointment compound after the art of the apothecary: it shall be an holy anointing oil. Exodus 30:23-25

The holy anointing oil was used one time only for the anointing of the tabernacle and all of its furnishings before they were put into use, thus, consecrating the tabernacle and its furnishings to the service of the Lord. It was also used for the consecration of Aaron, the high priest, and his sons. From that time on, the priests for all generations were to be anointed with this holy oil. (Exodus 30:26-33) This anointing oil is a type of the anointing of the Holy Spirit on the members of the body of Christ for the work of the ministry.

Jesus, our High Priest, had the special anointing of the Spirit of God. He said:

The Spirit of the Lord is upon me, because he hath anointed me to preach the gospel to the poor; he hath sent me to heal the brokenhearted, to preach deliverance to the captives, and recovering of sight to the blind, to set at liberty them that are bruised, to preach the acceptable year of the Lord.
Luke 4:18-20

As Jesus came close to the time in which He would return to heaven, He instructed His followers to, "wait in Jerusalem until ye be endued with power from on high" (Luke 24:49). The Church of Jesus

Christ was born on the Day of Pentecost when the Holy Spirit descended upon the 120 followers who were waiting for the promise of the Father (Acts 2:1-4). In the age of the Church, the members of the body of Christ have this blessing available to them. We call it the Baptism in the Holy Spirit.

Remember the holy anointing oil was only to be used in the consecration of the priests. Peter says that we are a holy priesthood who offer up spiritual sacrifices (1 Peter 2:5). John says that we have the anointing of Him that abides in us so that we have the understanding of the Truth (1 John 2:27).

If the Church is filled with the Holy Spirit, it is endued with the same power with which Jesus was anointed. We proclaim the gospel of good news to the world; we lay hands on the sick and they recover; we give sight to the physical and spiritually blinded; we minister to the poor; we set the Satan-oppressed free! We preach—"Jesus is Coming Soon."

The number one thing that hinders the Church from going forth with power is disunity. When the Holy Spirit fell the first time, the disciples were all in one place and in **one accord** (Acts 2:1). Soon persecution came, and the disciples went back to the church body and asked for prayer from the believers for the boldness they needed. As they agreed together in prayer, the place was shaken and they were filled with the Holy Spirit (Acts 4:31). We can withstand any problem when we are in one accord, one mind—set on one purpose. Our purpose is to win the lost at any cost.

Disunity was a problem in the early days of the Church, and Satan has not changed his tactics of warfare. Going back to the holy anointing of Aaron—look at what David wrote in Psalms 133:

> Behold, how good and how pleasant it is for ***brethren to dwell together in unity***! It is like the ***precious ointment*** upon the head, that ran down upon the beard, even Aaron's beard: that went down to the skirts of his garments; as the dew of Hermon, and as the dew that descended upon the mountains of Zion: for there the Lord commanded the blessing, even life for evermore.

The anointing flows as believers come together in unity. How can you divide one body? I certainly would not want to cut off one of my limbs. How can we separate ourselves from each other with divisions, strife, warring, and fighting? We are the Army of the Lord. A military unit is only effective as it works together as one organism. How good it is when we come together in love and purpose.

I have one more thought that needs to be addressed. This is the fact that we are not to touch (hurt) God's anointed. Saul was anointed king over Israel, but he disobeyed God. Because of this disobedience, Samuel had anointed David to take Saul's place as king. Consequently, Saul wanted to kill David and pursued him all over the mountains. Two times David had the opportunity to kill Saul, but he would not stretch forth his hand against the Lord's anointed (1 Samuel 26:23). The same principal applies to the leaders of our local churches. We need to be very careful not to speak evil of these men and women of God, or that we in anyway discourage our pastors and leadership. If we do not agree with what they are doing, we need to lovingly speak to them and pray for them. They are anointed by the Lord to lead and guide the Church.

My Prayer: The anointing You have placed upon me is so blessed, yet it is such a great responsibility. I seek Your face that I may go forth into a dying world with the power You have placed in my heart. Remind me always that I am part of the body of Christ; therefore, I must walk in unity and love with the other members. Guard my mind from any critical thoughts. Guard my lips from any hurtful things that Satan would tempt me say about the chosen ones that You have assigned to shepherd Your Church.

AMPLE SUPPLY OF WATER

A fountain of gardens, a well of living waters, and streams from
Lebanon. Song of Solomon 4:15

The Bride is a garden fountain that has enough water for many
gardens. The supply is unlimited. A well of living waters, cool and
fresh, is the only thing that will satisfy the thirsty soul. This is different
from the **sealed up fountain** we talked about in verse twelve of this
chapter. The **sealed up fountain** spoke to us of her purity and her dedication to Christ alone. She is able and willing to share this **living water** with other gardens that are thirsty and dry. "Blessed are they which
do hunger and **thirst** after righteousness: for they shall be filled" (Matthew 5:6). Anyone who is thirsty for the things of God will be filled.

The streams from Mount Lebanon are well known for being
cool and clean. The source of water is the melting snow from the high
mountaintops. The streams of Lebanon are the source of supply for the
fountain and the well in the garden.   Our source of supply is Jesus
Christ and the Holy Spirit. "The glory of Lebanon shall come unto
thee, the fir tree, the pine tree, and the box together, to beautify the
place of my sanctuary; and *I will make the place of my feet glorious*"
(Isaiah 60:13). I am His temple during this dispensation of grace. My
heart is **the glorious place** prepared for His nail scarred feet.

There is joy and gladness from the bubbling water within our
souls. "There is a river, the streams whereof shall make glad the city
of God, the **holy place of the tabernacles** of the most High. God is in
the midst of her; she shall not be moved: God shall help her, and that
right early" (Psalms 46:4-5). We are the city of God—the holy
tabernacles during the age of grace. Water flows from the throne of
God to cheer us and makes our hearts joyful. "The joy of the Lord is
your strength" (Nehemiah 8:10).   This is truly living water. Without
this water, our hearts become dry and dead.

When the children of Israel were in a dry and weary land, they
cried out for water. The Lord supplied gushing rivers: "He clave the
rocks in the wilderness, and gave them drink as out of the great
depths. He brought streams also out of the rock, and caused waters to
run down like rivers" (Psalms 78:15-16). Paul tells us in 1 Corinthians
10:4 that the rock was Christ Jesus.

The Church needs the refreshing of the Spirit from time to
time. "The times of refreshing shall come from the presence of the
Lord" (Acts 3:19). It is so easy to get busy with all kinds of activities

and to neglect coming into the presence of our Lord. We must set time aside to renew our spirits, so that we remain fresh and not dry up.

I had three uncles who liked to do a little amateur prospecting in the Arizona mountains. On one of their excursions, they had trouble with their Jeep and could not get it to start. They were about twenty miles from the highway. They had to walk out of the desert to find help. It was not long until the canteens ran out of water. I can recall how they described the unimaginable thirst that came over them. Out there with the rattlesnakes and other undesirable creatures, there was absolutely no shade. My uncle, Clifford, told how his tongue actually stuck to the roof of his mouth, and his lips were so dry they cracked and bled. They thought they could die out there, and nobody would discover their bodies for days. Needless to say, it was quite some time before they ventured out into the desert again. There was no amount of gold or silver that was worth the suffering they had gone through.

Church, we live in a dry, thirsty, dying world that needs Jesus. We know the source of living water. How can we be selfish and hold on to it without sharing? I pray we are the Bride of Christ that John saw in his revelation:

> The Spirit and the bride say, Come. And let him that heareth say, Come. And let him that is athirst come. And whosoever will, let him take the water of life freely.   Revelation 22:17

My Prayer: Thank You, Lord, for Your joy and Your refreshing in my soul. Cause me to come and drink from Your river each day. I pray that my fountain will bubble up and spill over to a lost and dying world. Holy Spirit, use me to gather the thirsty into the kingdom of God.

BLOW ON MY GARDEN

Awake, O north wind; and come, thou south; blow upon my garden,
that the spices thereof may flow out. Let my beloved come into his
garden, and eat his pleasant fruits.
Song of Solomon 4:16

Come Holy Spirit and breathe on my garden. The north wind is strong with conviction that causes me to draw near to my King. It may bring trials to refine me, but let it blow. I become stronger in my faith as I learn to yield to Your Holy Spirit's work in my life.

Come Holy Spirit and breathe on my garden with the gentle south winds of Your comfort. In the south winds of summer, You allow times of refreshing and renewal.

Whatever winds blow on my life, I am content knowing that You are in control. "And we know that all things work together for good to them that love God, to them who are the called according to his purpose" (Romans 8:28). Just as Paul declared, "I have learned, in whatsoever state I am, therewith to be content. I know both how to be abased, and I know how to abound: every where and in all things I am instructed both to be full and to be hungry, both to abound and to suffer need. I can do all things through Christ which strengtheneth me" (Philippians 4:11-13).

Many times it takes the wind of adversity to blow upon my garden, so as to stir up the fragrance of my spices—spices of my crucified life, my extravagant worship, my prayers ascending to the Father, and my holy anointing oil which causes me to reach out to others. Most of all, it takes the wind and the breath of the Holy Spirit to quicken me and make me alive. (John 6:63, Ezekiel 37:9) Come Holy Spirit as a rushing mighty wind and fill me with power from on high. (Acts 2:2)

Come Holy Spirit and produce the fruit that is pleasing to my King. May my love for Jesus and others be foremost in my life. The same love that produces the other fruits that You delight in—joy, peace, longsuffering, gentleness, goodness, faith, meekness and self-control (Galatians 5:22).

Amen

CHAPTER 5

COME AND DINE

I am come into my garden, my sister, my spouse: I have gathered my myrrh with my spice; I have eaten my honeycomb with my honey; I have drunk my wine with my milk: eat, O friends; drink, yea, drink abundantly, O beloved. Song of Solomon 5:1

The great "I AM", the ruler of the universe, is the gardener of my heart. Before He found me, I was just a piece of dirt—a weed infested lot. Then Jesus took possession, began to dig, cultivate, and plant the seed of His precious Word within my heart. Now I am His garden, and He comes to harvest the crop. He has invited His friends, for there is an abundant supply. Jesus told His disciples in John 15:13-16 that He would call them friends if they would do His commands. When we plant a garden, there is usually more produce than we can eat alone so we share with our friends. It is the same with the Lord's garden—more than enough. Let's share!

What He has planted, He is now gathering—for it all belongs to Him. He has worked hard on my life to bring it to this point of return. I am confident that "*He who began a good work in you* [and me] *will carry it on to completion until the day of Christ Jesus*" (Philippians 1:6, NIV).

Note the "*my*" in the verse we are contemplating in the Song of Solomon denotes Jesus, the Beloved King. Jesus comes to His garden and gathers His myrrh—my crucified life. He comes to eat His honey—all my sweet and encouraging words. He drinks of His wine—which is the Holy Spirit who causes me to walk after the ways of God and not my flesh. He drinks of His milk—the Word of God that I use to nurture the newborn babes in Christ. The fruits my garden produces are ultimately His; I produce nothing without Him.

I am Christ's sister and His spouse. I am His garden. My invitation is: "Come to my garden party and dine with me my Beloved King." "Bring all Your guests and friends, for there is plenty." I will "*go out into the highways and hedges, and compel them to come in, that my* [Christ's] *house may be filled*" (Luke 14:23).

My Prayer: Lord, have Your way with me. Cause me to yield to Your shovel, Your pruning, Your wind, and Your rain; thereby, I may yield much fruit for Your kingdom. Come, Lord Jesus—dine and commune with me. I love to be in Your presence.

MY BELOVED KNOCKS

I sleep, but my heart waketh: it is the voice of my beloved that knock-eth, saying, Open to me, my sister, my love, my dove, my undefiled: for my head is filled with dew, and my locks with the drops of the night. Song of Solomon 5:2

This verse is the beginning of a new stanza in the Song of songs. The Bride is half-awake and half-asleep. She is not sure if she is dreaming, or if she is really hearing the knock on the door and the voice of her Beloved asking her to open up. As she begins to wake up, she hears Him quietly calling out all of His favorite names for her: "my sister, my love, my dove, my undefiled." Her heart starts to pound, and now she is really starting to wake up.

She realizes in that split second that He has added another special name—"my undefiled." This name reminds her that she is pure, cleansed, and set apart for a holy purpose. The Holy Spirit has anointed her for use. Nevertheless, she is still so sleepy. Is this a picture of the Bride resting in her past experiences? Yes, I believe she is in her comfort zone and does not want to be moved out of it. The Lord requires her to move, and He wants her to give her service in a different, perhaps frightening, place.

The Lord is speaking to the Church from outside of its walls. His head is damp from the dew. The dew falls while it is still dark but just before daybreak. He has been outside all night laboring. She knows His voice, but she is so warm and tired. Besides, she feels no compassion for those out in the night—in the darkness of sin.

The Lord wants us to open our heart's door, and to share His heart's longing. We need to look out upon the world and see the harvest field. The laborers are few. We must pray! We must go! The Lord's desire is for souls, and that must become the Church's overwhelming desire (Luke 10:2).

The Lord speaks to the church of the Laodiceans in Revelation 3:14-22. He commends them for their past works, but they had become lukewarm. They were very comfortable with the wealth of goods, and they thought they did not need anything else. Our Lord wanted to stir them up. Consequently, He rebuked them severely and disciplined them saying: "As many as I love, I rebuke and chasten: *be zealous therefore, and repent. Behold, I stand at the door, and knock*: if any man hear my voice, and open the door, I will come in to him, and will sup with him, and he with me. To him that overcometh will I grant to sit with me in my throne, even as I also overcame, and am set down with my Father in his throne" (Revelation 3:19-20).

Wake up Church! This is not the time to be comfortable and content with past victories. Open the door. Invite Jesus to come in, and He will share His vision and purpose for the Church and for each of our lives. There will be plenty of time to relax when we have overcome.

My Prayer: Lord, what can I do? Where can I go? Stir my heart until I am wide-awake to your call. Shake me and discipline me if that is what I need. I want to be ready to move out of my slumber at Your command on a moments notice.

EXCUSES

I have put off my coat; how shall I put it on? I have washed my feet; how shall I defile them? Song of Solomon 5:3

The Bride is so comfortable and warm—tucked in her blanket of self-righteousness and the quilts of status quo. She starts to question why would her Beloved want her to get up. She has already taken off her coat, and it will be cold when she opens the door. Why would He want her to get her feet dirty? After all, didn't He just call her, "the undefiled"?

Can we, as the Church, become so involved with the righteous activities of the church that we sometimes only see other Christians? We never open the door and look at what is happening outside of our comfort zone. Do we only move in a sheltered, restful type of situation?

Jesus laid aside His heavenly robe and took on the robe of flesh. He got His feet dirty on the filthy roads of humanity. He mingled with sinners. He was accused of being a friend of sinners by the righteous people of His day (Mark 2:16). We need to follow His example and move out into the night.

The Church (our brothers and sisters in the Lord) are important, and they are not to be neglected. We need the comfort and love we give and receive in the church setting, but we also need compassion and a desire to move out into the dirty world and win the dying that walk in darkness. The local church should be a place of growth; equipping the believer for ministry. Then we are ready to go out into the world and minister to them the message of hope and light. We need to tell them the wonderful story of love, which is the theme of our song.

Day will break when our Lord returns to Earth again. I want to be working when He comes. I do not want to be giving Him excuses for why I was too comfortable or too tired to do His bidding.

My Prayer: Lord, I thank You for loving me so much that You took off Your royal robes and walked up the dusty road that led to Calvary. Help me to spread this message of love to a sinful and hurting world. Lay souls upon my heart and give me a burden for the lost.

I'M COMING LORD

My beloved put in his hand by the hole of the door, and my bowels were moved for him. I rose up to open to my beloved; and my hands dropped with myrrh, and my fingers with sweet smelling myrrh, upon the handles of the lock. Song of Solomon 5:4-5

The precious hand of Jesus reaches out and touches the hole (lock) by the door. He has been knocking, and now He tries the lock to see if I may have responded to Him. He will not force His way into my heart, for He is a gentleman. I am reminded that His hands are nail-scarred for me. This stirs a deep longing within me to see His face once again. My love moves me right down to the pit of my stomach. My bowels of mercy and compassion are awakened (Colossians 3:12).

I rise up to open the door and to do His bidding. Whatever He wants me to do; wherever He wants me to go; I am ready. I am willing to take up my cross and follow Him. My hands are covered with the myrrh of surrender. My fingers are dripping with sacrifice and praise to my Beloved.

There is such urgency now, for I have been so slow to heed His call. Have I missed His will for my life completely? Oh, why didn't I shake off the sleep when He first knocked? Why have I been so afraid of change? Forgive me Lord for not responding as soon as You called. My fingers must turn the door handle, but they are slippery and I cannot get a grip on it. I must call on His name; He will strengthen me. Please wait Lord—I'm coming!

I am going to open every door of my heart to You, Lord. I am not going to try to keep anything hidden. I will not live any longer for myself, but I will live for You because You have died for me. (2 Corinthians 5:15)

My Prayer: Lord, I know I have been slow to answer Your call. Please forgive me for not responding as soon as You knocked on the door of my heart. I have been so foolish to think that I could silence the Holy Spirit's tug on my soul.

GRIEVE NOT THE SPIRIT OF THE LIVING GOD

I opened to my beloved; but my beloved had withdrawn himself, and was gone: my soul failed when he spake: I sought him, but I could not find him; I called him, but he gave me no answer.
Song of Solomon 5:6

She flung open the door to the One she loves so much! Let Him be the King of all! He shall reign upon the throne of her heart. She has moved out—ready to do His will.

Oh, no! Where is He? He has withdrawn Himself. She is faint with worry and fear. Now, there is doubt about His will in the secret recesses of her heart. Had He really desired her to move out of her safe position? Would it be right to go out into the night and leave her warm bed and the safety of her bedroom chambers? If she could only hear Him speak again—He would answer her questions.

I know how she felt. When I (Ginger) was a teenager, I drifted away from my Lord. I was not in deep sin, but I was being very disobedient to my parents and doing things behind their backs, which I knew they would not approve. My affections were set on a certain boy who was not serving the Lord. I knew I was not pleasing the Lord by the way I was living, but I wanted my own way. I was weary of all the demands—the do's and the don'ts of the church. The relationship with my boyfriend suddenly ended in heartbreak. I was devastated, but it was for my good. I cried out to the Lord for His forgiveness. I made things right with my parents. Then I expected to have the witness of the sweet presence of Jesus come back into my life, right away, but that did not happen. I prayed and read my Bible, but it seemed like heaven was closed. The Word of God consoled me, for He promised that if I confessed my sin, He would be faithful and just to forgive that sin (1 John 1:9). I prayed as David did, "Restore unto me the joy of thy salvation; and uphold me with thy free spirit" (Psalms 51:12). About a month went by before the answer to my prayers came. My friend, Mary Ann, and I stayed at church after everyone had gone home. We bombarded heaven for the restoration of His Spirit. That night I was refilled with the Holy Spirit and spoke in tongues. [1] Immediately, the joy of my salvation was restored. I cannot describe the emptiness I had felt before that restoration. I never want to grieve the Holy Spirit again by my selfish actions.

I believe this is the Bride's situation in the scripture we are examining here in the Song of Solomon. The Spirit of our Lord was

145

grieved because she took so long to respond. The Lord is grieved by the hardness of our hearts: "And when he had looked round about on them with anger, *being grieved for the hardness of their hearts*, he saith unto the man, Stretch forth thine hand. And he stretched it out: and his hand was restored whole as the other" (Mark 3:5-6). Paul admonishes us to, "Quench not the Spirit" (1 Thessalonians 5:19).

The Lord chastises us for disobedience. For a time, He may seem to remove His presence from us. He does not really forsake us; however, we cannot feel the sweet fellowship as before.

The Bride is afraid, but she takes on fresh courage. She must find her Beloved. Communication has been broken—she must restore it. She regrets that she did not answer His first call. She has learned to answer, "Here am I; send me" (Isaiah 6:8). She now knows that the Beloved will not move out into new areas of ministry without her. The Church is the hands, the feet, the mouth, and the eyes—Jesus is the head—the Commander and Chief. He must use His Church to reach out to the world.

Just as the Bride has learned this hard lesson—we learn obedience. We learn this obedience through our failures, trials, and tribulations. We learn to walk by faith when the feelings are not there. Trust and obey.

My Prayer: Lord, help me to obey You and walk in faith. Help me not to grieve the Holy Spirit as He leads me and guides me. When it seems like You are not there, help me to realize that You will never leave me nor forsake me. Although I really do not find pleasure in chastisement, I am willing to submit as I learn the lesson You are teaching me. I praise You Lord, for Your Word that causes me to trust and obey.

[1] See Acts 2:4; Acts 10:46; Acts 19:6. Note that speaking in an unknown tongue is the evidence of the infilling of the Holy Spirit.

Ginger as a teenager

Living in Arizona

PRIDE GOES BEFORE A FALL

The watchmen that went about the city found me, they smote me, they wounded me; the keepers of the walls took away my veil from me. Song of Solomon 5:7

Again, she goes out into the streets to search for her Beloved. (Refer to Chapter 3, verse 3) The watchmen that go about the city (the darkness of the world) find the Bride. They hate her, for she stands for holiness. They throw blows of false accusations and half-truths at her. They are wolves in sheep's clothing, and they are acting like angels of light. (Matthew 7:15; 2 Corinthians 11:14) They are the false prophets of this world. They are people who claim to be looking out for her best interest, but they do not love her.

As she rested upon her bed, she had been so spiritually proud and self-satisfied with her accomplishments done in the name of the Lord. The scripture warns, "Woe to them that are at ease in Zion" (Amos 6:1). When she finally moved out into the night, she found that the Lord had removed Himself. She should have known better than to go into the enemy's territory without the Lord's protection. She becomes frightened, and once again, turns to man for help.

The keepers of the wall take away her veil. The veil was a symbol of her sanctification. [1] She, being wounded and weak, yields to sin. Spiritual pride and self-satisfaction will bring us into a great deal of distress. The scripture warns us: "Pride goeth before destruction, and an haughty spirit before a fall" (Proverbs 16:18).

We must be vigilant at all times; otherwise, Satan will take advantage of us. If we neglect our reading and meditating upon the Word of God and do not spend time with the Lord in prayer, as a rule, we will stop attending church. Our spirits become cold and indifferent. How careful we must be to maintain our dedication to Jesus.

Rather than looking into her own heart and getting right with her Lord, she went to people. There is no peace for the child of God who turns to man for help. Only Jesus is able help us, and He is so willing to respond to our call for help.

You will call upon Me and go and pray to Me, and I will listen to you. And you will seek Me and find Me, when you search for Me with all your heart. I will be found by you, says the Lord, and I will bring you back from your captivity.
Jeremiah 29:12-14, NKJV

My Prayer: Lord, help me to remember that You alone are my source of peace. I find help by searching for You and making my heart right with You. Thank You for being so longsuffering toward me. Thank You for not giving up on me.

(1) Sanctification: To sanctify means commonly to make holy, that is, to separate from the world and consecrate to God.
(From International Standard Bible Encyclopedia, Electronic Database Copyright © 1996, 2003, 2006 by Biblesoft, Inc. All rights reserved.)

HEALING FOR THE WOUNDED

I charge you, O daughters of Jerusalem, if ye find my beloved, that
ye tell him, that I am sick of love.
Song of Solomon 5:8

The Bride finally turns back to the church (the daughters of Jerusalem). Many times, when we have lost that intimate relationship with the Lord, we turn to the church for guidance and prayer. We share our problems with those of like, precious faith. She begs, "Please, if you contact my Beloved, tell Him that I still love Him, and I want to get back into fellowship with Him." She is sick with love and, oh, so sorry for her waywardness. Now she is hurt and wounded by trying to make it on her own—trying to solve her own problems.

The church is a place for family and prayer: "Brethren, if a man be overtaken in a fault, ye which are spiritual, restore such an one in the spirit of meekness; considering thyself, lest thou also be tempted. Bear ye one another's burdens, and so fulfil the law of Christ" (Galatians 6:1-2). The wounded desperately need the comfort, forgiveness, and healing of their brothers and sisters. The church is tempted, at times, to be harsh and to exile the one who has fallen, but we are to restore the one who is hurt. We must remember that we could be in the same place if it were not for the grace of God.

She has found that the world is very cold and cruel. The desire to return to the covering of the believers is overwhelming! We need the fellowship that the church offers. The next problem that our Bride encounters is that her sisters are not very spiritual; therefore, they are not very much help. The ideal church body is made up of very spiritual leaders and concerned, praying members. Needless to say, this is not always the case. There are some problems, habits, and hurts that only Jesus is qualified to heal. She has to find Him!

My Prayer: Thank You for the fellowship of the believers. How I covet their prayers. I cannot make it on my own. Help me not to let my spiritual pride separate me from other members of Your body, even if some do not understand what I am going through.

MY BELOVED IS LORD

What is thy beloved more than another beloved, O thou fairest among women? What is thy beloved more than another beloved, that thou dost so charge us? Song of Solomon 5:9

Her fellow believers ask twice, "*What is thy beloved more than another beloved?*" In other words, "What is it you see in the Beloved King that we have not seen?"—Or— "What makes your lover so special?" Her fellow believers must be coming from that same complacent place where she had been dwelling a few verses ago. They are questioning why she is so enthusiastic—even fanatical—about the relationship that she wants to restore.

Her friends are in the church, but they have not caught the vision of how absolutely wonderful Jesus is. Perhaps they are satisfied with just attending a service on Sunday morning, which makes them feel like they have fulfilled their religious duty. They do not feel the need to draw closer to the Lord by attending Bible studies and prayer meetings. They do not seek the Holy Spirit's infilling. This type of believer is being cheated out of the fullness Christ has for them by following the religious traditions of men:

Beware lest anyone *cheat* you through philosophy and empty deceit, *according to the tradition of men*, according to the basic principles of the world, and not according to Christ. For in Him dwells all the fullness of the Godhead bodily; and you are complete in Him, who is the head of all principality and power.
Colossians 2:8-10, NKJV

The Bride, the fair one, who is reflecting the Savior of her soul is about to give an answer just as Peter says we must be ready to do:

But in *your hearts set apart Christ as Lord*. Always be prepared to give an answer to everyone who asks you to give the reason for the hope that you have. But do this with gentleness and respect.   1 Peter 3:15-16, NIV

I believe her attitude is different from her sisters because she has truly fallen completely in love with her Lord. She has determined that Christ is Lord (King) of her life. Every action—every thought—every

151

good work that she does is because He is ruling and reigning in her life.

She is about to give her sisters the description of her Beloved, and she is going to explain why He means so much to her in the next verses. He is the fairest of ten thousand—the bright and morning star. He is to be loved above all men who ever walked the earth.

Her veil has been taken away. The watchmen had removed it for evil purposes, but the Lord is going to work out all things for her good. She is coming out of this time of grief seeing clearer than ever before. The Holy Spirit is giving her liberty that frees her from the traditions of men. "Stand fast therefore in the liberty wherewith Christ hath made us free, and be not entangled again with the yoke of bondage" (Galatians 5:1).

We can draw others closer to the Lord by the way we live and speak. Love, excitement, and spiritual renewal are contagious. Let the praise of our Beloved King be on our lips continually: "The branch of the Lord be beautiful and glorious" (Isaiah 4:2). "Whoso offereth praise glorifieth me" (Psalms 50:23).

My Prayer: Keep me, Lord, ever excited about Your love and Your work within my life. Let Your sweet Holy Spirit continually change me so that I am moving from glory to glory. I desire to reflect Your glory. I desire to show others how special You are. I enjoy the freedom of Your Spirit. May my love and enthusiasm show others what they are missing when they do not allow You to be Lord of their lives.

WHITE, RED, AND BLUE

My beloved is white and ruddy, the chiefest among ten thousand.
Song of Solomon 5:10

The Bride is now going to describe her Beloved to the daughters of Jerusalem. I can still remember when I first fell in love with David, my husband. Although he had graduated a year earlier than I had, he had to come back to high school to make up for one class he had not completed. My heart would almost burst with pride as my girlfriends saw him enter the halls of our school. He was very handsome and tall, with dark wavy hair, and the biggest—bluest eyes—you have ever seen. He had to wear his work uniform because he only took a break from work to attend this class. His muscles showed under the white shirt, and he looked so sharp.

The Bride's Beloved is the chief among ten thousand. There is none to compare with Him, for He is Jesus. King David had the women singing his praises: "the women answered one another as they played, and said, Saul hath slain his thousands, and David his ten thousands" (1 Samuel 18:7-8). How much more the Bride of Christ sings the praises and extols the beauty of her King of kings.

The first distinctive feature of our Beloved King is that He is white. White is always a symbol of holiness and purity. There is no flaw—no off color—no sin to mar the appearance of my Beloved. He is perfect in every way. This description is of His heavenly, glorified body. His earthly body was so beaten and bruised that He was not recognizable (Isaiah 53:2). Oh, what love He demonstrated to us!

The Hebrew word that is translated as "white" in this passage is like a dazzling, radiant, or bright white. [1] Daniel had a vision of the Lord in which he said the Ancient of Days' garments were white as snow (Daniel 7:9). On the mount of transfiguration, the disciples tell us that Jesus was, "transfigured before them: and his face did *shine as the sun*, and his raiment was *white as the light*" (Matthew 17:2-3). John describes his vision of Jesus as, "his countenance was as the *sun shineth* in his strength" (Revelation 1:16). I think it was very difficult for mere men to describe the glory that shines forth from Jesus. The best words they could find were "white", "shines as the sun", "white as the light", and "the sun shineth in his strength." Our eyes are not made to look directly into the sun. When we look upon our Beloved, he is too bright and shining for us to look directly at Him with our human eyes. With the eyes of the soul, we see our Lord high and lifted up and

153

shining in all of His glory. When we catch a glimpse of Him, all we can do is fall on our faces in humble adoration (Revelation 1:17).

My Beloved is ruddy. Ruddy denotes rosy cheeks associated with health and energy. David, as a young shepherd boy, was ruddy: "Now he was ruddy, and withal of a beautiful countenance, and goodly to look to. And the Lord said, Arise, anoint him: for this is he" (1 Samuel 16:12). This was a quality of good looks. Our Lord is alive and well. He is victor over death and sickness, and He is beautiful to behold. David was anointed King of Israel above all his older brothers. Jesus has been anointed King, Priest, and Prophet. The Psalmist sang of Him, "You are fairer than the sons of men; Grace is poured upon Your lips; Therefore God has blessed You forever" (Psalms 45:2, NKJV).

Jesus was a Nazarite: "Nazarites were purer than snow, they were whiter than milk, they were more ruddy in body than rubies, their polishing was of sapphire" (Lamentations 4:7). Various prophets saw visions of the throne of God, and they say that under His feet and around His throne is this beautiful, blue sapphire. (Exodus 24:10; Ezekiel 1:26, 10:1; Revelation 4:6) It speaks to us of heaven and the very throne room of God.

Jesus is the chiefest of ten thousand. He is not only superior to any other man, but He is the Captain of the hosts of heaven and earth. He comes with ten thousands of His saints. He loves the people. All His saints are in His hand. (Deuteronomy 33:1-4)

My Prayer: I stand in awe at Your holiness, Your beauty, and Your strength. I will boast in Christ my Savior, for He has done great things in my life. He loves me with an everlasting love. I am not ashamed to shout of Your excellence from the housetops. Wash me and I will be whiter than snow—just like You are. Bathe me with physical and spiritual health. My desire is to be like You in every way.

(1)   Biblesoft's New Exhaustive Strong's Numbers and Concordance with Expanded Greek-Hebrew Dictionary. Copyright © 1994, 2003, 2006 Biblesoft, Inc. and International Bible Translators, Inc. OT:6703, OT:6705

GOLD AS THE SUN

BLACK AS THE RAVEN

His head is as the most fine gold, his locks are bushy, and black as a raven. Song of Solomon 5:11

My Beloved's head is as the finest gold. Gold speaks to us of His deity: "For in him dwelleth all the fulness of the Godhead bodily" (Colossians 2:9). Jesus was God in the flesh.

Who is the image of the invisible God, the firstborn of every creature: For by him were all things created, that are in heaven, and that are in earth, visible and invisible, whether they be thrones, or dominions, or principalities, or powers: all things were created by him, and for him: And he is before all things, and by him all things consist. And he is the *head of the body, the church*: who is the beginning, the firstborn from the dead; *that in all things he might have the preeminence. For it pleased the Father that in him should all fulness dwell.*
Colossians 1:15-19

His locks are black and bushy. Black hair indicates youthfulness, and bushy probably means wavy; therefore, we get the picture of a young man with thick, black hair. Jesus is from everlasting, yet He is full of youth and full of life—never lacking energy or health. "Jesus Christ is the same yesterday and today and forever" (Hebrews 13:8, NIV). He never changes, and He is always strong:

Hast thou not known? hast thou not heard, that the everlasting God, the Lord, the Creator of the ends of the earth, fainteth not, neither is weary? there is no searching of his understanding. He giveth power to the faint; and to them that have no might he increaseth strength.   Isaiah 40:28-29

Oh, how we need to draw from the everlasting Creator, who is the head of the Church, the physical and spiritual strength we lack when we find ourselves weak and faint.

The locks are also compared to being as black as a raven. The raven is an unclean bird, and it is quick to spot death. Jesus took upon His sinless head the sins of the world. "For he hath made him to be

155

sin for us, who knew no sin; that we might be made the righteousness of God in him" (2 Corinthians 5:21). My beautiful Lord became my substitute and took my punishment for sin. I am the one who deserved to die, but He took my place. "For the wages of sin is death; but the gift of God is eternal life through Jesus Christ our Lord" (Romans 6:23). My uncleanness was laid upon His holy head, so that I could become united with Him. "But he that is joined unto the Lord is one spirit" (1 Corinthians 6:17).

My Prayer: Oh Lord, my Lord, how wonderful You are. You are my Creator, my Lover, my Strength, and my Deliverer. You have released me from the penalty of sin by taking my sin upon Yourself. I can never praise You enough. When I am weak, You are strong within me. I worship Your Deity—I worship Your love for me.

FORGIVING EYES

His eyes are as the eyes of doves by the rivers of waters, washed with milk, and fitly set. Song of Solomon 5:12

How could she have been so stupid? She had fallen right into the trap of the religious men of the town. They knew that she would be entertaining one of her men clients that day. They had not acted like they paid any attention to her sinful activities before this day, but now they wanted to make a spectacle of her because of the new teacher. Here she stands before the teacher and all those angry men who want to stone her. She closes her eyes and awaits the first stone to hit. All is quiet, so she opened her eyes—keeping her gaze humbly downward. She can only see the teacher. He has knelt down, and he is writing something on the ground. The silence is broken by shouts of the angry men again, "What shall we do with her?" The teacher stands upright and says, "He that has no fault; let him cast the first stone." Then He goes back to writing on the ground. The religious leaders had seen His piercing eyes and felt the Holy Spirit's conviction. One-by-one they left. The woman did not dare to look around, for she knew she was guilty. When all had left, Jesus asked her, "Where are your accusers?" She answered that no one was left to condemn her. Jesus looked directly into her eyes. She saw mercy and love flow from His eyes, as He said, "Neither do I condemn thee, go and sin no more." Just one look into His eyes had changed her life completely. (John 8:3-11)

We have seen before that the dove is a symbol of the gentle Holy Spirit. It is difficult for us to look straight into the eyes of our parents when we have been naughty, or to look at someone that we have lied to, or to look at someone we have gossiped about, or look at someone we have mistreated. This is because we have a guilty conscience, and the Holy Spirit is convicting us of the wrong that is in our hearts. The eyes of the Lord are tender, gentle—and yet piercing. Our loving heavenly Father uses eye contact to bring us back into the way we should go. They say to us, "Come and wash in the river of the Holy Spirit and the Word of God. Be refreshed and renewed. Go back to the basics and drink from the milk of the Word."

I am so thankful for the forgiveness and freedom we experience in Christ. "There is therefore now no condemnation to them which are in Christ Jesus, who walk not after the flesh, but after the

Spirit" (Romans 8:1). We are so fortunate to live in this Day of Grace while the waters of forgiveness flow freely.

At the end of this age, the Lord's eyes will change to eyes of judgment. John's vision of the Lord was very different, "His eyes were as a flame of fire" (Revelation 1:14). "I tell you, *now is the time of God's favor, now is the day of salvation*" (2 Corinthians 6:2-3, NIV). Now is the time to seek His forgiveness. Now is the time to experience joy and peace. Come to the waters, drink, and be renewed in the Holy Spirit.

My Prayer: "The eyes of the Lord are over the righteous, and his ears are open unto their prayers" (1 Peter 3:12). I am righteous only because You have cleansed me. May You always hear my prayers. Thank You for the rivers of water that are Your sweet Holy Spirit. I love the milk of Your Word. It causes me to come and draw new strength. Let Your tender, compassionate eyes ever be upon me.

SWEET JESUS

His cheeks are as a bed of spices, as sweet flowers: his lips like lilies,
dropping sweet smelling myrrh.
Song of Solomon 5:13

I, [*Jesus*], gave my back to the smiters, and my **cheeks** to
them that plucked off the hair: I hid not my face from shame
and spitting. For the Lord God will help me; therefore shall I
not be confounded: therefore have I set my face like a flint, and
I know that I shall not be ashamed.   Isaiah 50:6-7

Why did Jesus have to endure the agony and shame of the
mockers and cruel soldiers even before hanging on the cross? In the
sixteenth chapter of Leviticus, it gives us the details of the offering
given on the Day of Atonement. Before Aaron, the High Priest, entered into the Holy of Holies where the mercy seat was located, he
would take a censer full of burning coals from off of the altar, fill his
hands with sweet incense that had been beaten small, and bring them
within the veil. When the incense was set on fire, it made a cloud that
covered the mercy seat, thereby, protecting Aaron from the justice of
God. Only then could he sprinkle the blood on the mercy seat.

The night before Jesus died, He was spat upon, the crown of
thorns was jammed into His forehead, His beard was pulled out of His
cheeks, His lips bled because the soldiers beat Him with their fist, and
He was beaten with many stripes. The incense of His love and submission ascended to His Father as Jesus' body was crushed. God was
watching all of this agony—ready to justify His Beloved Son by raising Him from the dead. Jesus entered into the heavenly tabernacle
with His own blood (Hebrews 9:23-24). This sacrifice satisfied the
justice of God; therefore, we are able to stand before Him without
shame, for Jesus bore our shame.

His lips dropped words of sweet myrrh as He prepared His disciples for the coming death and resurrection. Many times, He dropped
these words into their hearts: "I must die, but fear not, I will rise
again." (Luke 18:32-33; Mark 10:34) Even the words He spoke from
the cross were sweet to those whom He spoke to: "Father, forgive
them; for they know not what they do"—"Woman, behold thy son!"—
"Verily I say unto thee, Today shalt thou be with me in paradise."
(Luke 23:34; John 19:26; Luke 23:43)

[Jesus] Who did no sin, **neither was guile found in his mouth**: Who, when he was reviled, **reviled not again**; when he suffered, **he threatened not**; but committed himself to him that judgeth righteously: Who his own self bare our sins in his own body on the tree, that we, being dead to sins, should live unto righteousness: by whose stripes ye were healed.

1 Peter 2:22-24

Jesus did not speak a harsh word in His defense—all His words were **sweet as flowers**. How it breaks my heart as I meditate upon His suffering and death; yet it is sweet to me, for it purchased my salvation, my pardon, and my healing.

My Prayer: I remember the day You spoke to me, "Your sins are forgiven." From that time until now, I seek Your words as I would seek a hidden treasure. They remind me of Your suffering and my salvation. Your sweet words are in my mind as I awake in the morning, as I go about my daily tasks, and as I lay my head down to sleep. Speak Lord, for I am listening.

ENTRUSTED WITH AUTHORITY

His hands are as gold rings set with the beryl: his belly is as bright ivory overlaid with sapphires. **Song of Solomon 5:14**

The gold rings that are upon the Beloved's hands are very significant. They are signs of His status, wealth, and authority. He has so many rings on His fingers that they resemble rods when the fingers are outstretched. The rings are inlaid with precious stones.

My Beloved is very wealthy. He owns the cattle on a thousand hills. He also owns the hills with all the gold, silver, and precious stones that are hidden in them (Psalms 50:10). He will supply every financial need we have out of His abundant riches. Our needs of spiritual well being are supplied by the riches that are in Christ Jesus (Philippians 4:19).

The ring of a king carried with it the authority of the kingdom. Once a document was sealed by the use of the king's ring, it was a law that could not be broken. From time-to-time, kings have entrusted their ring with its authority to another man. Pharaoh gave his ring to Joseph, thereby, making Joseph the second in command of all Egypt (Genesis 41:42). King Ahasuerus (Xerxes) was sorry that he had given his ring to the evil Haman, for Haman tried to use it to exterminate the chosen people of Israel (Esther 3:10-13). After such a bad decision, King Ahasuerus took the ring from Haman and gave it to Esther's loyal uncle, Mordecai (Esther 8:2).

The son of a well-to-do family was honored when his father gave him the ring of authority. It meant that he could carry out his father's business. I feel so unworthy to be called, "a son of God." I relate to the prodigal son who had spent all his inheritance upon careless living in a far away land. He returned to his father's house thinking that it would be good just to be a servant there, but the father accepted this wayward son home with open arms. He put a ring on his son's finger, and he gave him a clean robe for him to wear (Luke 15:22). King Jesus has entrusted His Church with His authority; therefore, we may go forth with the power of the Holy Spirit doing the work of our Father. Jesus says:

Most assuredly, I say to you, he who believes in Me, the works that I do he will do also; and greater works than these he will do, because I go to My Father. And whatever you ask in My name, that I will do, that the Father may be glorified in the Son. John 14:12-13, NKJV

The Beloved's rings are studded with precious stones of beryl (sometimes interpreted as topaz). It was one of the stones assigned to the High Priest breastplate, and it is one of the stones within the foundation of the New Jerusalem. This precious stone was taken from the heart of the earth where it had been created under intense heat. Jesus was in the heart of the earth three days. He came forth with victory over death, hell, and the grave. His nail-scarred hands took away the keys of death from Satan. Jesus told John, "I am he that liveth, and was dead; and, behold, I am alive for evermore, Amen; and have the keys of hell and of death" (Revelation 1:18).

His belly is as bright ivory. Men have treasured ivory because it could be carved into very beautiful jewelry, ornate boxes, and sculptures. King Solomon made his throne out of ivory and overlaid it with gold (1 Kings 10:18). It is a shame that in order to harvest the ivory tusks, the elephant must give his whole body and die. King Jesus was found in the fashion of a man (took on the appearance of a man). He laid down His life to purchase our salvation. Now He is exalted to the throne and sitting on the right hand of the Father. (Philippians 2:2-11)

We have already noted that the throne of God is surrounded by the likeness of the sapphire stone. "And above the firmament that was over their heads was the likeness of a throne, as the appearance of a sapphire stone: and upon the likeness of the throne was the likeness as the appearance of a man above upon it" (Ezekiel 1:26-27). Our Beloved King gave up His place in heaven for a short span of time making all the difference in mankind's history. He took upon Himself the likeness of man, was obedient to the cross, and is now sitting down upon the throne. He has passed His authority on to the Church. His authority enables the Church to bring glory to the Father.

My Prayer: To think that You have entrusted me with Your authority. Who am I—that You have called me? When I stand before Your magnificent throne, may I hear You say, "Well done, my good and faithful servant."

162

PILLARS IN THE TEMPLE OF MY GOD

His legs are as pillars of marble, set upon sockets of fine gold: his countenance is as Lebanon, excellent as the cedars.
Song of Solomon 5:15

The legs of my Beloved are likened to strong, straight pillars that are made of the finest marble. The roofs of ancient buildings were supported by its pillars. An example of the structural importance of the pillars is seen in the story of Samson as he took his final revenge on the Philistines. He took hold of the pillars of the temple of Dagon, and as God renewed Samson's strength, he pushed the pillars apart causing the roof to collapse on all the people gathered there. (Judges 16:24-31)

Solomon had erected two bronze pillars to support the porch of the magnificent temple he had built for the Lord. "And he set up the pillars in the porch of the temple: and he set up the right pillar, and called the name thereof Jachin: and he set up the left pillar, and he called the name thereof Boaz" (1 Kings 7:21-22). I think the names that Solomon gave these pillars are significant. *Jachin* means "he that strengthens and makes steadfast." [1] *Boaz* means "in strength." [1] The Beloved has legs that are very steadfast, and they are full of strength.

Marble is a very strong material and often used as pillars. Although marble comes in various colors, this passage uses the Hebrew word that conveys the meaning of "white or bleached." [2] Therefore, the Beloved's legs are not only strong and steadfast, but they are also righteous and holy. The legs are grounded in gold, which signifies Jesus' divine nature. He is divine from head to toe. (See Song of Solomon 5:11- head of fine gold)

The Church is a building under construction. Paul says that since we have been reconciled to God through the cross of Jesus...

Now, therefore, you are no longer strangers and foreigners, but fellow citizens with the saints and *members of the household of God*, having been *built on the foundation of the apostles and prophets*, Jesus Christ Himself being the chief cornerstone, in whom the whole building, being fitted together, *grows into a holy temple in the Lord*, in whom you also are being built together for a *dwelling place of God in the Spirit*.
Ephesians 2:19-22, NKJV

163

The two foundational factors of this most holy temple are the apostles and the prophets. The apostle's teachings are foundational to the Church because the apostles were the eyewitnesses of Jesus' ministry. They heard the teachings of Christ and recorded them for the Church (1 John 1:1-4). The early church continued steadfastly in the apostle's doctrine daily (Acts 2:42). The other foundation is the prophets because they foretold the coming of our Savior. The apostles explained the meaning and fulfillment of the prophet's sayings as they applied to the Church of Jesus Christ. Even Jesus explained to the two disciples on the road to Emmaus how the prophets had foretold of His death and resurrection, and their eyes were opened to the scriptures (Luke 24:13-32). These are the strong, righteous legs we stand on as the Church of Jesus Christ.

You may say, "But I don't feel very strong at times." Neither was the Church of Philadelphia that Jesus gave this message to: "for thou hast a *little strength*, and hast kept my *word*, and hast not denied my name " (Revelation 3:8). Our strength rests on the Word of God and the Name of Jesus. He goes on to say that because they have kept His word with patience, He would keep them in the hour of temptation. He promises to come quickly, and He instructs this last day church to hold on to what they have been given. Holding on to the truth of the apostles and the prophets will give us the strength to overcome. Jesus says to the Church, "Him that overcometh *will I make a pillar in the temple of my God*, and he shall go no more out: and I will write upon him the name of my God..." (Revelation 3:12).

We are strong as we stand upon the Word of God and proclaim the Name of Jesus. We, as His Church and Bride, are built up in His strength, for without Him we can do nothing (John 15:5). Jesus answered Paul's prayer when he felt weak in body: "My grace is sufficient for thee: for my strength is made perfect in weakness" (2 Corinthians 12:9).

Let us go back to our verse in the Song of Solomon: "His countenance is as Lebanon, excellent as the cedars." If we look at the whole man from head to toe—we see Jesus Christ the divine Son of God and the Son of Man. Remember the woods of Lebanon are a symbol of his human nature. Therefore, He is the Son of Man, standing tall and straight, beautiful to behold, righteous altogether, strong in strength, and a sweet fragrance among the nations. (2 Corinthians 2:14; Hosea 14:6) He overcame every temptation; therefore, His Church is an overcoming Bride.

164

My Prayer: Lord, as I grow older, my body seems so weak at times. Satan would tempt me to just give up and let others continue the mission of the Church, but as long as You give me strength—I will never give up. I lean upon the pillars of the Word of God which was given to us by the apostles and the prophets. I am determined to be a pillar in the temple of my Lord.

ALL TOGETHER LOVELY

His mouth is most sweet: yea, he is altogether lovely. This is my be-
loved, and this is my friend, O daughters of Jerusalem.
Song of Solomon 5:16

Every word from my Beloved's mouth is most sweet. Even as
we have sought after the truth of this obscure book in the Word of
God, we have seen how the words, commands, prophecies, history,
songs, and letters of this Book of books all fit together to form the
whole truth of our Lord. From Genesis to Revelation, it feeds our
souls. Jesus rebuked Satan's temptation with, "It is written, Man shall
not live by bread alone, but by every word that proceedeth out of the
mouth of God" (Matthew 4:4). Jesus is the Word: "In the beginning
was the Word, and the Word was with God, and the Word was God"
(John 1:1).

God provided the children of Israel with manna sent from
heaven to feed them as they traveled the wilderness: "And the house
of Israel called the name thereof Manna: and it was like coriander
seed, white; and *the taste of it was like wafers made with honey*"
(Exodus 16:31). Notice that the manna was sweet to the taste buds.
Jesus said Moses did not provide this manna, but the Father sent it—
the Father has given Jesus, the Bread of Life, to the Church. This living Bread provides life to the world (John 6:31-33). It is the Holy
Spirit that helps us to digest the sweetness of His Word: "It is the
spirit that quickeneth; the flesh profiteth nothing: the words that I
speak unto you, they are spirit, and they are life" (John 6:63).

To the Church of Pergamos, Jesus said, "To him that overcometh will I give to eat of the hidden manna" (Revelation 2:17). We
need to search the scriptures, for in them are hidden treasures of wisdom. Jesus said, "Search the scriptures; for in them ye think ye have
eternal life: and they are they which testify of me" (John 5:39). He
will open His treasure of hidden manna to the upright: "His secret
counsel is with the upright" (Proverbs 3:32, NKJV). To the searching
heart that is dedicated to the Beloved, His words are more precious
than gold. Job, who was probably the first writer recorded in the Bible, writes: "I have esteemed the words of his mouth more than my
necessary food" (Job 23:12).

Yes, Jesus is altogether lovely. I experience His love by reading, studying, and meditating on His living words. He has become my
friend. I can confide in Him and share my deepest secrets, just as He

166

confides His secrets with me. There is such a wonderful companionship as He sticks to me closer than a brother (Proverbs 18:24). He has called me friend:

> Henceforth I call you not servants; for the servant knoweth not what his lord doeth: *but I have called you friends; for all things that I have heard of my Father I have made known unto you.* Ye have not chosen me, but I have chosen you, and ordained you, that ye should go and bring forth fruit, and that your fruit should remain: that whatsoever ye shall ask of the Father in my name, he may give it you.   John 15:15-17

Because He calls me *friend*, He shares all things that He has heard of the Father with me. He has chosen me and ordained me to go forth and bear much fruit. My fruit will remain until the end of time. Look at the last wonderful privilege of being His friend—*whatever I ask of the Father in Jesus name, He will give it to me*! Now that is what I call a friend. Can you imagine being the friend of the most influential man on earth, and he tells you that you can have anything you desire? My friend is the most influential person in heaven!

This is why our Bride is so excited about her Beloved. She says, "Oh, daughters of Jerusalem, don't you want to get better acquainted with my wonderful King, for He is altogether lovely." She loves all of the fellow believers, even if their eyes have not been enlightened to see Him in all of His beauty. Whatever truth Jesus is revealing to me, He is anxious to reveal to the entire church body.

My Prayer: How I love to search Your words and find the precious truths and wisdom in them. It is so sweet when You open my eyes to new revelations that were before hidden to me. Help me to understand what You are saying to the Church. Help me to share what I have learned with everyone I meet. Thank you for calling me, "Your friend."

CHAPTER 6

COMING OUT OF THE DARK TRIAL

Whither is thy beloved gone, O thou fairest among women? whither is thy beloved turned aside? that we may seek him with thee.
Song of Solomon 6:1

The Bride has painted such a wonderful picture of her Beloved that the daughters of Jerusalem are stirred up. They, too, want to seek after the Lord. They have never seen Him in the light that the Bride has just shown them. As the Bride spoke of her Beloved, the Holy Spirit revealed Jesus to her in a fresh way. Isn't this just like the Lord? Sharing the goodness of our Lord shows us how real and precious He is to us. As she recounts the dark trial that she has been going through, she gets a clear revelation of how much she needs Him. It also causes the daughters of Jerusalem to sense their need of an intimate relationship with Jesus.

I look back to the darkest time in my marriage. David and I were married right out of high school. The Lord called David to the ministry the night he was baptized in the Holy Spirit. We struggled through Bible College during World War II. During our first pastorate in a little logging camp in the mountains above Eureka, California, the Lord blessed us with a baby girl. We then went back to San Francisco to finish our Bible college training, and we ministered in a skid row mission at the same time.

David became very discouraged with the ministry, so he decided to work for a while as a truck driver. Even while driving a truck all week long, he kept an interdenominational Sunday School going in Happy Valley, California. By this time, we also were blessed with a son. We were living out in the country, surrounded by strawberry fields, when our fourteen-month-old baby boy drowned in an irrigation stream. David was totally broken hearted from the loss of his little boy. As a result, we gave up trying to minister at all. We moved to Richmond. I attended church, but David made himself very scarce and was not around very much. He used his work schedule as an excuse, but I later found out the truth that he was seeing another woman who worked as a waitress along his route.

When the truth surfaced, we tried to work it out for a while, but I later found that he kept going back to her. This is when I loaded up our car with my six-year-old daughter and a few belongings, and we went home to my Mom and Dad. My Mom, Rev. Gertrude Jones, was the pastor of a thriving church in Bisbee, Arizona. [1] I cried so hard on the drive to Arizona that I came close to having a bad accident. Needless to say, it was a terrible time in my life. David had been such a strong Christian; I never thought he would fall so far away from God. I made a few friends in the church who stood by me in prayer and travailed for my husband's soul.

We experienced a very heavy burden for David as we prayed around the altar one Sunday night. That same night, I had a dream about David. In my dream I saw him all dressed up, and he was standing beside a mailbox. He was trying to mail a letter, but every time he reached out to insert the letter into the slot, a dark cloud would envelop him. I knew that Satan was hindering him from getting back to God. I woke up praying so hard that I also woke my daughter who was sleeping beside me.

It was very late the next night when I heard a small cargo van drive up in front of the house. It was David. I went out to meet him as the entire household was sleeping. I did not know if my dad would even let him in the house because he was very angry with his son-in-law. David cried and told me how sorry he was to have hurt me, and how he had asked the Lord's forgiveness on the long drive down to Arizona. He said he had written a letter in which he had asked my forgiveness, but for some reason, he just could not mail it. That is when he jumped into the smallest vehicle in his fleet and drove to see me.

I have told you all of this in order to explain how God works through our darkest trials to show us how deeply we long for His presence. David was a changed man, and his ministry was totally changed. He had such compassion for those who had strayed away from their Savior. Jesus' death and forgiveness were so dear to him that it was almost impossible for him to serve the Communion without tears coming to his eyes. Time-after-time in the following years of productive ministry, he helped husbands to make things right with their wives. Countless marriages were saved because of the trial of our faith.

Do you see why the daughters of Jerusalem longed to experience the same Lord the Bride knew and loved? It takes someone who has gone through the fire to ignite the passion in others. Oh Lord, use me as your torch!

Peter declared: "We have not followed cunningly devised fables, when we made known unto you the power and coming of our Lord Jesus Christ, but were eyewitnesses of his majesty" (2 Peter 1:16). The apostles were blessed to have seen Jesus walk and talk, but we are even more blessed because we have also seen His power to change a life completely. We see His majesty in the scripture and in the Spirit as we draw near to Him (John 20:29).

Why would the daughters of Jerusalem ask the Bride where her Beloved has gone? They know that she was the one who was searching for Him. I believe they have seen her change right before their eyes as she has been extolling the beauty of her wonderful Lord. This has brought her full circle, and we will see in the next verse that she has the answer.

My Prayer: How my heart yearns for You. How my lips extol Your grace. Cause me to be so on fire with the message of Your loving kindness that others will be begging me to tell them more. I am sometimes tempted to keep my past failures to myself because I am ashamed. Help me to overcome my shame and tell of your goodness for all the world to see. I thank You for the dark trials of my life, for they have given me the testimony I need to minister to others.

[1] Even though Gertrude Jones is actually my Aunt, I call her and her husband Claude Jones, Mom and Dad because they raised me as their own child.

This picture is of Gertrude and Claude Jones with the Bisbee church. Gertrude was the preacher and Claude was the builder.

Bisbee Assembly of God Church was built by Claude Jones and other members of the church.

David, Vivian and Virginia (Ginger) during the early days of ministry.
Vivian is expecting Steven in this picture.

Ginger and Steven

Ginger 5 year old and Steven 1 year old

WHERE ELSE WOULD HE BE?

My beloved is gone down into his garden, to the beds of spices, to feed in the gardens, and to gather lilies.
Song of Solomon 6:2

"The word is **nigh thee**, even in thy mouth, and **in thy heart**: that is, the word of faith, which we preach;....Whosoever believeth on him shall not be ashamed" (Romans 10:8, 11b). When asked again, "Where would your Beloved go?"—the Bride thought of her Beloved's favorite places. It is similar to when we have misplaced one of our children—we start contacting the child's friends, the park, the school, and the library. It dawns on the Bride, "Of course, He would be where He loves to go." He has gone back to the garden of her heart. He was there all the time. All she had to do was to reach out in faith, and He would show Himself to her.

He had been listening to her praise as she shared her Lord with others. Her praise is her perfume of spices as they reached His nostrils. How He loves to hear us praise Him. He is enthroned upon the praises of His people (Psalms 22:3).

He was feeding upon the developing fruit that is growing out of the trial of her faith. He rejoiced when she realized just how much she loved Him, and how she needed Him above all else. He rejoiced when He saw how she was quick to share her love with others that were in the church. She was developing patience with them. More-over, she was gently causing them to come with her and to draw near to her Lord. He is not just feeding in her individual garden, but now has many gardens as a result of her fruit and ministry to others.

He was gathering lilies. Lilies are people who have been res-urrected from a life of sin and death. These people are walking testimonies of the new creature in Christ. Out of her trial, many have seen Jesus and have accepted Him as their Lord.

My Prayer: You are there all the time. Even though I may have to walk by faith while I am beset on all sides with trials and testing, I know You will never leave me. I praise You and I love You—My Lord and My God.

SECURE IN JESUS

I am my beloved's, and my beloved is mine: he feedeth among the lilies. **Song of Solomon 6:3**

The security we find in Jesus is so sweet. There is nothing that will keep a marriage growing more than the feeling of security. Marriages start to fail when there has been unfaithfulness, financial instability, or turmoil. We know that our Lord is always faithful even when we have failed and stumbled. As long as we come back with a humble and contrite heart—He will restore and heal.

> For thus says the High and Lofty One
> Who inhabits eternity, whose name is Holy:
> "I dwell in the high and holy place,
> With him who has a contrite and humble spirit,
> To revive the spirit of the humble,
> And to revive the heart of the contrite ones."
> Isaiah 57:15-16, NKJV

Jesus is the potter who is fashioning me into a masterpiece. The potter must break and smash the clay that is flawed. He applies water and starts all over again. If He allowed the imperfection to remain in the clay, it would break when pressure is applied. (Isaiah 64:8; Jeremiah 18:4-6; Romans 9:21) The breaking and molding are not always pleasant, but they are necessary. I am so glad He has the patience to mold me into His image.

He feeds among the lilies. We die to our sin and flesh as He molds us and breaks us, and then we are brought back to a renewed and restored life in Christ. We walk in newness of life (Romans 6:4).

I must admit, there were times I did not feel really secure. It is not that I doubted my salvation, but my mind has been plagued with insecurity as we ventured out, in faith, to do a work for the Lord. My husband was always more adventurous than I. He loved new places and new circumstances; whereas, I am really a home body and like to stay with the familiar.

We had been itinerating after being in the Marshall Islands for a couple years. In our denomination, the missionary has to raise their own funds, which include the monies needed for the work. We were not fully supported, as we were technically "too old"; therefore, we went to the foreign field under the status of "missionary evangelist."

The Lord had marvelously supplied all of our needs, and we had raised funds that would allow us to erect three prefabricated, metal buildings. These buildings were going to be our house. We rented a U-haul truck in order to transport the buildings from Arizona to California. There we would send them on a ship to Majuro. David was driving the truck, and I was following him in a car. We had to stop at the border of California and pay a $5.00 fee to take the truck across the line. David opened his wallet to pay the $5.00 fee, and he showed me that he only had a 5-dollar bill and a 1-dollar bill. That was all the money we had until our next missionary service, which was scheduled the next evening. Thankfully, we were going to stay with some friends when we arrived in Orange County. We were really hungry because we had been on the road since early morning and it was late afternoon by this time. The only place to buy food around there was a restaurant across the street. Reasoning between ourselves, we thought perhaps we could buy a couple dinner rolls. David opened his wallet to pay for the rolls and found that there was a 5-dollar bill instead of just the one-dollar bill. I'm not kidding you. I know there was only a dollar there a few minutes earlier. We sat down, gave thanks, and ate a whole sandwich, which had been miraculously supplied. We love to tell this story as we get so much enjoyment out of the confession of our faith. Safe and secure in Jesus!

He is mine and I am His. He keeps me in the hollow of His hand. I bring joy and satisfaction to my Lord when I trust and praise Him. How could I doubt that He loves me enough to take care of my every need? He has never failed me yet.

My Prayer: I feel so safe and secure in Your love. You are there in every situation. I have never gone hungry. Even when I have to be broken and reshaped, You are there doing what is best for me. I want to bring the same joy to Your heart as You have poured out on me.

Picture of Vivian and David

During their Missionary Days in the Marshall Islands

THE AWESOME ARMY OF THE LORD

Thou art beautiful, O my love, as Tirzah, comely as Jerusalem, terrible as an army with banners. Song of Solomon 6:4

Now it is the Bridegroom's turn to tell of the Bride's beauty again. The Church, and each of us as individual members of the Bride, is beautiful to the Lord because He loves us so much. It is said that, "beauty is in the eye of the beholder." Surely, this is the case with our relationship with Jesus. He has given us beauty for ashes (Isaiah 61:3).

He compares the Bride to the city of Tirzah. Tirzah was a royal city of the Canaanites, which Joshua and the army of Israel conquered. (Joshua 12:24). It must have been beautiful with its palaces and such because the Bridegroom goes on to say the Bride is as comely as Jerusalem. Jerusalem was the royal city of King David and Solomon. There were beautiful buildings in the city of Jerusalem including the king's palace and the magnificent temple. Nevertheless, it is nothing compared to the City of the Bride:

> *"Come, I will show you the bride, the Lamb's wife."* And he carried me away in the Spirit to a great and high mountain, and showed me the great city, *the holy Jerusalem*, descending out of heaven from God, having the glory of God. Her light was like a most precious stone, like a jasper stone, clear as crystal.
>
> Revelation 21:9-12

Read the rest of Revelation chapter 21 to see all the details on twelve great pearl gates, twelve foundations of precious jewels, and streets paved with purest gold. The Lamb is the light and the temple of the city. All will be at peace in that city. This is the eternal home that Jesus is preparing for His Bride.

She is awesome in beauty like an army with banners. The Church goes into the enemy's territory, wins the victory through the name of Jesus, and comes back with banners waving. The Lord delivers His Church from the strong enemy that hates us. Satan hates the born again—blood-bought—saint of God. He is too strong for us to conquer in our own strength, but our Lord delivers us from the attack of Satan and sets our feet on a large place of blessing. Jesus does this because He delights in His Bride. The meaning of the *Tirzah* is delightful. [1]

> He *delivered me from my strong enemy*, and from them which hated me: for they were too strong for me. They prevented me in the day of my calamity: but the Lord was my stay. He brought me forth also into a large place; he delivered me, *because he delighted in me*.   Psalms 18:17-19

We come back from the battle with the enemy with banners because victory has been won through the name of our God. Our banners are answered prayers.

> We will rejoice in thy salvation, and in the *name of our God* we will *set up our banners*: *the Lord fulfil all thy petitions*. Now know I that the Lord saveth his anointed; he will hear him from his holy heaven with the saving strength of his right hand. Some trust in chariots, and some in horses: *but we will remember the name of the Lord our God*. They are brought down and fallen: but we are risen, and stand upright.
> Psalms 20:5-8

If ever I felt like I had gone right into the heart of enemy territory, it was while we were home missionaries on the Apache Reservation in San Carlos, Arizona, from 1954-1956. We lived right next door to a medicine man (witch doctor). Sometimes we could hear his drums and chants all night long. There were times when we could feel the demonic oppression creep into our bedrooms. During those nights, we would get up and pray the evil spirits out, in the name of our Lord, and pled the blood of Jesus to cover and protect us. We witnessed the power of our Lord by many marvelous healings in our church services. We gave that medicine man a lot of competition as we prayed to our living, loving God.

Then there was the yearly Devil Dances that lasted for a whole week. This activity had a real hold upon the natives because it was steeped in culture and tradition. They would drink homemade liquor which they called *raisin jack*. It was horrible to see how intoxicated they became. We witnessed men coming into the church service staggering under the influence of raisin jack and within an hour walking out sober and praising God for salvation. It was wonderful to witness how the power of God transformed these men and

179

women who had been bound by superstition; who had danced to the Devil—totally changed and filled with the Holy Spirit instead of the evil spirits. We loved the people just as our Lord loved them. It was a delight to see how the Lord would set them free from the enslavement of this Devil worship. He that sets us free—makes us free indeed. There are no prisoners of war in our fight for the souls of men and women—there are only liberated freemen.

Church of God, let us not be timid to go into the enemy's territory and proclaim the name of Jesus. Marching out with prayer and fasting—returning with waving the banners of answered petitions. We are going home to the New Jerusalem that is being prepared for the Bride of Christ.

My Prayer: Lord, You have given us victory again-and-again. We raise our banners of answered prayers for all to see Your mighty power to save and heal. Surely, we are a delight to You as we obey Your every command and follow you into battle as the army of God throughout this world.

The Lord's command: "Go into all the world and preach the good news to all creation. Whoever believes and is baptized will be saved, but whoever does not believe will be condemned. And these signs will accompany those who believe: In my name they will drive out demons; they will speak in new tongues; they will pick up snakes with their hands; and when they drink deadly poison, it will not hurt them at all; they will place their hands on sick people, and they will get well." (Mark 16:15-18, NIV)

[1] International Standard Bible Encyclopedia, Electronic Database Copyright © 1996, 2003, 2006 by Biblesoft, Inc. All rights reserved.

San Carlos Assembly of God

The Thompson family with Vivian's parents
Gertrude and Claude Jones

Faithful, Apache women of the Church

HIS PERFECT WILL

Turn away thine eyes from me, for they have overcome me: thy hair
is as a flock of goats that appear from Gilead.
Song of Solomon 6:5

Why does the Lord say to, "turn away your eyes from me"? I thought we were supposed to have our eyes fixed on Jesus, the author and finisher of our faith. Instead of comparing her eyes to dove's eyes, He says that her eyes have overcome Him. (See Song of Solomon 1:15; 4:1) Looking at the words "overcome me" in the Hebrew, it enlightens us to the fact that now the eyes are urging severely, emboldened, and / or acting insolently.[1] This gives us a completely different picture of how the Bride is looking to her Beloved. It is not the gentle look of a dove, but an emboldened—aggressive look.

I believe that the Lord recognizes that she still has carnality in her life. Has she forgotten her humble beginnings when she saw herself as a shepherdess that was blackened by the sun? Perhaps she is asking with her eyes for more than He, in His wisdom, knows she is ready to handle. He loves her so much that He wants to give her anything her heart desires, but He knows that it may not be the best thing for her or it is not the correct time to grant her request. It is difficult to deny someone you love anything—especially when it is in your power to supply that desire. We need to remember in asking the Lord for things always to say and to mean: "Not my will, but yours be done" (Matthew 6:10).

Sometimes the modern day church is guilty of demanding the blessings of God to the point of being presumptuous. Yes, we are to ask in faith believing, but we must remember that He is God and His will is of utmost importance.

Again, the Bridegroom mentions her hair as being like a flock of goats that appear on the hillsides of Gilead. We have stated earlier that her long flowing hair was a sign of her consecration. Yet the long flowing hair reminds the Beloved of *goats*. Goats are symbols of the sinful nature, which we still struggle with, even though we have consecrated our lives to the Master. This is a paradox—how can she be so beautiful in her consecrated life and yet she can be so carnal.

As we search the Scriptures concerning Gilead, we find that it was first conquered by the Israelites just before it was time to cross over the Jordan River and take possession of the Promised Land. The two tribes of Gad and Reuben looked at this land and desired it, for they had many cattle and the land was good pastureland. They met with Moses and requested that their families should possess this land as their inheritance. At first, Moses questioned their motive and thought they did not want to fight with the rest of the army on the other side of Jordan. They assured Moses that they would send their fighting men with Joshua when it was time to conquer the rest of the Promised Land. Therefore, Moses granted their request to build cities and settle their families in the area of Gilead. Was this God's perfect will or His permissible will? It is hard to say because the plan was initiated by man—not God. I have heard Bible teachers who were of the opinion that Gad and Reuben should have waited until all of the land was conquered to claim their share. It seems that the tribes of Gad and Reuben got their way in spite of Moses' better judgment. (Numbers 32)

The crossing over Jordan is a type of going through a death to self and the flesh. The Jordan River reminds us of water baptism because that is where John was baptizing when Jesus began His ministry. Paul says this about baptism:

> Know ye not, that so many of us as were baptized into Jesus Christ were baptized into his death?" …… "Knowing this, that our old man is crucified with him, that the body of sin might be destroyed, that henceforth we should not serve sin.
> Romans 6:3, 6

Many Christians are constantly seeking prosperity and delight in the material blessings God provides for them, rather than seeking for God's will concerning a deeper walk with Him and the building up of His kingdom. We are to, "Seek ye first the kingdom of God, and his righteousness; and all these things shall be added unto you" (Matthew 6:33). What a pleasure it is when God rains His blessing on us just because we are pleasing Him. "He is a rewarder of them that diligently seek him" (Hebrews 11:6).

In the last verse, the Bride is compared to a victorious army. The Church is tempted to be satisfied with past victories and large church buildings and congregations. As the army of God, there is no time to get relaxed. "No man that warreth entangleth himself with the affairs of this life; that he may please him who hath chosen him to be a soldier" (2 Timothy 2:4). We constantly discipline ourselves to please our Commander and Chief, Christ Jesus.

My Prayer: Sometimes I wonder, Lord, do I pray amiss that I may be blessed? (James 4:3) Help me to remember that I want to do Your will more than obtaining any pleasure that will last for only a short time. I do not want to be a spoiled child who is determined to have my own way. I want to take up my cross and follow You. I want Your perfect will in my life.

(1)   Biblesoft's New Exhaustive Strong's Numbers and Concordance with Expanded Greek-Hebrew Dictionary. Copyright © 1994, 2003, 2006 Biblesoft, Inc. and International Bible Translators, Inc.
"OT:7292 bh^r* rahab (raw-hab'); a primitive root; to urge severely, i.e. (figuratively) importune, embolden, capture, act insolently:"

SINK YOUR TEETH INTO THE WORD

Thy teeth are as a flock of sheep which go up from the washing, whereof every one beareth twins, and there is not one barren among them. Song of Solomon 6:6

We discovered while chewing on these same words in chapter four, verse two, that teeth are for chewing and preparing food for digestion. We compared this to the assimilation of the Word of God into our spirit life. The teeth must be cleaned everyday or they will decay. Jesus said we are cleansed by the word that he has spoken (John 15:3).

We partake together of the bread of God's Word as a flock of sheep. The flock speaks of numerous sheep, just as we are many members in the body of Christ. We look to each other for the encouragement and fellowship around the Word of God.

The cup of blessing which we bless, is it not the communion of the blood of Christ? The bread which we break, is it not the communion of the body of Christ? *For we being many are one bread, and one body: for we are all partakers of that one bread.* 1 Corinthians 10:16-17

Just as each tooth has its twin, each scripture has its twin or mate. We need to compare scripture with other scriptures to be sure our interpretation is correct. We are admonished to, "Be diligent to present yourself approved to God, a worker who does not need to be ashamed, rightly dividing the word of truth" (2 Timothy 2:15, NKJV). This means that we are to apply ourselves to diligent study of the Word of Truth, so that we are able to handle it correctly. We do not use the Word of God to prove a doctrine that suits our beliefs, but we form our doctrines upon the solid foundation of the Word. Many of the cults have been formed by isolating a certain scripture and twisting it to fit their own belief system.

The Beloved sees a beautiful smile when our teeth have been cleaned. I have taught the Word to many men and women who are preparing for the ministry using the Berean Correspondence curriculum. Recently, I challenged my current class to memorize at least one scripture a week. One of my students came back to class a week later so anxious that he just could not wait to share his testimony. He said that he had been struggling with the studies; his studies were quite

difficult since English was his second language. Because of the diffi-
culty and the hard work it required, he had lost his joy of studying the
Word of God. As he memorized 1 Timothy 4:15-16 and began to
apply it to his life, the Lord had worked a miracle and restored joy in
his quest to know Jesus better. The Word had taken on fresh life.

> Meditate on these things; give yourself entirely to them, that
> your progress may be evident to all. Take heed to yourself and
> to the doctrine. Continue in them, for in doing this you will
> save both yourself and those who hear you.
>
> 1 Timothy 4:15-16, NKJV

The study of the Word brings joy to our hearts and a smile on our
faces. For by the Word, we will grow in our own spiritual walk, and
we will be able to confidently share it with others.

Meditate on the things of God—think about His words and
pray for the correct meaning. Give ourselves entirely to them. I am in
my eighties and have studied the Bible most of my life, but I never tire
of the Word. It is new and living every day. I have given myself
wholly to the study and teaching of His Word. I will continue to
preach the Word of God, for my joy comes from seeing souls rescued
from sin.

My Prayer: There is such joy in my heart as I meditate on Your Word
day and night. I am so blessed to have been exposed to the Word of
Truth early in my life. Lord give me the understanding of the entire
Word, and help me to pass on the knowledge that You have given to
me. May I leave a legacy of competent ministers who will continue to
teach the Word and win many souls for You.

MIND WARS

As a piece of a pomegranate are thy temples within thy locks.
Song of Solomon 6:7

The King repeats some of the same loving words that He had said in chapter four, verses two and three. Do you remember how she had been complacent and cold until she woke up only to find that He had withdrawn? Then she went out and frantically searched for Him and asked the daughters of Jerusalem if they had seen Him. It was only as she began exalting His beauty that she, once again, found Him in her garden. I believe He is now reassuring her that His love is still the same. She needs this reassurance. He repeats the necessary virtues that will make her the mighty army that He desires her to be.

We saw in our last verse that He reiterated her need for cleaning her teeth; therefore, her joy in the Word of God was restored. Now, He talks about the temples (her mind) being covered with locks of consecration. He says that her temples resemble a pomegranate cut in half; thereby, the pink fruit is exposed on each side of her head. Our minds are an open book to Him—He knows exactly what we are thinking. The mind plays such a vital part in our Christian walk, for as we think in our heart, so shall we be (Proverbs 23:7). We are prone to suffer discouragement and low self-esteem if we do not renew our minds with the expressions of His love and tenderness toward us (Ephesians 4:23).

The New Testament has much to say about our minds being in agreement with the mind of Christ. The Hebrew children failed miserably in keeping the law that was written on tables of stone, so God promised: "I will put my laws into their mind, and write them in their hearts" (Hebrews 8:10). Paul says, we "have the mind of Christ" (1 Corinthians 2:16).

What is the mind of Christ? It is a humble, loving, and forgiving mind. Paul's admonition on how to possess a mind like that of Christ's is to, "Let nothing be done through strife or vainglory; but in lowliness of mind let each esteem other better than themselves" (Philippians 2:3-4). He also says,

> Put on therefore, as the elect of God, holy and beloved,
> bowels of mercies, kindness, humbleness of mind, meekness,
> longsuffering; Forbearing one another, and forgiving one
> another, if any man have a quarrel against any: even as Christ

187

forgave you, so also do ye. And above all these things put on charity, which is the bond of perfectness.   Colossians 3:12-14

Do you see the fruit of the Holy Spirit revealed in such a mind? There is love, forgiveness, kindness, meekness, longsuffering, and the bond of peace among the brethren.

As we are observing the Bride as a mighty army, we see that the enemy wages war in the believer's mind.

> For the weapons of our warfare are not carnal, but mighty through God to the pulling down of strong holds; Casting down imaginations, and every high thing that exalteth itself against the knowledge of God, and bringing into captivity every thought to the obedience of Christ.
>
> 2 Corinthians 10:4-5

Our mind is the battlefield. We thank God, for He has provided weapons for us to defend our minds. They are the sword of the Spirit, which is the Word of God, and the power of the Holy Spirit indwelling our hearts and minds in Christ Jesus. By the Word, we cast down the imaginations planted by the enemy. These imaginations can be jealousy, doubt, anger, envy, covetousness, bitterness, and pride....just to name a few. Once these thoughts take root in our minds, they become strongholds. We must bring every thought into control and into obedience to Christ. Peter exhorts us to, "*prepare your minds for action*; be *self-controlled*; set your hope fully on the grace to be given you when Jesus Christ is revealed. As *obedient children*, do not conform to the evil desires you had when you lived in ignorance" (1 Peter 1:13-14, NIV).

I found that obedience to the Word of God is a key factor in bearing the fruit of the Spirit. The Lord made this so real to me (Ginger) in a situation I faced at work. A customer had complained that I had been disrespectful, and that I had not cooperated with his needs. Although this was not true, my immediate supervisor did not stand up for me when the complaint reached higher management. I especially resented one woman in management, for she made some remarks to me and to other people in the company about my performance that were very humiliating. Some of my closer friends said, "Why don't you stick up for yourself and set people straight?" The Lord checked me to keep quite. The Holy Spirit convicted me about the anger I felt toward her, but it hurt so bad—I could not get rid of this gnawing an-
188

ger. In my morning devotions, I came across this scripture: "Bless them that curse you, and pray for them which despitefully use you" (Luke 6:28). In shear obedience to God's Word, I began to pray for this woman and bless her in my prayers. After a couple weeks of praying in this manner, I found love in my heart for her and concern about her problems and salvation. That love was a gift from God, for it was not something I could conjure up with my own willpower. God was so gracious in that He made everything right and the truth came out about the situation. This woman and I had a wonderful working relationship for many years after this incident.

Only as we bring our thoughts and prayers into the obedience of Christ, do we break down the fortified walls that the enemy would build in our minds. Many times, we will not feel like being obedient—this is when we must press on beyond our feelings and just do what He says.

My Prayer: Lord, cleanse and renew my mind daily. Take control of my thoughts. Help be to be obedient to Your every command and to walk in faith. Cause me to bear the fruit of the Spirit in my life. Thank you for the assurances in Your Word that You love me.

MY PLACE IN THE KINGDOM

There are threescore queens, and fourscore concubines, and virgins without number. My dove, my undefiled is but one; she is the only one of her mother, she is the choice one of her that bare her. The daughters saw her, and blessed her; yea, the queens and the concubines, and they praised her. Song of Solomon 6:8-9

This verse in our Song is difficult to understand, and there is a variety of ways to interpret it according to the commentaries I consulted. Nevertheless, by looking at the customs of that era, I think we will come to a better understanding. It was customary, in Solomon's day, for kings to marry many women, thereby, making them queens. Some of the wives were foreigners, and some were even the daughters of other kings. Solomon collected multiple concubines who were slave-wives. Then there were virgins who serviced the court. All of these women were part of his royal court. Each woman had her specific duty and position in the house of her king. Solomon loved them all, but none of them compared to his dove—his undefiled one.

Just as Solomon surrounded himself with all these lovely women who were his comfort and joy, the Lord has surrounded His Bride with a great company of witnesses. (Hebrews 12:1) The eleventh chapter of Hebrews presents us with a list of these faithful men and women who have shown us how God wants to interact with His people. From the very beginning of time when Abel brought a pleasing sacrifice—to Abraham, who left his homeland to look for a city not made with hands—to Moses, who chose to be counted with his people—to the kings and prophets, who were firm in their faith unto the Lord—to the apostles, who were eyewitnesses of His majesty—to the pioneers and missionaries of the modern day church; they are the faithful observers who look down from heaven today and encourage the Bride of Christ to press forward and lay aside everything that would hinder her from drawing close to her King.

There are believers from the time of Adam and Eve clear through to the end of the Tribulation—including those in the future who will give their lives to be counted among the saints of all times. Everyone will have a place in the kingdom. Nevertheless, the Bride of the Lamb (the Church) will have a special place. I am not certain how the Lord will divide the kingdom authority among other dispensational saints, but I know He will be just and fair.

In Revelation chapters four and five, we see through John's eyes into the throne room of heaven. Around the throne are twenty-four elders. Many Bible scholars believe that these represent the twelve tribes of Israel and the twelve apostles, thus, uniting Old Covenant and New Covenant saints in the worship of God and the Lamb. [1] These twenty-four elders fall down before the Lamb. They have harps and golden vials full of sweet smelling prayers of the saints, and they proceed to sing this new song:

> Thou art worthy to take the book, and to open the seals thereof: for thou wast slain, and hast redeemed us to God by thy blood out of every kindred, and tongue, and people, and nation; And hast made us unto our God kings and priests: and we shall reign on the earth. And I beheld, and I heard the voice of many angels round about the throne and the beasts and the elders: and the number of them was ten thousand times ten thousand, and thousands of thousands; Saying with a loud voice, Worthy is the Lamb that was slain to receive power, and riches, and wisdom, and strength, and honour, and glory, and blessing.
>
> Revelation 5:9-12

The Bride of Christ will have this special place because she is His dove. Christ has filled her with the Holy Spirit of promise who has enabled her to spread the gospel to the uttermost parts of the earth (Acts 1:8). Purified by her trust in the blood of Jesus, she is undefiled. Paul said, "I am jealous for you with a godly jealousy. I promised you to one husband, to Christ, so that I might present you as a pure virgin to him" (2 Corinthians 11:2, NIV).

Although there are ten thousand times ten thousand and more that have put their trust in Christ, He still has the capability of treating each of us separately. "To him that overcometh will I grant to sit with me *in my throne*, even as I also overcame, and am set down with my Father in his throne" (Revelation 3:21). I believe that each person will be able to speak to the Lord one-on-one. It is marvelous to know that Jesus loves the Church as His corporate body, and still He gives each of us His undivided attention.

At the end of this verse in the Song of Songs, we see how all the daughters, the queens, and the concubines praised the chosen Bride. This was possible, for there is no selfishness or pride in the kingdom. There is no cause of jealousy, for Jesus loves each of us. He has given us gifts as He wills. When one excels in ministry, the entire church excels. All the glory belongs to Him, as it is not due to anything we could have done on our own. Therefore, everyone around the throne or (*in the throne*) will praise the other. We are one in the bond of love.

My Prayer: It is beyond my comprehension how You could single me out from all the other saints that You so dearly love. You have called me, chosen me, and gifted me to do Your will. You make me feel so special when I come to You with my needs and desires. I rejoice with my brothers and sisters, in the Lord, as they too find their special place in You. We must learn to work together, now, as we will some-day rule and reign with You in Your kingdom.

[1] From the study notes of The Full Life Study Bible, Donald C. Stamps, General Editor, Zondervan Publishing House, Grand Rapids, Michigan

THE RIGHTEOUS ARMY

Who is she that looketh forth as the morning, fair as the moon, clear as the sun, and terrible as an army with banners?
Song of Solomon 6:10

It is the Bride—the Church of Jesus Christ. She has come out of the darkness of her separation from her Beloved and her bout with the world, and she looks forward to the morning. "For his anger endureth but a moment; in his favour is life: weeping may endure for a night, but joy cometh in the morning" (Psalms 30:5). He has been faithful to her even in the night hours: "It is a good thing to give thanks unto the Lord, and to sing praises unto thy name, O most High: To *shew forth thy lovingkindness in the morning, and thy faithfulness every night*" (Psalms 92:1). As she sings the praises of her Beloved, her face shines with the glory of the Lord. She is a reflection of His loving-kindness.

She shines forth as a light to the sinful world. She is wise, for she has put on Christ's righteousness. "And they that be wise shall shine as the brightness of the firmament; and they that turn many to righteousness as the stars for ever and ever" (Daniel 12:3). She is turning many to righteousness as she shines the light of Jesus in this world. "That ye may be blameless and harmless, the sons of God, without rebuke, in the midst of a crooked and perverse nation, among whom *ye shine as lights in the world*; Holding forth the word of life" (Philippians 2:15-16).

Even in the middle of the night—the darkness of sin and trouble of the world—she is reflecting the light of Jesus the same way the moon reflects the sun. The Church is as clear day because her integrity is not clouded with half-truths or deception. She is blameless and harmless.

Commit your way to the Lord;
trust in him and he will do this:
He will make your righteousness shine like the dawn,
the justice of your cause like the noonday sun.
Psalms 37:5-6, NIV

The Church of Jesus Christ marches forward as an awesome army. Our cause is to set men and women free from the clutches of Satan. We fight for justice in a crooked and perverse world. The

193

world would not know what righteousness looked like if it were not for the Light shining through us. We speak hope and healing to the depressed and distressed people who grope in darkness. If we commit our ways to the Lord and trust in Him, He will do this—He will make us a triumphant army.

I think of Joshua and the children of Israel as they marched around the walls of Jericho. The priest carried the Ark of the Covenant. Its cover was of pure gold and the sides were overlaid with gold. Can you see the people of Jericho looking down from on top of the walls at the procession of people marching around their city day after day? The sun must have reflected off the top of the Ark with blinding light. On the seventh day, at daybreak, they marched around seven times. As the army of Jericho shook their heads at the ridiculous method of warfare and covered their ears at the trumpet blast, the walls tumbled down upon them. (Joshua 6) The world may shake their heads and think we are just a noisy bunch of Christians, but we have the victory. "Through God we shall do valiantly: for he it is that shall tread down our enemies" (Psalms 60:12).

Do not lose hope for your unsaved loved ones, for the battle is not over yet. Keep praying and working because God will tear down the walls of opposition. As the Lord told Joshua, "Be strong and courageous. Do not be terrified; do not be discouraged, for the Lord your God will be with you wherever you go" (Joshua 1:7, NIV). All the wars will be worth it at the end of the age when we come marching home, for, "the righteous will shine like the sun in the kingdom of their Father" (Matthew 13:43, NIV).

My Prayer: Lord, help me to be a strong and courageous warrior. I march under the banners of Your love and joy. Help me to be a shining light of righteousness in this perverse world. You may sometimes ask me to do things that the world would think a little crazy; nevertheless, if that is what it takes, I am not ashamed to put my reputation on the line. It will be worth all the sacrifice and struggles of this life when I see You face to face.

BROKEN SHELLS

I went down into the garden of nuts to see the fruits of the valley,
and to see whether the vine flourished, and the pomegranates
budded. Song of Solomon 6:11

We go through seasons in our physical and spiritual lives.
The Bride has gone through a winter season where she felt cold and
isolated from the warmth of her Beloved's embrace. Now she is on
the verge of spring. She and her Beloved go into the garden of her
heart to inspect the fruits. Will they find growth and new life forming
in her spirit?

The first thing they look for are the nuts. The nuts are probably fruits of the previous autumn—survived the winter and now at the
onset of spring have fallen to the ground. Nuts are usually considered
as a luxury. This was especially true in Bible times before chocolate
was discovered. During the great famine when Jacob sent his sons to
Egypt, they lacked the staples of wheat and corn. They had some nuts
left over from previous years. Jacob thought the nuts, along with
some honey, balm, and spices, would be a pleasing gift for Pharaoh.
(Genesis 43:11) Thus, we see that nuts are an example of fruit that
remains for a long period of time.

The only problem with the nut is the hard shell that has to be
broken before anyone can enjoy the goodness inside. My granddaughters lived in a rented house that had a macadamia nut tree in the
neighboring yard. I can remember my two granddaughters, ages six
and four, endeavoring to crack the shell of these extremely hard nuts.
They were so determined to get the precious meat out that they
devised a way to put the nut between two pieces of thick cloth to
stabilize the perfectly round nut, and then they would hit it with a
hammer as hard as they could. Their dad thought this looked dangerous for little fingers, so he showed them how to use a vise. It was cute
to watch them work so diligently to get to the delicious heart of the
nut. All of their struggles were worth the reward.

If we are not careful, a bitter shell encases our spiritual fruit.
This fruit is absolutely of no worth until that shell is broken. I
(Ginger) once went through some hurtful criticism at a church where
we were diligently working for the Lord. After patiently enduring and
continuing to work in that church for over a year after the criticism,
which had wounded my spirit, the Lord moved our family to another
location.

195

We started attending the new church during a week of revival services. Our souls were so thirsty and hungry for a fresh touch from God. I was surprised that after a few nights of sitting in the pew with people all around me experiencing the blessing of God, I could not enter into worship as I had in the past. Sunday morning came and our dear pastor, Rev. Eva Bloom, spoke from the passage in Hebrews 12:15: "Looking diligently lest any man fail of the grace of God; lest any root of bitterness springing up trouble you, and thereby many be defiled." The Lord showed me—through the eyes of the spirit—that I had built up a brick wall of bitterness around my heart. I was trying to shield myself from any more hurt. I realized, with the Holy Spirit's help, that I must push down the wall in order for His presence to penetrate my heart. I wept and prayed my way through that wall and forgave the people who had hurt me—and the glory fell. [1]

Being placed under the hammer and submitting to being broken is not a pleasant experience, but it is worth the results. Out of our brokenness comes pure worship for our Beloved Lord. Out of our brokenness comes compassion for others. Out of our brokenness comes new growth in our spirit.

The Lord is looking for new growth out of every trial that we go through. He is checking out the fruits that are developing from our valley experiences. He is checking to see if the vine is flourishing. Our vine will put forth new shoots as we abide in Him. (John 15:5)

Are the pomegranates of our mind budding—showing new growth? A stagnate mind is the Devil's playground. We must always be teachable and be willing to learn new things so that our minds will be fruitful. [2]

My Prayer: Sometimes I want to cry out ,"Ouch"! Lord, help me not to run away from the hammer that would break me, for I know You are only taking away the bitter and useless shells from my life. I desire to be a productive, fruitful Christian that is always abiding in the vine. Jesus, You are my source and my strength.

[1] Ginger's personal testimony- Read Jeremiah 23:29
[2] See Song of Solomon 4:3 which explains the pomegranate representing our mind.

My granddaughters, Colleen (3years old) & Sharon (5 years old)

They are the "nut crackers" -- Ready for Sunday School in this picture.

WILLING PEOPLE

Or ever I was aware, my soul made me like the chariots of Amminadib. Song of Solomon 6:12

It caught the Bride off guard. All of a sudden, the Lord had given her soul a ride on the chariots of a willing heart. **Amminadib** means a "willing people." [1] Isn't it wonderful when the Lord suddenly and miraculously changes our attitude? Out of our brokenness and desire to be fruitful, the Lord makes us willing to be of service. He desires that we perform our service out of a cheerful, willing, and generous spirit. Paul's prescription concerning giving with the correct attitude is, "Every man according as he purposeth in his heart, so let him give; not grudgingly, or of necessity: for God loveth a cheerful giver" (2 Corinthians 9:7). Paul's instructions not only apply to monetary offerings, but it also applies to any offering of helps, time, or talents. Only Jesus can change our natural inclination of being self-centered.

Notice that is it a willing **people**—people meaning a group such as a tribe, a nation, or in our application, the Church of Jesus Christ. We accomplish so much more by working together than we would by working alone; each member of the body exercising their own God-given talents.

Sometimes the Lord will ask us to take the humble, servant's place in the body to accomplish His plan. David and I worked every muscle and exerted every ounce of our physical strength to fulfil the Great Commission while stationed in the Marshall Islands. The Youth Department of the Assemblies of God had donated a 42-foot diesel vessel through their Speed-the-Light program. The name of this vessel was *The Ambassador II.* It was David's dream and mission to be the captain of this vessel. My husband was a jack-of-all trades. It not only took a navigator to captain this vessel, but it also took a mechanic to keep it running properly. When we would arrive at the island of destination, he would put on his "preacher's hat" and perform weddings, a baptismal service, and preach the good news.

We taught in the Calvary Bible Institute during the school year, but in the summer, we actually put all the training to the test. It was time to take the students to other small islands where they could practice teaching, testifying, and building churches. The students scrambled aboard the vessel with high hopes of winning souls for Jesus and planting churches on the outer islands. The excitement was

198

short lived as the boys and girls hung their heads over the side of the boat and vomited until there was nothing left in their stomachs. Our trips were not very pleasant. Almost every one got seasick (including me). The deck and hole of the boat were covered with grease and vomit. It became my duty to clean up at every port as soon as everyone disembarked (the young people were too sick to clean up this mess). I would get out a scrub brush, get down on my hands and knees, and scrub every inch with gasoline. Looking back at it, I wonder how I managed to do such a job with a willing heart. Only by the grace of God can we perform such tasks without complaining. The Lord had given David and me the privilege of spreading the gospel to the far reaches of this world, and this lowly task was just a necessary part of that mission. He indeed carries us along in chariots of willingness.

Satan would fight us by placing grumblings and complaints in our minds, but I have the mind of Christ. The body of Christ is made up of willing people who are janitors, babysitters, painters, cooks, mechanics, bus drivers, carpenters, and the list goes on. The Church of Christ serves by a different beat of the drum. Its beat is:

Take up your cross and follow me.
Deny yourself.
Lose your life for the sake of the gospel.
Put your life on the line.
Go into all the world and preach the gospel.
Put God first.
Love, love, love!
Pray, pray, pray!
Give, give, give!
Serve, serve, serve!

Are you marching to the heartbeat of heaven? Songs and praise play a major role in our learning to worship; however, giving of oneself completely, with a willing attitude, completes the training.

My Prayer: Lord, ever include me as part of the company of Your chariots—swift to do Your work. May I take no thought for my ease or care for my life. Thank You for the glorious privilege of being part of Your Kingdom. I will go where you want me to go, say what you want me to say, and do whatever task is needed to build Your Church. Gladly! Cheerfully! Willingly!

Vivian, David, and crew on The Ambassador II

The Sophomore Class of Calvary Bible Institute, Majuro

Building materials supplied by churches across the U.S.

Men are putting up the frame of a new church building on the
Island of Ailuk

Inside of the new church building

DON'T LOOK BACK

*Return, return, O Shulamite; return, return, that we may look upon thee. **Song of Solomon 6:13a***

The Bride of Christ has left the daughters of Jerusalem behind as she gallops off in the chariots of willing service. They call after her, "O Shulamite, return, return." I wonder if they are trying to bring her down to earth by calling her a ***Shulamite***—reminding her of her humble beginnings. Many people, even religious folks, would question why God would ask us to be totally committed and to pay such a costly price to fulfill the Great Commission. Some of the questions and comments that I have heard are:

> Why are you so fanatical?
> Why are you leaving family and friends?
> Why endure hardship?
> It's not safe, you could get hurt!
> Why aren't you concerned about your health?
> Have you considered retirement?
> Don't you think you are getting too old?
> Return, Return, Return!

Come home to a life of ease and take care of yourself. These people may claim to have our best interest in mind, but they have not seen the full picture. They, like the daughters of Jerusalem, say to the Bride, "we want to look at you." Do they really miss the committed Christian's presence, or are they selfishly missing the blessing of God that spilled over on them? Many Christians live under the shadow of blessing that God bestows on His dedicated child. We sometimes grumble that the church is dead and there is not the moving of the Holy Spirit in our services. There is a price to pay for the presence of God. We love the mothers and fathers of our churches who spend many hours on their knees praying for the Holy Spirit's move. The younger generation has to see the importance of total dedication and surrender to the will of the Father, as well. Only then will our churches continue to experience the blessing.

The Bride of Christ is composed of just ordinary people with the determination to fulfill the unordinary call of God upon their lives. There is an example in Second Kings about an ordinary woman who the Bible only identifies as the "Shunammite." She lived in an ordinary village. The only eventful thing that happened in this town was that the man of God often passed through. She recognized the spirit and power of Elijah and told her husband, "Let us make a small room for the prophet where he can rest from his travels." She willingly and graciously served Elijah every time he came her way. Her house was his house. Her food was his food. Elijah wanted to repay her in some way because he was thankful to have this refuge. He asked her what she needed, but she refused any type of reward. Elijah's servant suggested a child since the woman was barren. Elijah told her, "You will have a child." She thought he was teasing her, but in due time she birthed a child of promise.

It was a wonderful day when the baby boy arrived in the home of this elderly couple. There were tears of joy shed as they received the blessing of God. They watched the boy take his first steps, say his first words, and shared all the joys of a growing child. One day when he was old enough to go out in the fields with his father, the boy was working in the hot sun when he cried out in pain from a severe headache. His father carried him into his mother, and she held the boy close until he died in her arms. It was such a shock that she did not even want to tell her husband. She took the boy up to the prophet's room and laid him on the bed.

What was she to do? Why had God given her this blessing—only to take it away? She saddled up a donkey. She and her servant went as fast as they could to Mount Carmel where Elijah was working. Elijah sent his servant to meet them as they were coming up the road. When the servant questioned her as to the welfare of her family, she only insisted on speaking directly to Elijah. Elijah did not know what was wrong at first, for the Lord hid the knowledge from him. She questioned, "Did I desire a son of my lord? Did I not say, Do not deceive me?" (2 Kings 4:28) Elijah realized that the son had died. He sent his servant ahead with his staff. The boy did not come to life when the staff was placed on him. When Elijah arrived at the house, he went up to his room…He [Elijah]…

shut the door on the two of them and prayed to the Lord. Then he got on the bed and lay upon the boy, mouth to mouth, eyes to eyes, hands to hands. As he stretched himself out upon him, the boy's body grew warm. Elisha turned away and walked back and forth in the room and then got on the bed and stretched out upon him once more. The boy sneezed seven times and opened his eyes. 2 Kings 4:33-35, NIV

This ordinary woman, from an ordinary town, willingly opened her home to the servant of God; consequently, she received the desire of her heart. She thought the promise had been taken away, but God rewarded her with a miracle resurrection. (2 Kings 4:8-37) Nothing is able to stop the Church of Christ from taking back what the enemy has stolen. There is no reason for any of us to look back to our old ways. We are determined to follow Jesus all the way.

My Prayer: Lord, cause me to be more than a conqueror. Help me to have a willing heart. Help me not to despise the small things You ask me to do. I know You will reward every task and duty that is part of Your plan for the Church. If I do receive some favor or miracle, help me to continue to serve You with all of my heart. If You should decide to remove that blessing, help me to continue to have faith.

CHAPTER 7

SHOES OF PEACE

What will ye see in the Shulamite? As it were the company of two armies. How beautiful are thy feet with shoes, O prince's daughter! the joints of thy thighs are like jewels, the work of the hands of a cunning workman. Song of Solomon 6:13b, 7:1

Let us look at the way verses 6:13b and 7:1 are translated in the New King James Version. I believe it will give us more insight.

The Shulamite (inserted identification, NKJV)
6:13b What would you see in the Shulamite — As it were, the dance of the two camps?

Expressions of Praise -The Beloved (inserted identification)
7:1 How beautiful are your feet in sandals,
O prince's daughter!
The curves of your thighs are like jewels,
The work of the hands of a skillful workman.
Song of Solomon 6:13-7:1, NKJV

The daughters of Jerusalem are watching the Church dance up and down between two camps. Shulamite is the feminine version of Solomon. *Solomon* means Prince of Peace; thus, *Shulamite* would mean the daughter of peace or the Princess of Peace. We do not think of peace in association with armies, but the Church is a messenger of the Prince of Peace.

There was once a wall between the Israelite nation and the rest of the nations. The wall that separated them was religion because God had revealed Himself to Israel by giving them the Law, but the Gentile nations were without the true God. There was also a wall of sin between the sinner and God. Jesus has broken down both of these walls by His atoning work on the cross.

At that time ye were without Christ, being aliens from the commonwealth of Israel, and strangers from the covenants of promise, having no hope, and without God in the world: But now in Christ Jesus ye who sometimes were far off are made nigh by the blood of Christ. For he is our peace, who hath made both one, and hath broken down the middle wall of partition between us...   Ephesians 2:12-14

The Church is a messenger to our Jewish friends that we, Jews and Gentiles, do not need to be separated by walls, for Jesus has broken down the wall that has divided us throughout the centuries. The Church is the messenger to the nations of this world that they no longer need to be aliens from God's grace. Jesus paid the price for the Gentile's adoption into the family of God.

The feet of the Church are beautiful, for they carry the gospel of peace to a war-torn world:

> How beautiful upon the mountains
> Are the feet of him who brings good news,
> Who proclaims peace,
> Who brings glad tidings of good things,
> Who proclaims salvation,
> Who says to Zion,
> "Your God reigns!"
> Isaiah 52:7, NKJV

The spiritual armor of the Church has the feet shod with the preparation (or readiness) of the gospel of peace. It has loins (waist and hips) girded about with truth. Both speak to us of strength and readiness to share the truth and peace of our Commander and Chief. The Church is skillful since her Maker is the Master Craftsman. (Ephesians 6:14, 15; 2:10)

Paul said we are to stand firm in the armor that our Lord has provided. He concludes this passage in Ephesians 6:16-17, requesting that the Church would pray for him that he would be able to share the mystery of the gospel without fear and in all boldness.

Jesus has paid the price for our peace. (Isaiah 53:5) He is our peace, and He has broken down the wall between God and man. With shoes of peace, the Church dances between the camp of Satan and the camp of God. We dance because there is peace and joy in our spirit. We are bold because our weapons are the Word of God and prayer.

My Prayer: I will be swift, bold, and powerful in my beautiful shoes of peace. I dance for joy in my salvation. I call to the world, "Come dance with me"; "Come live in the peace that surpasses all understanding." Thank you, Lord, for working in my life to make me strong, graceful, and well equipped for the battle.

MOVING IN THE SPIRIT

Thy navel is like a round goblet, which wanteth not liquor: thy belly is like an heap of wheat set about with lilies. **Song of Solomon 7:2**

The King is extolling the beauties of His Beloved again, but this time He begins His lavish portrayal from her feet traveling up to the top of her head. It is as if He is sitting on the sidelines watching her dance and serve. His eyes watch her swift and graceful feet as they weave in and out of the crowd—spreading peace and comfort to all she passes. Then His eyes travel up to her strong legs that support the truth of the gospel. Jesus must love to watch His body, as the members work together like a well-coordinated dancer. He orders each step, and each movement of the Church body is in perfect rhythm with His will.

Now His eyes are upon her stomach. In the center of her stomach is the navel. It is round and reminds Him of goblet or wine glass which is not lacking for wine. I would like to compare this to the "new wine" of the Holy Spirit. Out of our innermost being flows the wine of the Spirit, which brings joy and satisfaction to all that drink of it. It is called *new wine* for it was a new experience reserved for the New Testament believer. The infilling of the Holy Spirit opens up various new avenues of ministry for us. The Bride, filled with the Spirit, can serve the Church with healings, miracles, faith, and divine insight and knowledge. Paul tells us, "Don't be drunk with wine, because that will ruin your life. Instead, be filled with the Holy Spirit, singing psalms and hymns and spiritual songs among yourselves, and making music to the Lord in your hearts" (Ephesians 5:18, 19, NLT). The thought here is to be "continually filled" with the Spirit. It is not just a one-time experience, but it is a daily supernatural walk with our Lord.

Working out from the navel, He comes to the belly or abdomen. It is like a heap of wheat. Wheat usually denotes a harvest in Bible times. Out of the overflowing wine of the Holy Spirit comes a great harvest of souls. People are searching for the reality of God. When they are exposed to a Church, which is filled with the Spirit of God, they will receive the gospel. On the day a Pentecost, Peter stood up and preached His first Holy Ghost anointed message and three thousand souls repented of their sins (Acts 2:41). Jesus had promised power from on high after the Holy Spirit's infilling, and Peter believed it (Acts 1:8; Luke 24:49).

208

I will never forget one of the greatest revivals we ever experienced. It was in a small farming community of Wilcox, Arizona. We were truly in the middle of a great harvest. It all started with one young Mexican man, Joe Bedolla. He and his wife were having marital problems, and he was searching for help when he heard a radio broadcast from First Assembly of God in Tucson. He gave his heart to the Lord and brought his family to our church. God saved his wife and children, healed his marriage, and delivered him from alcohol and cigarettes. His mother and many of his brothers and sisters came to church out of curiosity, for they saw change in Joe's life. They, too, received Jesus as Savior. Our church services were pretty noisy as people were being filled with the Holy Spirit every night. Prayer went into the late hours of the night, and our neighbors were complaining about the noise—even threatened to shut us down.

One night as everyone gathered around the altar, crying and praying unto the Lord, Joe's mother was lying on the floor. We really were not alarmed because many people would just lay before the Lord in prayer and worship as they were seeking for a closer walk. Joe looked at his mother, and he became concerned for she did not seem to be praying—only lying very still. He went to check on her and found that she had no pulse. Joe immediately called for David, and he verified that she was not breathing. David and Joe called out on Jesus to raise this dear woman up. Even as David was praying, he was thinking of what a reproach it would be to the Lord if this town discovered that we had someone die at our altars. We had so boldly proclaimed healing to all who lived around us. As the church bombarded heaven, Sister Bedolla inhaled and came up shouting. All heaven broke loose! There was no doubt that the Lord was in the house. Sister Bedolla had heart problems before that night, but she was completely healed and lived to be over ninety years old. The harvest continued for many years in this town. We grew from a congregation of 30 people to approximately 250. We sent out workers into other harvest fields who are still proclaiming the good news that "Jesus saves."

There is one more detail about the Bride's stomach that we have not addressed in the verse we are studying. This is her hipbones surrounding her abdomen about with lilies. Remember lilies always speak to us of the crucified and resurrected life. There will be many sacrifices made to obtain a harvest of souls. Our will is crucified time-and-again. We must deny ourselves, take up our cross, and follow Him. I want to go back to my story about the harvest in Wilcox.

209

When we took the pastorate of that church, it had been through a deep trial of church division. Many people had left the church, and the ones who remained were deeply hurt. We asked the Lord what we could do to bring the people out of the pit they were in, and He spoke to us to have prayer meetings. I gathered the women of the church together, and we began to pray almost every morning. It was a struggle at first, but it was worth it when we saw the fruits start to come in a few months later. The Church has to be willing to set time and comfort aside if we are to gather the harvest.

The Lord of the harvest seeks a Church who is willing to sacrifice time, talents, and finance to see His kingdom built. He has empowered us with the Holy Spirit to do whatever is necessary.

My Prayer: Oh Lord, fill me with Your Spirit. Fill me every day with fresh wine. Give me boldness and empower me to gather many souls into Your kingdom. May the signs and wonders that followed Your ministry and that of the apostles, follow my ministry. Not for my glory, for all glory belongs to You. I pray for miracles that will point others to Jesus.

LABOR OF LOVE

Thy two breasts are like two young roes that are twins.
Song of Solomon 7:3

As we noted before, the Church is to put on the breastplate of faith and love (1 Thessalonians 5:8). Paul's introduction to his letter to the church of Thessalonica states that he was, "Remembering without ceasing your work of faith, and labour of love, and patience of hope in our Lord Jesus Christ, in the sight of God and our Father" (1 Thessalonians 1:3).

To the new mother, nursing a baby can be a trying experience. It is a work of faith as she simply trusts that milk will come as the newborn begins to suck. It is a labor of love as she suffers soreness the first days. It takes patience on mom's part to believe that it will get easier as she gets used to it. She will persevere because she believes with all of her heart that the milk her body produces is the best nourishment for her precious child. Our works of faith and labor of love, for Christ, takes the same kind of persevering attitude. Most times a mother will keep this hardship to herself because it is a private matter. Comparable to this is some of the works that we do for Christ.

In Matthew, chapter six, Jesus teaches us to give our assistance to the poor in such a way as to not draw attention to ourselves. He went so far as to say, we should not let our left hand know what our right hand is doing. In His teachings about prayer and fasting, He said we are not to pray for man's approval, but to go to our room and pray in secret. We should not put on the appearance of fasting, but we are to comb our hair and put on a fresh change of clothes. We all enjoy the corporate times of worship and prayer in the congregation. It is a time for edifying the Church. Our united prayer blesses the Lord, but there are times when we need to get alone with God. In the private prayer time, we pour our heart out and intercede for others.

Dorcas is a wonderful example of the labor of love. Her name means a "female roe-deer"- (note that our verse compares the Bride's breasts to two young roes with twins). *Tabitha* was the Hebrew version of this Greek name. This Christian woman was full of good works and the widows were her benefactors. She made garments for the poor of her town—never expecting any reward or payment for the clothing, she carefully sewed. She must have invested quite a bit of money into the supplies, as well as her labor. When she died, they sent for Peter who was in a neighboring town. It must have taken

211

Peter a few hours to get there. He found the widows and the poor gathered in the house weeping and clutching onto the clothes that Dorcas had made for them. He sent everyone out of the room where Dorcas had been laid; he knelt by her bedside and prayed. Then he turned toward the body and said "Tabitha, arise." She rose up from the dead and Peter gave her back to the church. Her gift was so important to the saints that they were at a loss without her. Recognition was not her motivation for service. (Acts 9:36-42)

Jesus said that we are not to seek for praise from our fellow servants. He knows the giving and praying that is done in secret, and He will reward (Matthew 6:1-18). The roe or deer is a gentle animal and pleasant to be around. I remember as a girl, we would visit the National Parks in California. I loved to feed the small deer as they would come up and eat out of my hand. I could hardly feel the deer's touch when it took the bread out of my hand. God's people should be as gentle and kind to one another as the touch of the deer.

Just as a mother scoops up her child and holds it close to her breasts, we need to be protective of each other. Loving and caring for those who are weak, those who need spiritual milk, and those who just need to know that someone cares. Any mother will tell you that her life is not her own from the time her baby first cries. Her life from that point is wrapped up in the care of her child until the day when that child matures to adulthood. In the same way, we as the Church must nurture and care for the newborn believer until the day that he can stand firm on the Word.

My Prayer: Lord, I seek Your face for the love and faith that is so desperately needed to fulfil Your commission—making disciples of all nations. Forgive me for sometimes growing weary of caring for others. Help me not to look for recognition for the works of faith and labors of love that I perform. I would much rather wait for the rewards that You have in store for me.

WISDOM, UNDERSTANDING AND DISCERNMENT

Thy neck is as a tower of ivory; thine eyes like the fishpools in
Heshbon, by the gate of Bath-rabbim: thy nose is as the tower of
Lebanon which looketh toward Damascus.
Song of Solomon 7:4

Just as Jesus set His face toward the suffering of the cross and would not be deterred from the Father's will, so the Church has purpose and direction. Her neck is compared to a tower of ivory. Her neck represents her will as we saw in chapter four, verse four. The secret of her confidence, as she goes about the Father's business, is her trust in the Lord. "Trust in the Lord with all thine heart; and lean not unto thine own understanding. In all thy ways acknowledge him, and he shall direct thy paths" (Proverbs 3:5-6). We do not wander about aimlessly, for He gives us the wisdom to know His plan and purpose for our individual lives, as well as for the corporate life of the Church.

The Beloved looks into the eyes of His Bride and sees them now as fish pools in Heshbon by the gate of Bath-rabbim. **Bath-rabbim** means "daughter of a large company or multitude." [1] We are not alone in our efforts to further the gospel of Christ. Multiple missions of the church are impossible to accomplish unless we pool our resources. For example, it would be impossible for one Christian or even one church family to send out foreign missionaries or to meet the need of world hunger. The Lord blesses the Church with wisdom so that we are able to join into a mighty multitude who builds His Church: "Through wisdom is an house builded; and by understanding it is established..." (Proverbs 24:3-4).

The meaning of **Heshbon** is "intelligent, clever, or understanding." [2] The Bride's eyes are open to the truth. She is full of wisdom. Solomon's instructions pertaining to wisdom: "My son, let not them [*words of wisdom*] depart from thine eyes: keep sound wisdom and discretion: So shall they be life unto thy soul, and grace to thy neck" (Proverbs 3:21-22). The Holy Spirit endows the Church with the ability to discern right from wrong. We pray even as Paul did:

That the God of our Lord Jesus Christ, the Father of glory, may
give unto you the spirit of wisdom and revelation in the

213

knowledge of him: The eyes of your understanding being enlightened; that ye may know what is the hope of his calling, and what the riches of the glory of his inheritance in the saints.

Ephesians 1:17-18

Lord, give us clear eyes of understanding—eyes of wisdom, revelation, knowledge—knowing your calling and directions in our lives. Help us to have the discernment of any evil that Satan may be plotting to bring against us.

The King compares her nose to a watchtower on the high mountain of Lebanon. From this high tower she can see a long ways off, even into Damascus. Such a nose can sense any approaching evil. Noses have the sense of smell. With the wisdom the Lord bestows on the Church, we can smell when something is not of God. "Dead flies putrefy the perfumer's ointment, And cause it to give off a foul odor; So does a little folly to one respected for wisdom and honor" (Ecclesiastes 10:1, NKJV). We have to guard the Church from anything that would spoil the ointment of the Holy Spirit's anointing. A little sin or indiscretion on the part of the leaders that we respect as being wise can devastate a congregation.

My Prayer: Give me wisdom and understanding to know the path You have planed for me. May the revelation of Your Word and Your will be constantly leading me. Give me a discerning spirit that will sense anything that is going to harm or bring reproach upon the gospel.

(1) Jamieson, Fausset, and Brown Commentary, Electronic Database. Copyright © 1997, 2003, 2005, 2006 by Biblesoft, Inc. All rights reserved.
(2) Easton's Bible Dictionary, PC Study Bible formatted electronic database Copyright © 2003, 2006 Biblesoft, Inc. All rights reserved.

214

CROWNED WITH JOY

Thine head upon thee is like Carmel, and the hair of thine head like
purple; the king is held in the galleries.
Song of Solomon 7:5

David spent many years as a fugitive from Saul, king of Israel. During this period of his life, David had several hundred men
who paid allegiance to him. He hid in Gath, Moab, and the wilderness of En-gedi. At one point, he and his men stayed at Carmel,
which was a place of orchards and fruit gardens. The enemies of
Israel did not harass them, nor did they take advantage of the farmers
and shepherds that dwelt in the same area because of their fear of
David and his mighty men. Nabal was one of the wealthiest men of
that area who benefited from David's watchful eye. When it came
time to shear the sheep, David sent ten young men to Nabal. They
courteously requested some provisions in return for the protection
they had given his shepherds. Nabal was a crude and stingy man, and
he flat out denied the request. He was very rude to the young men.
When David's men reported what had happened, David was ready to
put on his sword and lead his men into battle with Nabal.

Abigail, Nabal's wife, was a woman of good understanding
and beautiful as well. She had suffered with this wicked husband and
had learned to bite her tongue when she was around him. Some of the
servants had witnessed how Nabal had answered David's men. They
went to Abigail and explained to her how David had protected them,
and how Nabal had been so rude. She went into action immediately
and had the servants gather bread, wine, meat, corn, and even some
dessert of raisins and figs. She set off to meet David who was on his
way to destroy her family. She found favor in his sight and averted a
war. Nabal celebrated and got drunk that night. The next day Abigail
told Nabal that she had persuaded David not to avenge himself—
Nabal dropped dead. (1 Samuel 25:2-42)

When David found out that Nabal was dead, he went to the
woman of great understanding—the one he had fallen in love with—
Abigail—and took her for his wife. We were servants of a cruel
taskmaster, Satan—then Jesus came. Many of us thought there was
no escape from the bondage—then Jesus came. King Jesus has been
protecting us, from a far off, even when we were not aware of it.

I can see how the Lord protected me even during my early
childhood. My twin sister, Virginia, and I were abandoned by our

mother when were babies. My father had been killed a few months earlier in a suspicious accident. The Lord caused my aunt, Gertrude Jones, to find us lying in the middle of the bed. I shiver to think what would have happened to us if God had not led my aunt to come over that day. It was during the Depression and money was so tight that our family decided to split Virginia and me up. Aunt Gertrude was a preacher and would have taken both of us, but her family was already struggling to keep food on the table for their own two daughters. It was my lot to go with Uncle Babe who was not a Christian. He and his wife did not get along very well, and their goal in life was to make money.

When I was about four years old, I was struck down with polio. My left side was paralyzed, and I could hardly swallow because of the swelling in my throat. The doctor told my uncle there was nothing he could do—just to put me in a dark room and hope I could get better. Aunt Gertrude sent a prayer cloth to put under my pillow. I was too young to understand what was happening. I started to feel better, and I would get up and play when nobody was watching. I thought Uncle Babe would get mad if he saw me out of bed. They soon caught on to my trick. The family gave God the glory for my healing.

I had such a longing to go to church that I would walk whenever possible to a near-by church. When I was in the fourth grade, Uncle Babe and his wife divorced. Aunt Gertrude and her family took me home, and I learned all about Jesus. Even though I was not aware of the Lord's protection during those early years, He was there. When I was asked the question that Elijah posed to the children of Israel, on top of Mount Carmel: "How long halt you between two opinions? If the Lord be God, follow him: but if Baal, then follow him"—I chose God. (1 Kings 18:21)

King Jesus has brought me out of the slavery of sin and freed me from the evil taskmaster, the Devil. He has brought me into His kingdom and set upon my head the crown of life and joy. (James 1:12; 1 Thessalonians 2:19) My hair is like the royal tapestry of rich purple. Moreover, the wonder of it all is that King Jesus in enthralled and held captive by my tresses of hair! I have royal hair, for I am a daughter of the King! My locks or tresses of hair display my love, submission, and consecration to my Beloved King! It is true, for the glory of God has turned my wilderness to a blooming field of joy.

The wilderness and the wasteland shall be glad for them,
And the desert shall rejoice and blossom as the rose;
It shall blossom abundantly and rejoice,
Even with joy and singing.
The glory of Lebanon shall be given to it,
The excellence of Carmel and Sharon.
They shall see the glory of the Lord,
The excellency of our God.
Isaiah 35:1-2, NKJV

My Prayer: I thank You, Jesus, for blessing me with the understanding of Your love and protection. I would be lost if You had not found me. I praise You because You knew me even before I was born, and You caused me to come into the knowledge of Your saving grace. May I reflect Your glory, and may others see Your excellency through me.

Twins –Vivian and Virginia reunited after living apart during the early years

Approximately 12 years old

Graduation Pictures

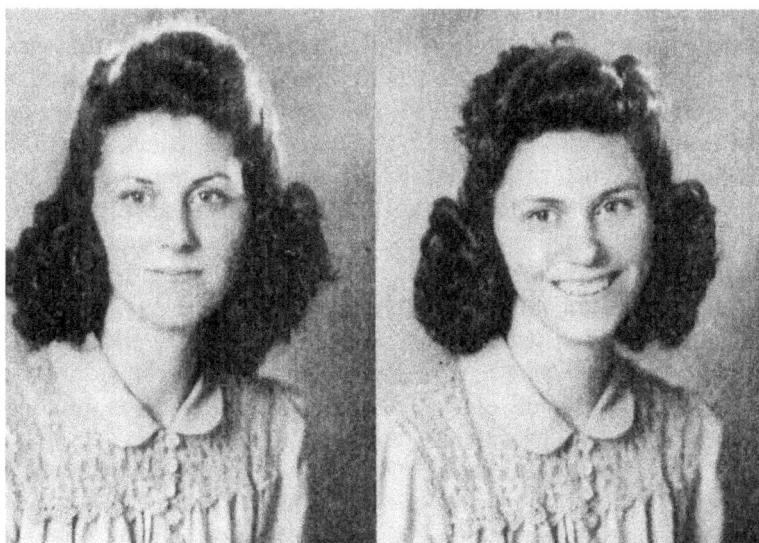

Vivian and Virginia

Age 17

BEAUTY OF JESUS IN ME

How fair and how pleasant art thou, O love, for delights!
Song of Solomon 7:6

This is the seventh time the Beloved addresses the Bride as His fair one. [1] Seven is the number of perfection—it is God's divine number. We are made perfect by His work within us. In the Sermon on the Mount, Jesus said that we are to be perfect even as the Father in heaven is perfect (Matthew 5:48). We think to ourselves, "How can I ever obtain perfection?" We need to learn to be patient and let the Lord continue to mold us into His perfect work. "Knowing this, that the trying of your faith worketh patience. But let patience have her perfect work, that ye may be perfect and entire, wanting nothing" (James 1:3-4). The word "perfect" is also interpreted as "mature."

Through the eyes of Jesus, we are fair and pleasant. He sees us through the eyes of love, and He is delighted with us. It certainly is not because we are the elite of the earth. If we go back to the first part of this song, we see that the Shulamite girl described herself as being a hardworking shepherdess. The sun had blackened her skin. She was an outcast in her family assigned to the vineyards. She was from very humble beginnings. (Song of Solomon 1:5-6)

It reminds me of the story of Esther. She was an orphan and a descendent of the captive Jews within a foreign land. She was only one of many girls brought into the house of women within the palace of King Ahasuerus. Right away, she caught the eye of the chief custodian, Hegai. He saw her as fair and beautiful. Could it be that the spirit within Esther made her unique? It is not just the outward appearance that our King is looking for, but also the reflection of Himself which beams forth as we allow the Holy Spirit to mold us and make us into His image. Peter told the early Christian women:

Your beauty should not come from outward adornment, such as braided hair and the wearing of gold jewelry and fine clothes. Instead, it should be that of your inner self, the unfading beauty of a gentle and quiet spirit, which is of great worth in God's sight. For this is the way the holy women of the past who put their hope in God used to make themselves beautiful.

1 Peter 3:3-5, NIV

This instruction does not only apply to the women, but also to men, as we are all part of the Bride of Christ. We need to be submissive to our husband, Jesus. Our beauty should come from the gentle and quiet spirit within us. Our spirit is quiet and content as we put our trust in Jesus as our provider and maker.

Esther became the queen after going through twelve months of purification, beauty treatments, and long soaking baths of myrrh. Does this sound like the process the Church must go through to get ready for our Beloved? We are being purified and made holy. We are bathed with the myrrh of suffering so we can become more like Jesus. Esther came out of all this preparation the most glorious from all the other women. (Esther 2)

Not many of the chosen people of God came from grand beginnings. He chose the foolish things of this world to confuse the wise. He chose the weak ones to confuse the mighty ones of this world. Why? His purpose was, "That no flesh should glory in his presence. But of him are ye in Christ Jesus, who of God is made unto us wisdom, and righteousness, and sanctification, and redemption: That, according as it is written, He that glorieth, let him glory in the Lord" (1 Corinthians 1:29-31).

There is no beauty in us other than that which He has given to us. We are a delight to the Lord when He sees a right spirit within us. The right spirit is a humble spirit; a hungry spirit; a righteous spirit; a spirit of integrity. "The steps of a good man are ordered by the Lord: and he delighteth in his way" (Psalms 37:23).

My Prayer: I pray that I will delight You, my Lord and King. Thank You for loving me so much that You see me as Your perfect child. I desire to live my life in a manner that will be pleasing to You, and that others will see Your goodness through me. I am nothing without Your grace and beauty.

(1)   See Song of Solomon 1:15; 2:10-13; 4:1; 4:7; 4:10, 6:10, 7:6.

STANDING FIRM AND TALL

This thy stature is like to a palm tree, and thy breasts to clusters of grapes. **Song of Solomon 7:7**

The Beloved King now looks at her entire appearance and sees her standing slender and tall like a palm tree. During our missionary days in the Marshall Islands, we came to appreciate the coconut palm tree more than you can imagine. Little else grew upon the coral atolls of the Pacific. Some of these trees grew to be sixty feet tall. During typhoon season, the islands were subject to severe storms and typhoons. Just looking at these tall slender trees, you would think that they would be uprooted and blown away during these storms; on the contrary, they would bend in the wind almost to the ground but never be uprooted. In the morning when the storm had passed, they would be standing tall again. Even though the branches were stripped away, there was no permanent damage to the trees.

The Church is to stand firm when the storms of persecution or trial come her way. Paul says, "Wherefore take unto you the whole armour of God, that ye may be able to **withstand** in the evil day, and having done all, to **stand**" (Ephesians 6:13). Jesus said that the life built upon His words would stand the test of the storm (Matthew 7:24, 25). Material things may be stripped away during the test, but our faith is grounded in the Rock.

The tall coconut palms were a welcome sight when we had been out on the ocean all night—with only the stars to guide us. Morning would come, and we would be straining our eyes to see if we were near land. Usually one of the young men would be the first to see a glimmer of the treetops. He would cry out, "Iling O" (land ho), and everyone would rush to that side of the boat to see if he really saw the trees. We would all break out in praise, joy, and relief that we were safe.

Does the weary, lost soul rejoice when he sees the trees of the Lord standing tall—showing him the direction to salvation? This is our mission as the Church of Jesus Christ. Blinded souls are straining to find direction in their lives. They are searching for relief from the sin and oppression of the evil one. We, as the Church, must stand out from the crowd—pointing the way to safety.

The Bride's breasts are a very prominent feature on her slender, tall body. They remind the Beloved of a cluster of grapes. We have seen that her breasts are the twin fruits of faith and love. As the

222

Church grows strong in the Word of God, it produces much spiritual fruit—not just a scrawny grape or two, but it produces a whole cluster of succulent fruit.

When the Holy Spirit is in control, our tree will be strong and full of fruit. Love produces joy, peace, longsuffering, gentleness, goodness, meekness, and self-control in our spirit and in our attitudes (Galatians 5:22, 23). Faith produces the prayers, witnessing, good works, and the courage to go where Christ sends us. Whatever the Lord calls us to do, He will cause us to prosper. (Psalms 1)

I am so glad that palm trees do not stop bearing fruit when they get old. The mature Christian is still green, and he is still declaring that the Lord is good.

> The righteous will flourish like a palm tree, they will grow like a cedar of Lebanon; planted in the house of the Lord, they will flourish in the courts of our God. They will still bear fruit in old age, they will stay fresh and green, proclaiming, 'The Lord is upright; he is my Rock.'   Psalms 92:12-15, NIV

My Prayer: Oh Lord, I pray for strength to stand tall and firm when the winds of adversity blow upon me. I pledge to meditate upon Your Word so that I will be standing upon the Rock of my Salvation. May I direct the lost to You. May I be bearing much fruit, and may I be blessing others with my love and faith until the day You call me home.

PALMS BRANCHES OF PRAISE

I said, I will go up to the palm tree, I will take hold of the boughs thereof: now also thy breasts shall be as clusters of the vine, and the smell of thy nose like apples; Song of Solomon 7:8

The Bridegroom says, "I will go up to the palm tree and I will take hold of its branches" (Song of Solomon 7:8, NKJV). The palm tree is difficult to climb, as it is so tall and straight up. This does not hinder Jesus from cutting and pulling down the branches, which are signs of victory. He lives within the praises of His people. He purchased our victory as He hung on the old rugged tree.

God initiated the custom of waving palm branches. He instructed the Israelites to celebrate a Feast of Tabernacles each year as a commemoration of their exit out of Egypt. On the first day of the Feast, they were to cut down branches and rejoice in the Lord (Leviticus 23:40). To the Christian, this is a type of our release out of Satan's kingdom, thereby, becoming citizens of Christ's kingdom.

When Jesus came into Jerusalem riding on the colt of a donkey, the people could not contain their praise. They waved palm branches and sang out, "Hosanna: Blessed is the King of Israel that cometh in the name of the Lord" (John 12:13). Jesus longs to hear us spread the good news of salvation through our praises. The religious leaders were jealous of the praise given to Jesus, and they demanded to know why He allowed it. Jesus replied, "I tell you that, if these should hold their peace, the stones would immediately cry out" (Luke 19:40).

Is it possible to be part of the kingdom of the Christ, the anointed one of the Father, and hold our tongues? As we remember what the Lord has done for us, the Spirit of God starts to churn within our innermost being, and before we know it, His praises are flowing from our mouths. If praise is not coming out of our mouths, we need to stir up our memory of what God has done for us (2 Peter 3:1).

Our verse continues, "The fragrance of your breath like apples" (Song of Solomon 7:8, NKJV). Can you remember the smell of fresh baked apple pie? Words of praise and thanksgiving are as pleasant as the smell of apples to the Lord. These pleasant words are pleasing to everyone we speak to. I recently entertained a guest in my home who was a stranger. She blessed me with one victory story after another. My faith was increased, and my heart was full of joy from just listening to what the Lord had done for her. She had recently lost

224

her daughter to cancer; nonetheless, she had given even this— her most precious possession—into the hands of a loving Father.

The palm tree and the apple were symbols of joy to the Israelites (Joel 1:12). The palm is a symbol of victory to the New Testament Church. This will be our song around the throne of God.

> After this I beheld, and, lo, a great multitude, which no man could number, of all nations, and kindreds, and people, and tongues, stood before the throne, and before the Lamb, clothed with white robes, and *palms in their hands;* And cried with a loud voice, saying, Salvation to our God which sitteth upon the throne, and unto the Lamb.
>
> Revelation 7:9-10

Have we surrendered our lives and our speech so completely that the Lord feels free to use us to sing His praises? Do we bless Him and magnify His name in every conversation? "Give unto the Lord the glory due unto his name; worship the Lord in the beauty of holiness" (Psalms 29:2).

My Prayer: Oh Lord, climb my tree of praise and take whatever branches of thanksgiving You can use. Use me to spread the good news of Your salvation, healing, and Your soon coming to everyone I meet today. My love overflows in testimony and song of Your marvelous works. Keep me from having the bad breath of complaint and worry.

THE BEST WINE EVER SPOKEN

And the roof of thy mouth like the best wine for my beloved, that goeth down sweetly, causing the lips of those that are asleep to speak. Song of Solomon 7:9

The servants were in a panic as they whispered the shameful news to each other, "We've run out of wine." The reply was, "Oh, no, how can we save face for the bridegroom?" Word was spreading fast among the servants. One of the servants confided in Mary, mother of Jesus, that the wine had run out. Mary may have been helping in the kitchen, and the servants must have looked to her as a problem solver. This problem was beyond her ability to solve. She did not have the money to go down to the store, even if there was a fast way to purchase more wine. What could they do? She went to her son, Jesus, and stated the problem. "Dear woman, why do you involve me?" Jesus replied. "My time has not yet come" (John 2:1, NIV). Mary did not answer Him back. She just told the servants to "do whatever Jesus tells you to do." Jesus took charge of the situation and told the servants to fill six large water vessels with water. Then He told them to dip into the vessels and take a sample to the governor of the feast. The governor exclaimed, "This is the best wine, how is it you have saved it for last?" The wine that Jesus made was purer and sweeter than the original wine. (John 2:1-11)

When we taste of the heavenly wine (the Holy Spirit) that Jesus offers to us, it is satisfying to our souls and quenches our spiritual thirst. The gift of the Holy Spirit is to be shared with others. Mary did not have the answer, but she knew Jesus. When the Church runs out of answers—Jesus is the answer. As we depend upon the Holy Spirit, He causes the sweet essence of Jesus' love to come forth out of our mouths; thereby, the Holy Spirit gives us the divine knowledge needed to solve whatever dilemma. Just as the Lord promised Jeremiah the prophet, "Behold, I have put my words in thy mouth" (Jeremiah 1:9), so Jesus promised His disciples:

Therefore settle it in your hearts not to meditate beforehand on what you will answer; for *I will give you a mouth and wisdom* which all your adversaries will not be able to contradict or resist.   Luke 21:14-15, NKJV

226

He not only gives us the answers to those who would question our faith and persecute us; He also gives us answers for the weary of this world.

A man hath joy by the answer of his mouth: and a word spoken in due season, how good is it!   Proverbs 15:23

The Lord God hath given me the tongue of the learned, that I should know how to speak a word in season to him that is weary.   Isaiah 50:4

We are ambassadors for Christ, *as though God were pleading through us*: we implore you on Christ's behalf, *be reconciled to God.*   2 Corinthians 5:20, NKJV

Our God given assignment is to plead with the person who is asleep—dead in sin—to wake up and be reconciled to God. What a monumental day it was when Jesus told Mary and Martha of Bethany, "I am the resurrection and the life." He told them to remove the stone from Lazarus' tomb, and after offering a short prayer thanking God the Father for hearing Him, He said in a loud voice, "Lazarus, come forth." Lazarus woke up from the "death" sleep and came stumbling out of the grave bound up in grave clothes. Jesus ordered, "Loose him and let him go" (John 11:25-44).

Jesus has given His Church the authority to loose men and women from the death of sin. (Matthew 16:19; 18:18) As we speak the sweet words (*the best wine*) of our Beloved Lord, men and women will *awake* from their spiritual *sleep* and *speak*—declaring the wonderful works of the Lord. (Psalms 40:2-5)

My Prayer: Lord, cause my lips to speak sweet, healing words of life to the lost and dying of this world. Use me to pray deliverance for those who are bound by the Wicked One—those who have been blinded to the truth. Give me wisdom to speak the right word at the right time.

HE DESIRES ME?

I am my beloved's, and his desire is toward me.
Song of Solomon 7:10

It is the Bride's turn to speak, "I am my beloved's." She is asserting her absolute love toward her Beloved. As we come into the intimate relationship with our Redeemer King, we become totally committed to the One who has purchased our redemption. We are not our own anymore, for He has bought us with the greatest love ever known to humankind. In the New Living Translation this verse reads, "I am my lover's, and he claims me as his own."

This reminds me of the beautiful love story of Ruth. Ruth was an idol worshiper from Moab until she converted to the God of Israel. She loved and respected her mother-in-law, Naomi. Naomi and Ruth went back to Naomi's hometown of Bethlehem with nothing but the clothes on their backs. As the custom was for widows, Ruth went out to glean (pick up the leftovers) in the fields to provide food for herself and Naomi. She just "happened" to go to a field belonging to a kinsman of Naomi's whose name was Boaz. Boaz took a liking to Ruth right away, and he told his men to leave a generous portion of grain behind for her. As time went on, Ruth desired Boaz as a kinsman redeemer to take her under his covering (protection, care, and support) and marry her. To show Boaz her devotion, she boldly laid at his feet one night after the men had finished threshing the grain. Boaz would have complied to her request immediately, but there was a problem because there was an even closer kinsman than he who would have the right to claim Naomi's daughter-in-law and her land. Boaz had to go through the proper procedure of offering this other kinsman the first chance to redeem Naomi's land. The other kinsman declined the offer, for he did not want to marry the Moabitess. Boaz purchased the right to Naomi's land, which also gave him the right to take Ruth as his wife.

This is a picture of how Jesus purchased our salvation and redeemed us out of the clutches of Satan. He is our kinsman redeemer, for He has already paid the price for our redemption. Ruth had to be willing to step out in faith and ask for the protection of Boaz. Likewise, we have to step out in faith and believe that Jesus is our Redeemer. Ruth was willing to put her pride on the line. She came under Boaz's love and authority. We must turn everything over to Jesus, knowing that He loves us so much that He will only bring good into our lives.

Just before that awesome day when Jesus laid down His life for His own, He ate the Passover Supper with His disciples. He told them: "*I have eagerly desired* to eat this Passover with you before I suffer. For I tell you, I will not eat it again until it finds fulfillment in the kingdom of God" (Luke 22:15-16, NIV). "My beloved's desire is towards me" (Song of Solomon 7:10). His desire is that I accept the price that He paid for my redemption—His shed blood. His desire is that I would commune with Him and partake of His broken body. His desire is that I join Him in His kingdom and dine at the Marriage Supper of the Lamb. "Blessed are they which are called unto the marriage supper of the Lamb" (Revelation 19:9). Blessed, happy, fulfilled—there are not enough words to describe the glory that awaits the Bride of Christ. The most wonderful thing that will happen when we sit down and drink of the fruit of the vine will be seeing Jesus face to face—never to be out of His presence again. To think that He desires to be with me for eternity is far more than my finite brain can comprehend.

My Prayer: My Redeemer, I humbly bow before You—I lay myself at Your feet. How I love You, for You first loved me, and You bought me with Your own blood. You are my covering and protection while I walk this earth. You deliver me from evil. Your love surpasses any love that has ever been sought after; nevertheless, You so freely give it to all who believe on Your name. I long for the day when Father God tells Jesus, "It's time—call your Bride home." It will be the most joyous wedding feast ever known to man, when I see You face to face.

INTO THE VILLAGES

Come, my beloved, let us go forth into the field; let us lodge in the villages. Song of Solomon 7:11

The Bride is not willing to go anywhere alone. She is saying, "Come with me, my Beloved, Jesus." We are partners with Christ as we go out to work in the harvest fields of this earth. We can do nothing without Him, and He must use our humble vessels to carry His glorious gospel (1 Corinthians 3:9). It is a great privilege to spread His Word to every small village of the earth—no matter how remote. It is usually the working class people or the poor who live in the small villages. They are sometimes more receptive to the Word than the rich and famous. Jesus said that He was anointed to preach the gospel to the poor (Luke 4:18). This is not to say that the gospel is not for the rich; it is only to say, it may be more difficult for the rich to humble themselves and become poor in spirit (realizing their need of salvation). (Matthew 19:23-26; Matthew 5:3)

Jesus said that before He returns for His Church, the gospel must be preached to the entire world (Matthew 24:14). We should not discount the importance of a place because it is far away, or because there are not many people living there. The Lord's commission includes every little village.

When we went to the island of Majuro, we did not expect the land mass to be so small. It was as if God had flung out tiny bits of coral in a vast expanse of ocean. The islands are arranged in chains of islands, which are called atolls. It is like a necklace with water in between the pearls. The runway was located on the main island in the Majuro chain. There was a 30-mile road on one side that connected several of the islands, but the other side could only be accessed by a small boat. In the middle of the atoll was a huge lagoon. The waters were very difficult to navigate where the seawater would meet the water in the lagoon.

It was a burden on our hearts to get over to islands not accessible by vehicle, for we knew some of the people had heard the gospel but did not have a steady minister. Our children shipped an 18-foot outboard motor boat to us, so that we could go across the lagoon and minister to these small islands. We had purposed to go to an island where we knew there were some Christians, but the Lord had another plan.

The weather was perfect and the ocean was calm on the day we made our first venture to the other side of the atoll. As we approached a 100-foot passage where the ocean and lagoon water met, David sped the boat up. We were right in the middle when a huge wave came out of the ocean side and landed inside the boat. It broke the fiberglass windshield directly over my head and blood was streaming down my face. We sat there stunned for a few minutes, for it took us completely by surprise. We decided to go back along the shoreline. Soon we came to a small grass hut. We stopped and went onto the island. We were greeted by the one and only family that lived on that island—Mom, Dad, two daughters, and five grandchildren. They were so happy to see us, and as they listened to the message of Jesus' love, they accepted Him as their Savior. Our Lord ordered the change in direction, for we would never have gone to that particular island on purpose. My injury was minor. Thank You, Jesus, for being in the boat with us.

Jesus set the pattern for us in sending out his disciples two-by-two—instructing them to go into every village telling the residents that the kingdom of God was at hand. He empowered them to heal the sick and to set the demon possessed free. (Luke 10:5, 9, 17) Paul and Silas followed this pattern in their missionary journeys. They went into a town, dwelt there, preached the gospel, planted a church, and then they moved on as the Lord led them. (Acts 16 and 17) Lord, give us the wisdom we need, and help us as individual members and as a corporate body to fulfill Your commission to:

> Go therefore and make disciples of all the nations, baptizing them in the name of the Father and of the Son and of the Holy Spirit, teaching them to observe all things that I have commanded you; *and lo, I am with you always*, even to the end of the age. Amen.   Matthew 28:19-20, NKJV

My Prayer: The harvest field is so large that sometimes it seems overwhelming, but I know that nothing is impossible with You. It is said that we live in a Global Village since communications and travel have become so commonplace in our world. I do thank You for the communications of television and the internet that are reaching all over the world. Nevertheless, I know that the most effective witness is usually the one-on-one, person-to-person witness. Direct the Church as we plant more churches in more neighborhoods. Help us to reach the tiniest village in the remote areas of the world.

Picture of our prayer of dedication for God to use this 18-ft boat.

Picture of the family that was on the small island, David in the back and 2 of our students in the front

EARLY TO RISE

Let us get up early to the vineyards; let us see if the vine flourish, whether the tender grape appear, and the pomegranates bud forth: there will I give thee my loves. Song of Solomon 7:12

Every day I wake up and sense the sweet presence of Jesus. His mercies are new every morning, and He is so faithful. (Lamentations 3:21-23) "My voice shalt thou hear in the morning, O Lord; in the morning will I direct my prayer unto thee, and will look up" (Psalms 5:3). Farmers usually get up before daybreak. They eat breakfast, and then they are ready to go out and tend the fields as soon as the sun comes up. Solomon warns against being lazy. He says a little sleep and a little slumber, a little folding of the hands will lead to poverty (Proverbs 6:9-11). The Christian who procrastinates and is slack concerning the work of the Lord will be spiritually poor.

I am so glad that the Lord saved me and called me early in life. I have had many fruitful years of ministry. I delight to go back in time, with my Lord, and check out the fruit. I relate to Paul when he said that the souls that had been saved under his ministry were his joy (Philippians 2:17, 18).

It was my privilege to go back to Majuro some thirty years after David and I were missionaries there. I was sent as a temporary replacement for a missionary who needed a break, and I was placed at the very same Bible school where we had previously taught. The word quickly spread that Sis. Thompson had returned to the island. One-by-one my former students came knocking at my door and asked, "Do you remember me?" Of course, everyone had matured so much, it was hard for me to recognize them right away. As they told me their names and reminisced about the past, the remembrance flooded back. Each one had been serving the Lord and fulfilling their call. Several were ministers and leaders of the fellowship there in the islands. They told me of others who had gone out to various islands to preach the gospel. Other former students owned businesses such as a bakery and a fabric store. All of them were precious fruit for the Master. There have been countless souls saved due to their testimony of God's amazing grace.

"They that sow in tears shall reap in joy. He that goeth forth and weepeth, bearing precious seed, shall doubtless come again with rejoicing, bringing his sheaves with him" (Psalms 126:5-6). I bring my *loves* and present them to my beloved Master. Yes, there have been many tears sown in prayer and hardship, but it will be worth it all when I stand before Him with the precious fruit of ministry.

You may say, "But I am not a missionary like you, how can I bring my *love* to Jesus?" Each one of us has our own mission field. It may be your family, the neighborhood, or children in your local church. Whatever He calls you to do, get busy and do it. Do not put it off until tomorrow. Caring for the young Christian and making sure that they are becoming fruitful is a special work of love. Caring for the children and teaching them to love Jesus is also demonstrating our love for the Lord. James wrote, "Religion that God our Father accepts as pure and faultless is this: to look after orphans and widows in their distress and to keep oneself from being polluted by the world" (James 1:27, NIV). Jesus loved the children: "Jesus said, 'Let the little children come to me, and do not hinder them, for the kingdom of heaven belongs to such as these.' When he had placed his hands on them, he went on from there" (Matthew 19:14-15, NIV).

Fruit inspection—checking the tender grape and the pomegranate that is just budding is comparable to the believer checking on the new convert who is being transformed into the image of Christ, and checking on the young child whose tender mind and conscience is being formed. By these acts, Jesus knows that we are in love with Him.

My Prayer: It is such a privilege to be included in the planting, watering, and harvesting of souls. Help me to be diligent about checking on the tender grapes and the budding pomegranates—the young convert, the child, and the widow. I want to have baskets full of fruit to present to You as a token of my love.

BEARING PRECIOUS GIFTS

*The mandrakes give a smell, and at our gates are all manner of pleasant fruits, new and old, which I have laid up for thee, O my beloved. **Song of Solomon 7:13***

There is some speculation as to what a mandrake is. Some scholars believe it is a fruit about the size of an apple, and that it had a stimulating effect on a person. Some call it a *love plant* or *love apple*. [(1)] In modern terms, it was a love potion. The only other time mandrakes are mentioned in the Bible is in Genesis 30:14-16. Rachel traded with Leah a night with Jacob for some mandrakes. Therefore, we can conclude that they were probably rare and precious. Based on this, we understand that the Bride is saying that she is bringing rare and precious gifts to the Beloved, which demonstrates her deep love for Him. Not only is she bringing mandrakes, but also she has stored up all manner of pleasant fruits—new and old.

The Church is comprised of many members, but each of us is our own distinct person. God created each of us as a unique treasure. Every person has a distinct offering of fragrant praise for the King. Knowing how different we are, He leads us and deals with us on a personal basis.

What is the Lord doing in your life? Have you opened your heart in such a way that He can change you and guide you in His paths of righteousness? God will open the gates of heaven for those who have walked according to His ways. Even during this walk, He gives perfect peace when we put our trust in Him. He is the stable Rock of our faith, and He holds us steady as we pursue His ways.

Open the gates to all who are righteous;
allow the faithful to enter.
You will keep in perfect peace all who trust in you,
all whose thoughts are fixed on you!
Trust in the Lord always,
for the Lord God is the eternal Rock.
Isaiah 26:2-4, NLT

But for those who are righteous,
the way is not steep and rough.
You are a God who does what is right,
and you smooth out the path ahead of them.

235

Lord, we show our trust in you by obeying your laws;
our heart's desire is to glorify your name.
All night long I search for you;
in the morning I earnestly seek for God.
For only when you come to judge the earth
will people learn what is right.
Isaiah 26:7-10, NLT

God is so gracious that He goes before us making our paths smooth. We can look back to the times of sickness or distress and see how God has prepared us for even these hard times. We, in turn, show our trust in Him by obeying His commands. He knows when our heart's desire is to glorify His name and to seek after Him above all else.

We are storing up treasures in heaven while we serve our Beloved King. Jesus instructed His believers to:

Lay not up for yourselves treasures upon earth, where moth and rust doth corrupt, and where thieves break through and steal: But lay up for yourselves treasures in heaven, where neither moth nor rust doth corrupt, and where thieves do not break through nor steal: For where your treasure is, there will your heart be also.   Matthew 6:19-21

I am so unworthy of any rewards that I may store up in heaven, for it is only by the grace and love of my Lord that I can even stand in His presence. Nevertheless, His delight is to prepare a place for me with all kinds of treasures. "Come, ye blessed of my Father, inherit the kingdom prepared for you from the foundation of the world" (Matthew 25:34).

My Prayer: How I long for the day when You call me to enter into the celestial gates. I do not want to be empty handed. I want to be able to present precious fruits of all kinds—works and deeds that I have unselfishly done while I walked in Your path. I want to bring men, women, and children that I have led to You; those whom I have discipled with Your strength and Your wisdom.

CHAPTER 8

CLOSER THAN A BROTHER

O that thou wert as my brother, that sucked the breasts of my mother! when I should find thee without, I would kiss thee; yea, I should not be despised. Song of Solomon 8:1

The betrothed Bride of olden times was to be chaste and modest. It was unacceptable to publicly display her love to the man she was to marry. Therefore, the Bride is daydreaming as to what it would be like if he were her brother. In that case, it would not be shameful to just go up and kiss him, for he would be part of the family—with the same mother. Jesus has become our elder brother in the sense that we share the same father—our loving Father God. We share the same inheritance. Still, our love for the Lord draws us even closer than a brother. Our relationship is designed to go deeper than even the closest of friendships. It is wonderful to know that Jesus is our brother and our friend; nevertheless, Jesus would draw us into a more intimate relationship—His Bride—His Lover. The relationship between lovers holds no restrictions, and every thought and action is shared when the two persons have become one.

I found this to be true in marriage. I can be thinking about something that my husband and I have not spoken about, and all of a sudden, he will comment on the very thing I was thinking. This is what Paul meant when he said we should be so close to Jesus that we have the same mind. We share the same thoughts, the same desires, and the same ambitions (1 Corinthians 2:16; Philippians 2:5). Most of all, we just yearn to be near each other and let love flow freely.

Most of the people of the world do not mind if we are religious as long as we keep our beliefs to ourselves. There are many who do not understand our obsession with drawing closer to Jesus. Jesus told the disciples not to be surprised when the world around them did not understand them. The majority did not understand Him—some even hated Him (John 15:18). The beloved disciple, John, understood this when he said, "Marvel not, my brethren, if the world hate you" (1 John 3:13).

Jesus was despised and rejected—a man of sorrows and acquainted with grief (Isaiah 53:3). Jesus warned his followers to beware when all men speak well of you, for there must be something wrong with what you are teaching if everyone agrees with it (Luke 6:26). Even those within the church will not always understand why we are so emotional and excited about our love for the Lord.

238

A few months ago, we established a Healing Room on the Leeward side of Oahu. This place is separate from the church and located in an office type building where anyone can walk in and request prayer. Claudia came for prayer because she desired a closer walk with the Lord. She also had a burden for her husband to be healed since he was in constant pain. He refused to come with her for prayer. God saw her hunger and baptized her in the Holy Spirit according to Acts chapter 2. She was so happy and just bubbling over with excitement. She went home and started praying in her heavenly language. Her husband thought she was crazy, and he was worried that she was getting *too religious*. Her regular church was uncomfortable about her sharing this new experience with other members and politely requested that she keep it to herself.

The other day, Claudia attended a conference on healing. She was so blessed by the teaching that she just wanted to go home and find a quiet place with the Lord. Her husband was asleep, so she crept into the house trying not to wake him. She went into a room far away from her husband and began to worship the Lord. All of a sudden, she had a flashlight shining directly into her eyes. Her husband had used a flashlight instead of turning on the lamp. He asked her, "What are you doing?" She replied, "I'm praying for you." He shook his head and said, "You are really weird!"

As the Bride, we must be respectful of other people. Peter said that we should always be ready to give an answer to those who are seeking for God with gentleness and respect (1 Peter 3:15). Nevertheless, we must not be ashamed of our relationship with our Lord (Luke 9:26). There will be times when the Holy Spirit will lead us to speak out boldly so that people will see the joy and the reality of having Jesus live within us. Other times, we are to find the secret place in our prayer closet to commune privately with the Lover of our souls.

My Prayer: Jesus, I love You so much that Your goodness and blessings are always on my lips. I seek Your face in the quiet of my prayer closet. I find so much joy and peace speaking to You and expressing my love to You. Help me to have wisdom as to how I can draw Your people into a closer walk with You.

WHO IS LEADING WHOM?

I would lead thee, and bring thee into my mother's house, who would instruct me: I would cause thee to drink of spiced wine of the juice of my pomegranate. Song of Solomon 8:2

In our zeal, we must be careful not to take the lead. Here the Bride is saying, "**I would lead you**." "**I would** have **my** mother instruct you." "**I would cause** you to be blessed by spiced wine of the juice of **my** pomegranate." The focus is upon what she would do for the King. It is our deep desire to see the kingdom of God advance, but we must follow our Lord's leading and timing. We are to learn of Him—not thinking that our human mind will do a better job. Beware of the idea of "all is well that ends well." In the Lord's economy, the destination is often less important than the means we use to arrive there. Notice that the Bride is not offering just fresh fruit but special spiced wine. It is as if she thinks that her way will result in even greater blessing than what He has produced in the past. The God of all gods said: "For my thoughts are not your thoughts, neither are your ways my ways...For as the heavens are higher than the earth, so are my ways higher than your ways, and my thoughts than your thoughts." (Isaiah 55:8-9)

The relationship we have with Christ is so similar to that of the natural husband and wife relationship. (Ephesians 5:32-33) It is the temptation of every wife to get the job done whatever it takes. How many of us wives have become impatient with our husbands when a task was not done as soon as we thought it should? How many times have we decided that we will just do it ourselves? Then we proudly expect our husbands to thank us for a job well done. As I have found out through experience, my husband is able to do a much better job. If only I had been patient and let him do it, there would not have been any hurt feelings between us. I have also been guilty of getting ahead of God's plan.

One example of this was the time I decided to prove that we could pay for the building of a new sanctuary. It was true that we really needed a new building as the congregation had outgrown the old one. We were holding Sunday School classes in every room of our parsonage, which was attached to the church. Even though we had grown in numbers, the offerings were still too small for such a venture. David, being the financial wizard of the family, found out about a program the General Council of the Assemblies of God of-

240

fered to assist churches to build called the Church Extension Plan. This plan allowed members to take out certificates of insurance that would provide loans to the Church for building purposes, and at the same time, it provided life insurance for the families. It was ideal for our needs. Nonetheless, some members doubted that we could make the monthly payments.

That is when I decided to take matters into my own hands. I came up with a fund raising idea and enlisted the help of four other women. There was no bakery in our town, so we made donuts and sold them around town at the banks and office buildings every Wednesday. I would wake up at 4:30 a.m. and mix the dough for the first batches. My faithful helpers would arrive a little later and help me roll out the dough and fry. We had donuts rising everywhere, even on the beds that we had covered with boards. We fried and fried, and glazed and frosted. We worked our fingers to the bone and were very exhausted by the time the last dozen was delivered. We made the payments on the building with donut money for the first 2 years of the loan.

At the time, I felt like I was working hard for the Lord and that I was pleasing Him. As I look back on this experience, I can see that my attitude was not right. I was tired of hearing the grumblings and complaints of people, and I was just determined to show them that God would provide. I think we all missed a blessing by not allowing the Lord to guide us in the way He would show His power and provision. This is not to say that I am against all fund raising but only to point out that after searching my motivation—I was not operating in His will.

The Church and its members should always move with the Holy Spirit's direction. We must wait patiently for the Lord to answer our prayers and to give us His divine guidance. Paul would have gone into Asia, but the Holy Spirit led him instead to Macedonia. Paul was willing to change his plans, for he knew that God's divine wisdom far surpassed his earthly wisdom.

My Prayer: Lord, help me to seek Your ways and thoughts before I venture out to do Your work. You are always to be the leader and the planner. I do not want to miss the blessing and provision that You have planned for Your Church. "Surely goodness and mercy shall follow me all the days of my life: and I will dwell in the house of the Lord for ever" (Psalms 23:6).

REST IN HIS ARMS AND SEEK HIS FACE

His left hand should be under my head, and his right hand should embrace me. Song of Solomon 8:3

Yes, we *should** be resting in His embrace. In verse six of chapter two, we saw the love and protection afforded to us in His embrace. In this position of rest, she cannot lead the Lord. He is carrying her. Sometimes we feel so close to our Lord that we think we know what is best without carefully consulting Him. We must always rest in the Lord and never rush ahead of Him.

Our loving Shepherd holds us tenderly in His arms. If we do not jump out of His arms like a naughty child, we will never be separated from His love. The Good Shepherd says, "I give unto them [*his sheep*] eternal life; and they shall never perish, *neither shall any man pluck them out of my hand.* My Father, which gave them me, is greater than all; *and no man is able to pluck them out of my Father's hand*" (John 10:28-29). No person is able to take us out of the loving arms of our Savior.

This position is very submissive for the Bride, for she must lean upon the King's arms. She has to put her trust in His strong arms. She has to trust that He will not let her fall. As the Church of Jesus, we need to fully trust in His wisdom, love, and protection in order to rest in His embrace.

In this position, with His left hand under her head and His right hand holding her in an embrace, her face is turned upwards. Thus, she is gazing into His face and into His eyes. The phrase, "seek my face" is found many times in the Word of God. It does not mean that we are looking into His face with our physical eyes, but it means that we are humbly seeking His expression of love and care. It is a verbal expression of how much we want to draw near to Him—seeking His will and purposes.

We seek His face through prayer: "If my people, which are called by my name, shall humble themselves, and pray, and seek my face, and turn from their wicked ways; then will I hear from heaven, and will forgive their sin, and will heal their land" (2 Chronicles 7:14). Humbling ourselves, praying, and seeking His face will give us peace.

The scriptures command us to seek the Lord and His strength continually. (1 Chronicles 16:11; Psalms 105:3, 4) When David felt like everyone had forsaken him, he prayed:

242

Hear, O Lord, when I cry with my voice!
Have mercy also upon me, and answer me.
When You said, "Seek My face,"
My heart said to You, "Your face, Lord, I will seek."
Do not hide Your face from me;
Do not turn Your servant away in anger;
You have been my help;
Do not leave me nor forsake me,
O God of my salvation.
When my father and my mother forsake me,
Then the Lord will take care of me.

Psalms 27:7-10, NKJV

It is when we are not resting in His arms, and when we are busy solving problems by our own understanding that we get into trouble. That is when we come back to the arms of Christ—just like the Bride in our Song of Solomon did, reminding herself, "I should have been resting and trusting in my Lord."

My Prayer: Lord, here I am again. So many times, You have forgiven me for trying to do things my way. I humbly seek Your face for restoration. I never want to be out of Your arms of love. I am so safe in Your arms, looking into Your face, and feeling Your sweet presence surround me. You are my peace, my rest, and my strength. You are my all in all.

*Note: the word **should** is only found in the King James Version. Should is not in the original language but inserted by the translators to make it easier to understand in our language.

HE WILL STAND UP

I charge you, O daughters of Jerusalem, that ye stir not up, nor awake my love, until he please. Song of Solomon 8:4

We sometimes feel the need to admonish other members of the Church concerning stirring up the Lord. The daughters of Jerusalem represent the Church. All who **believe** (have faith, rely on, trust with your life) on the Lord Jesus Christ, and believe that He died and rose again are a part of this Church. Christ is the head of the Church. He is the One who should be making the decisions and guiding the body in the way to deal with the spiritual needs of people. Let us always remember that His time is the best time.

We are so bound up in time. Many of us work at jobs where we are pressed to meet deadlines. We rush to get to appointments. We live in an "instant" world of fast food, fast travel, and quick fixes. We are conditioned to think that the Lord should answer every prayer with an immediate response. Just because we do not get an immediate response does not mean that our Lord is asleep or that He has not heard us (Psalms 121:4). We must learn to wait upon the Lord for answers.

The Church sees the signs of the end times, and we are anxious for the Lord's second coming. We pray, "Come soon Lord Jesus, oh, come right now!" Jesus has charged us to occupy (keep working) until He comes (Luke 19:13). It is our earnest desire to be caught up to our heavenly home, but as we see the end approaching, it should quicken us to hurry and spread the gospel.

When the time does come for our Lord's return, nothing will hold Him back. His coming will bring joy to the believer, but it will also usher in a time of great judgment for the unbeliever. Jesus is seated at the Father's right hand, but one day He will arise—stand up and say, "That's enough." God will pour out His wrath upon this sinful world.

> Therefore wait ye upon me, saith the Lord, until the day that I *rise up* to the prey: for my determination is to gather the nations, that I may assemble the kingdoms, to pour upon them mine indignation, even all my fierce anger: for all the earth shall be devoured with the fire of my jealousy.
> Zephaniah 3:8-9

When the Lord *awaked as one out of sleep*, and like a mighty man that shouteth by reason of wine. And he smote his enemies in the hinder parts: he put them to a perpetual reproach.

Psalms 78:65-66

Believers do not need to fear that day, "For God hath not appointed us to wrath, but to obtain salvation by our Lord Jesus Christ" (1 Thessalonians 5:9)

In view of the wrath to come, we have the strong motivation to pray for mercy upon our loved ones. The Lord is waiting for us to persuade as many lost ones to follow Him as possible. Peter tells us that the Lord is not delaying His coming because He is not aware of the gross sin that covers every corner of our earth. He is delaying because of His "longsuffering to us-ward, not willing that any should perish, but that all should come to repentance" (2 Peter 3:9).

I sometimes wish I could leave all the toils, heartache, and pain of the world behind, but I am not going to ask the Lord to rush my homecoming. As Paul so eloquently put it:

For to me, to live is Christ, and to die is gain. But if I live on in the flesh, *this will mean fruit from my labor*; yet what I shall choose I cannot tell. For I am hard-pressed between the two, having a desire to depart and be with Christ, which is far better. *Nevertheless to remain in the flesh is more needful for you*. And being confident of this, *I know that I shall remain and continue with you all for your progress and joy of faith*, that your rejoicing for me may be more abundant in Jesus Christ by my coming to you again. Philippians 1:21-26, NKJV

My Prayer: I long for Your return or for Your call for me to come home; nevertheless, I am willing to wait if there is a lost soul that I can win. I pray that I will encourage those who feel weak. I pray that everyone that I meet as I sojourn will escape the day of Your wrath. May You find me faithful to the end.

LEANING UPON MY BELOVED

Who is this that cometh up from the wilderness, leaning upon her beloved? I raised thee up under the apple tree: there thy mother brought thee forth: there she brought thee forth that bare thee.
Song of Solomon 8:5

"Who is this coming up from the wilderness, leaning upon her beloved?" (Song of Solomon 8:5, NKJV) It has to be none other than the Bride. Who else would be leaning upon her Beloved?

She is coming up out of the wilderness (dry wasteland of the world). The Children of Israel were delivered out of Egypt and from its bondage by the strong arm of the Lord. This is likened to the sinner being delivered out of the bondage of sin. It was in the wilderness that the Israelites learned to know their God and walk with Him day-by-day. It certainly was not a pleasant experience at times, although God did provide for their every need and blessed them with many miracles along the way. The Church goes through the wilderness of trials and hardships, which draws us closer to our Lord and teaches us to trust Him. The majority of the Israelites did not learn to rest in God's love because they had unbelief in their hearts (Hebrews 3:18). The Bride of Christ has learned to enter into His rest; she has ceased from her own works; she rests upon the Word of her Lord. The Bible is her road map and Jesus is her high priest; therefore, she is bold to enter the Holy of Holies and find help in time of need (Hebrews 4:9-16).

"I awakened you under the apple tree" (Song of Solomon 8:5, NKJV). We discovered in chapter two, verses three and four that the apple tree is the refreshing shade from the hot sun and the apples are the tasty morsels of God's promises. Jesus woke us up while we were finding shelter from the enemy of our souls, and He shook us with the truth of His Word. The seed of the Word of God and His precious promises of eternal life raised us from death and gave us new birth. "Being born again, not of corruptible seed, but of incorruptible, *by the word of God*, which liveth and abideth for ever" (1 Peter 1:23).

Our mother is the New Jerusalem that is made up of all the believers: "ye are come unto mount Sion, and unto the city of the living God, the *heavenly Jerusalem*, and to an innumerable company of angels, To the general assembly and *church of the firstborn*" (Hebrews 12:22-23). The Church has birthed us by opening our understanding of the Word of God.

The Church has also birthed us by the prayers and supplications she has made in our behalf. The mother of a child has to go through the labor and pain of childbirth to bring forth new life. Paul said that he travailed—suffered birth pains—to bring forth the salvation of those he preached to (Galatians 4:19). We cannot enter into the Kingdom of God without the new birth (John 3:3). Therefore, the mothers (this does not exclude men) of the Church travail in prayer for the sinner. Most of us can look back in our lives and find one or more persons who took our salvation very seriously. They did not let go of God until you and I were born again. It may have been a mother, father, aunt, uncle, or a friend. You can be sure there were tears shed before you came into the joy of salvation.

That dear mother, the Church, gently cared for us as newborn babes in Christ. Teaching us the word of God and praying with us through every difficult situation.

Let me ask you a question as we come close to the end of this study. Have you found the rest of knowing that you are in God's care? Jesus says,

Come to me, all you who are weary and burdened, and I will give you rest. Take my yoke upon you and learn from me, for I am gentle and humble in heart, and you will find rest for your souls. For my yoke is easy and my burden is light.
Matthew 11:28-30, NIV

Jesus simply desires that you accept His death on the cross as atonement for your sins; believe that He was raised from the dead on the third day; repent of the sin in your life and ask Him to give new life to you. The peace of the Lord will fill your heart and life and you will become a new creature. After you have prayed this initial prayer to the Lord, find a Bible believing church where you can be nurtured and taught the Word. Read the Bible for yourself and ask the Holy Spirit to guide you into the truth. Pray and trust Him to guide you all the way to heaven.

My Prayer: Lord, I am tired of trying to live my life my own way. Forgive me for my stubbornness, and help me to yield to Your plan for my life. I believe that You have died to cleanse me from all my sin. I rest in the Word of God and in Your love for me.

ULTIMATE LOVE

Set me as a seal upon thine heart, as a seal upon thine arm: for love is strong as death; jealousy is cruel as the grave: the coals thereof are coals of fire, which hath a most vehement flame.
Song of Solomon 8:6

The seal is an engraving upon metal or precious stone that carries with it the signature of ownership. The Bride is asking the King to set her as a permanently engraved signet (seal) upon His heart and His arm. She has made up her mind that she belongs to Him only.

The same Hebrew word, "chowtham" which is interpreted *seal* here in our song is interpreted *signet* in Exodus chapters twenty-eight and thirty-nine. In these chapters in Exodus, God instructs Moses as to the holy garments to be worn by the High Priest. There was the ephod, which was worn as the top layer of clothing upon the upper part of his body. The shoulders were to be joined with two onyx stones, one on each side. On each onyx stone were engraved six of the names of the tribes of Israel. The breastplate of the ephod was foursquare double thick pieces of fine woven linen with all kinds of beautiful threads woven throughout it. On top of this breastplate of judgment (the ephod) were twelve stones. Each unique stone had one of the names of the twelve tribes. The purpose for these stones upon the shoulders and the heart of the Priest was: "So Aaron shall bear the names of the sons of Israel on the breastplate of judgment over his heart, when he goes into the holy place, as a memorial [*a remembrance*] before the Lord continually" (Exodus 28:29, NKJV). Therefore, we see that the High Priest wore the seals engraved with God's chosen people's names upon his arm and upon his heart as he entered the Holy of Holies.

Our Great High Priest, Jesus Christ, has entered into the Holy place in heaven. He comes before God the Father with his chosen people's names written upon His heart. "For Christ is not entered into the holy places made with hands, which are the figures of the true; but into heaven itself, now to appear in the presence of God *for us*" (Hebrews 9:24). He holds us up in remembrance before the Father constantly. "But this man, [*Jesus*] because he continueth ever, hath an unchangeable priesthood. Wherefore he is able also to save them to the uttermost that come unto God by him, seeing he ever liveth to make intercession for them" (Hebrews 7:24-25). He knows each one of us by name. He intercedes for us before the throne of grace.

The reason the Bride wants the Bridegroom to put her seal upon His heart is because "love is as strong as death." As the Bride remembers the willing sacrifice of her Beloved Savior, she too, is willing to give her all for Christ. Thousands of faithful believers have been martyred for the sake of the gospel and for the love of Christ throughout the Church age.

The Church is jealous for the Lord's name and righteous anger will arise when the believer is confronted with the one who would speak evil of the Lord—when the supposedly educated person refutes that our Lord is , "The way, the truth, and the life" (John 14:6).

Her heart is set on fire with the coals of sanctification. "He will baptize you with the Holy Spirit and with fire. His winnowing fork is in his hand, and he will clear his threshing floor, gathering his wheat into the barn and burning up the chaff with unquenchable fire." (Matthew 3:11-12, NIV) "Our God is a consuming fire" (Hebrews 12:29). The Church has hearts on fire—fueled by the love of the Lord who purifies us for His service.

Our Lord has extreme love for His people. He is a jealous God not wanting His people to seek after any other god. Whoever would touch us is touching the apple of His eye (Zechariah 2:8). Whoever would try to fight against the Church is fighting against Jesus (Acts 9:4-6). Not even the gates of hell will prevail against the Church (Matthew 16:18).

Christ also loved the church and gave Himself for her, that He might sanctify and cleanse her with the washing of water by the word, that He might present her to Himself a glorious church, not having spot or wrinkle or any such thing, but that she should be holy and without blemish. Ephesians 5:25-27, NKJV

He first loved us, and in turn, we have learned to love Him. He fights our battles as we take our stand against every high thing that would exalt itself against Him (2 Corinthians 10:5). His promise is, "No weapon that is formed against thee shall prosper; and every tongue that shall rise against thee in judgment thou shalt condemn. This is the heritage of the servants of the Lord, and their righteousness is of me, saith the Lord" (Isaiah 54:17).

The Lord will honor the overcoming believer with a white stone that has his new name engraved on it. That seal will be the ultimate sign of Jesus' love for me. It will be more exciting than an engagement ring.

"He who has an ear, let him hear what the Spirit says to the churches. To him who overcomes I will give some of the hidden manna to eat. *And I will give him a white stone, and on the stone a new name written* which no one knows except him who receives it.'"   Revelation 2:17, NKJV

My Prayer: My love for You grows stronger each day. It is like a burning fire within my innermost being. I am jealous for Your name's sake. I cast down every imagination and high thought that would raise its ugly head above the knowledge of You, my Lord Jesus, and above the Church for which He has died.

Thank You for always fighting my battles. Thank You for interceding for me before the throne of grace. One day I will stand before Your throne as an overcomer, and I will receive the white stone in which You have engraved my new name. Words cannot express how much I long for that day.

LOVE THAT CANNOT BE QUENCHED

Many waters cannot quench love, neither can the floods drown it: if a man would give all the substance of his house for love, it would utterly be contemned. Song of Solomon 8:7

In my lifetime, I have witnessed many disasters such as floods, tornadoes, and hurricanes. How many times have we seen reports on television of people sifting through the rubble that was once their beautiful home? There is always one who will say, "It is just material things, but I thank God that all my family is safe." We truly value our family above every earthly possession. This is because we love our family more than things, which can be replaced. A man will give up all his substance to keep those he loves safe. He would pay any price demanded for the return of a kidnapped child.

Many waters cannot quench (or put out the fire) of love. Love is the most powerful force on earth besides the power of God. Love will motivate us to do what is good and right. Love will cause us to sacrifice our own desires for the desire of another. I treasure the promise of Isaiah 43:1-2, for it tells me of my Father's love.

> But now thus saith the Lord that created thee, O Jacob, and he that formed thee, O Israel, Fear not: for I have redeemed thee, I have called thee by thy name; thou art mine. When thou passest through the waters, I will be with thee; and through the rivers, they shall not overflow thee: when thou walkest through the fire, thou shalt not be burned; neither shall the flame kindle upon thee.

This verse tells us not to fear, for Jesus has redeemed us out of the clutches of the enemy of our souls. Although the floods of water pass over us, He will be with us. As He was present when the three Hebrew children were thrown into the fiery furnace, He will be with us through the fiery trials that would strip us of everything. (Daniel 3:23-25)

Every time we launched our boat out into the vast ocean, while we were missionaries in the Marshall Islands, we would pray for the Lord's protection and guidance. It was a fearful thing to plunge into the chasm between waves that were taller than our vessel. As we launched out of port, we would sing, "Jesus Baca Jin ial"— "Jesus Savior Pilot Me...over life's tempestuous sea...unknown waves

251

around me roll." [1] Jesus never failed to be with us and brought us safely to shore. No matter what kind of sea we are riding, whether they be waves of emotions, fear, doubt, sickness, or grief, Jesus is with us all the way.

The perfect love of God casts out all fear. We do not have any fear of the judgment of sin because we abide in His love. God is love. He has taught us to love even as He loves.

> God is love, and he who abides in love abides in God, and God in him. Love has been perfected among us in this: that we may have boldness in the Day of Judgment; because as He is, so are we in this world. There is no fear in love; but perfect love casts out fear, because fear involves torment. But he who fears has not been made perfect in love. We love Him because He first loved us.   1 John 4:16-19, NKJV

My Prayer: Lord, help me to be made perfect in Your love. When it seems that circumstances would overwhelm me, help me to look to You. When the storm arose upon the Sea of Galilee, You spoke, "Peace be still" (Mark 4:39). Speak peace to my heart. I pledge my love to You forever. Thank You for loving me. Your love is more precious than silver.

[1] *Jesus, Saviour, Pilot Me*, by Edward Hopper and John E. Gould 1816-1888

MY LITTLE SISTER

We have a little sister, and she hath no breasts: what shall we do for
our sister in the day when she shall be spoken for?
Song of Solomon 8:8

As the Bride of Christ, we may express concern and dismay when we look at immature Christians. The sign that they have not matured is that they have not developed breast of faith and love. They are little sisters who claim Christ as their brother, but they do not produce the fruit that proves that they are part of the kingdom.

Rather than working in the harvest field, the little sister is content to sit back and watch others work. She enjoys the good feelings she has when she is surrounded by the praise and worship of the saints, but she is not willing to grow up and take responsibility. Her love for the Lord and others is too undeveloped to motivate her into service.

What will happen to this little sister? The Word does not give us a pleasant answer to this question. "If a man abide not in me, he is cast forth as a branch, and is withered; and men gather them, and cast them into the fire, and they are burned" (John 15:16). Those who do not bear fruit are to be cut off. "Wherefore by their fruits ye shall know them. Not every one that saith unto me, Lord, Lord, shall enter into the kingdom of heaven; but he that doeth the will of my Father which is in heaven" (Matthew 7:20-21). Doing the will of the Father is performing the work of faith and the labor of love (1 Thessalonians 1:3). It is not enough to call Jesus our Lord—we must develop fruit.

I am so thankful that we serve a God of second chances. In Luke chapter 13, Jesus told a parable about a landowner who planted a fig tree. When he came and checked on the tree for the third year, it still had not produced any fruit. He told the caretaker of the vineyard to cut it down. The caretaker pleaded with the owner to let him try to dig around the tree, fertilize it, and give it another year's grace to bear fruit. The mature Christian, with the guidance of the Holy Spirit, is the caretaker. We must do everything possible to encourage the immature to bear fruit. We have to stir up the soil, praying conviction of the Holy Spirit into the heart of the immature. We have to fertilize it with the words of life.

The mature Christian must have the attitude of blessing and nurturing, rather than of judging. We always remember that if not for

253

the grace of God and the love and care of the saints, we could be in the same situation (Galatians 6:1-2). We restore the weaker one with patience and love. If need be we will go so far as to *provoke* the weaker one to produce fruit. "Let us hold fast the profession of our faith without wavering; (for he is faithful that promised;) And let us consider one another *to provoke unto love and to good works*" (Hebrews 10:23-24).

I feel so sorry for those who do not surrender all to the King. He longs to develop fruit in their lives. We brought a Marshallese couple with us on one of our trips home to Hawaii. After seeing the largeness of the island, the richness of the land, and the prosperity of the people, they asked David this question: "Does God love Hawaii more than the Marshall Islands?" David explained that God does not love one area of the world more than another area. Nor does God love one person more than another person. He does not judge according to size, wealth, or outer appearance. God would have every Christian to be beautiful and bearing plenty of fruit—His abundance is available for all of His children. Likewise we, as the body of Christ, must love and care for the little sister who has not developed the fruit of faith and love. What can the Church do to correct this growth problem?

My Prayer: Lord, help me to bear fruit for You. Help me not to criticize or judge my little sister who has not developed faith and love. Help me to have the patience and take the necessary time to stir up the immature. Help me to pray when my body is weary. Help me to speak to the one who needs encouragement. Cause me to love with impartial love—just as You do.

LOVE AND PROTECTION FOR MY LITTLE SISTER

If she be a wall, we will build upon her a palace of silver: and if she be a door, we will inclose her with boards of cedar.
Song of Solomon 8:9

What should we do for our young sister? The mature, nurturing mothers of the Church feel the responsibility to do something to protect this young sister.

If she is a wall means that she is still closed up, innocent, and virgin like. She has not willfully gone into sin. This would describe the young Christian who is trying to prepare herself for the Bridegroom, but she lacks the fruit and wisdom that comes with maturity. *We* [the Church] *will build a palace*[1] *of sliver* around her for protection. This will protect her from the temptations of the enemy and the false teachers who would try to lead her astray.

The tower or battlement, which is built to protect her, is made of silver. Silver represents redemption. She must first come to the understanding of the precious price the Bridegroom paid for her. How Jesus has rescued her from the hand of the enemy. Then she and the Church will be able to build upon this foundation of Truth. Once she appreciates what the Lord has done for her, she will be prepared to grow breast of faith and love.

How does the Church build this redemptive protection? We teach over-and-over the foundational truths of the gospel. Build on the foundation of the prophets, apostles, and Christ. You may say, "We have repeated the message again-and-again, why do some people still not understand?" Anyone who has raised children can tell you that you do not instruct a child only once or twice as to how to brush their teeth, tie their shoes, or take out the rubbish. You have to guide them and remind them repeatedly. Some children learn faster than others do. We love the slow learners just as much as the children who leap ahead to more difficult tasks. We will surround this sister (the immature Christian) with love, prayers, and living examples. We will disciple her on a one-on-one basis.

If the little sister *is a door* means that she has opened her life to Satan's temptations and succumbed to sin. "But if she is promiscuous, like a swinging door, we will block her door with a cedar bar" (Song of Solomon 8:9, NLT). The cedar boards or bar which we will enclose her in will shut the door of temptation and sin. We have seen many times as we have studied this song that the cedar wood represents the human body of Jesus and the sacrifice of that body upon the Cross. The Church will prevail upon the promiscuous sister to repent and shut the door to the sin that has overtaken her, thereby, applying the atonement of Jesus upon her heart. The Church will do whatever possible to keep her from falling again—boarding her up—by covering her with the protection of the blood of Christ and the power of the Holy Spirit.

The Bride will pray and intercede for the immature and unfruitful brother or sister. She is like the mother who will not neglect feeding her child. Christ will never forget the weak one even if some Christians give up on them. The promise of the Lord is that our sons and daughters will come back. Do not give up, for one day we will wear each of them as jewels. They will be part of our glorious wedding garment.

> "Can a mother forget the baby at her breast and have no compassion on the child she has borne? Though she may forget, I will not forget you! See, I have engraved you on the palms of my hands; your walls are ever before me. Your sons hasten back, and those who laid you waste depart from you. Lift up your eyes and look around; all your sons gather and come to you. As surely as I live," declares the Lord, "you will wear them all as ornaments; you will put them on, like a bride."
>
> Isaiah 49:15-18, NIV

My Prayer: Lord, help me to be a prayer warrior who would intercede for the weak in faith. I pray for those who seem to have so little love for others. Many times they cause division and hurts, but they are my brothers and sisters. May the feeble walls of flesh be enclosed by redemption power. May the doors of loose living be closed. Help them to see what a stumbling block they can be when they profess to be Christians and still continue in sin. I will come rejoicing in the day when I am adorned with jewels (little brothers and sisters). A Bride ready for her King.

[1] Palace is interpreted various ways in other translations. NIV, towers; NKJV, battlement.

HIS EYES OF FAVOR

I am a wall, and my breasts like towers: then was I in his eyes as one that found favour. Song of Solomon 8:10

The Bride is testifying of herself, "I am a wall." Yes, I am still a wall of flesh and bone, but I am indwelt by the glory of the Lord and Christ encompasses my life. (See Song of Solomon 2:9) I have consecrated my love to Jesus.

The difference between the Bride and the little sister is that she has well developed breasts. Breasts that are fruitful, and breasts that are like towers. They are strongholds of faith and love. The enemy will have a difficult time sneaking up on her, for she is ever watchful. The Holy Spirit has given her the gift of discernment so she is able to try the spirits and detect the stranger's voice. Of course, this is all made possible because Christ is the Bride's "shelter and a strong tower from the enemy" (Psalms 61:3)

Before I can become the Bride of Christ, I must be His true disciple. Jesus said if I am planning to build a tower, I must sit down and count the cost first (Luke 14:28). He said, "So likewise, whoever of you does not forsake all that he has cannot be My disciple" (Luke 14:33, NKJV). To build the towers of faith and love, it will cost a yielded life, a crucified life, and a surrender of my will to the will of the Lord.

It is when I give up and let Jesus live in and through me that I find favor in His eyes. The angel told Mary, the mother of Jesus: "thou that art highly favored, the Lord is with thee" (Luke 1:28). Mary was a tower of faith accepting the word of the Lord. She believed the angel when he told her that she would carry the Son of God in her womb. Mary rejoiced to be used by the Almighty God in giving birth to her Lord and Savior. She was favored because she was willing to give up her plans and become an instrument of blessing.

Just as Mary carried the babe conceived of the Holy Spirit, I gladly carry the gift of the Holy Spirit within my soul. I will shine as a beacon light to point others to Christ. I will love the Lord; I will love the sinner; I will love the unlovely; I will love the little sisters; I will love the gossiper and backbiter; I will love....love... love! He loved me while I was black with sin and picked me up out of the pit. He has cared for my growth and fruit persistently—and yet gently. He has been my constant companion through every trial. How could I not love Him with everything that is within me?

257

My Prayer: When I remember what You have done for me, my heart overflows with love to You. I am still living within this human body, but I also carry the sweet Holy Spirit within my soul. May my life be a tower of faith and love. May there be banners of victory flying high on top of those towers for all to see Your goodness. I am Yours Lord, completely Yours. Take me and use me for whatever purpose You see fit.

FAITHFUL SERVANT

Solomon had a vineyard at Baal-hamon; he let out the vineyard unto keepers; every one for the fruit thereof was to bring a thousand pieces of silver. Song of Solomon 8:11

King Solomon had a vineyard. The King of kings owns the whole world. His vineyard was named **Baal-hamon**, meaning "the Lord of the multitudes." Jesus is the Lord of the multitudes, for He has purchased a great multitude that cannot be numbered from every tribe, tongue, people, and nation (Revelation 5:9). King Jesus has let out this vineyard to His keepers. His keepers are the members of His blood-bought Church. As His managers, we are to produce fruit and care for His interest here on earth.

At the Judgment Day, each of us will be called to give an account of the deeds done in our body. We are all accountable to bring a thousand pieces of silver. Wow! Isn't that a lot? No, for the thousand represents the victories we have over Satan. "One man of you shall chase a thousand, for the Lord your God is He who fights for you, as He promised you" (Joshua 23:10-11, NKJV). We are going to rule and reign with Christ a thousand years (Revelation 20:6). Every Christian is victorious over Satan as we allow the Lord to fight the battles for us.

Jesus, knowing He would shortly return to His Father, told a parable to His disciples in order to prepare them for ministry. He said that the kingdom of heaven is like a man who has to go on a long journey. This man distributes his wealth to his trusted servants. He gives one servant five talents, one servant two talents, and the last servant only one talent—to every man according to his ability. He returned after a long time and asked for a report on their management of his finances. The servant, who started with five, had gained five more. The servant, who started with two, had increased his to four. However, the servant, who started with one, only had the one. The wealthy man was displeased with the one who had not increased his talent. The unfaithful servant had just buried his talent. The owner was very pleased with the servants who had taken what he had given them, put it to work, and thus doubled the original amount.

Jesus has gone away into heaven for over 2,000 years. He has left the Church as stewards of precious gifts and abilities. He expects a return on His investment into our lives—the fruit, which we produce for Him and the souls we win for Him. He does not want us to hide the gifts He has given for ministry, nor the testimony of what He has done for us.

One-by-one, we will be called before King Jesus. Did you bear any fruit? Have you been faithful? I want to be the one who says, "Yes, Lord, I used what You gave me and I doubled it." Then I will lay a thousand pieces of silver at His feet. It will be in silver because silver stands for redemption that comes from grace alone. The King will have accomplished it all. He has won all my battles, and He has given me the victory over the enemy of my soul. He alone gives me the power to have anything of worth to bring back to Him. "Not unto us, O Lord, not unto us, but unto thy name give glory, for thy mercy, and for thy truth's sake" (Psalms 115:1).

All I long to hear are His words, "Well done, thou good and faithful servant: thou hast been faithful over a few things, I will make thee ruler over many things: enter thou into the joy of thy lord" (Matthew 25:23).

My Prayer: It is such a blessing and privilege to work in Your vineyard. There is great joy and peace at the end of each day knowing that I have done my best for the Master. Help me to be faithful until the end.

MY VINEYARD

My vineyard, which is mine, is before me: thou, O Solomon, must have a thousand and those that keep the fruit thereof two hundred.
Song of Solomon 8:12

Remember in chapter one, verse six, the Bride said that her family had made her the keeper of their vineyard—but her own vineyard she had not kept. She has matured since then, and now she has learned to take care of her own heart and her own salvation.

I am responsible for my own life and work. Paul said that I am to "work out your own salvation with fear and trembling. For it is God which worketh in you both to will and to do of his good pleasure" (Philippians 2:12-13). My life *is before me*, so I need to search myself and be sure that I understand the cost of following the Lord, My King.

I am required to bring one thousand pieces of silver as a return upon His investment in my life. I am not my own, for He has purchased me with His blood. All glory belongs to Jesus who has changed me, cleansed me, and has prepared me to live eternally with Him. I bring abundant fruits of giving, praying, and winning of souls to His feet.

The Bride says she is going to give two hundred pieces of silver to those who have been keepers of her fruit. Who are these keepers of fruit? I believe it is referring to the various members of the Church who have worked in the vineyard of her life to make sure that she matured, and that she bore the fruit worthy for the King.

He Himself [*Christ*] gave some to be apostles, some prophets, some evangelists, and some pastors and teachers, *for the equipping of the saints for the work of ministry*, for the edifying of the body of Christ, till we all come to the unity of the faith and of the knowledge of the Son of God, to a perfect man, to the measure of the stature of the fullness of Christ.
Ephesians 4:11-13, NKJV

So many faithful men and women have invested time and talents into our lives. They are the apostles that were called to plant mission stations and churches. They were the Sunday School Teachers who showed us how to study God's Word. They were the Pastors who have counseled us when our marriages were on the rocks. They have anointed us and prayed for our healing. They have sat by our hospital beds when we were near death's doors. They were the men and women that spoke faith and hope into our gifts. They were the evangelists who stirred us to get back on fire for our Master.

The call goes out, "Bring the whole tithe into the storehouse, that there may be food in my house" (Malachi 3:10, NIV). We are instructed to be faithful in our tithes so that the storehouse (the Church), and those who minister therein would not lack or want for anything. Most of us are well acquainted with the tithes as being a tenth of our earnings. We feel like we have fulfilled our obligation if we tithe that tenth—but we also need to bring offerings. We all love the promise that comes with this verse in Malachi:

> "Test me in this," says the Lord Almighty, "and see if I will not throw open the floodgates of heaven and pour out so much blessing that you will not have room enough for it. I will prevent pests from devouring your crops, and the vines in your fields will not cast their fruit," says the Lord Almighty.
> Malachi 3:10-11, NIV

The Bride, in our song, says she is not going to stop at the tenth tithe. She is going to give two hundred to the keepers of her fruit. That is **double** tithes! This kind of cheerful giving pleases the Lord. Would He not open the floodgates of heaven and pour out a blessing on such generous hearts? 1Timothy 5:17 says, "Let the elders that rule well be counted worthy of **double** honour, especially they who labour in the word and doctrine."

I would have fallen along the wayside, many times, if the elders of the Church had not encouraged me. The body of Christ has given me opportunities to cultivate my talents. I have learned to bear the fruit of the Spirit through friendship and relationships with other believers. I not only owe them my money, but I owe them my life!

My Prayer: Jesus, I am so thankful for the salvation You so freely gave. I praise You, that You have planted me within a body of believers who have worked the ground of my heart. Thank You for the pastors and teachers You have brought into my life to assist me in the cultivation and growth of my fruit. Each one is truly worthy of his/her hire. Help me to be generous with my money, talents, gifts, and time for the furtherance of the kingdom. As others have invested in my life, so I will invest in the lives You bring my way.

262

MANY GARDENS

Thou that dwellest in the gardens, the companions hearken to thy voice: cause me to hear it. **Song of Solomon 8:13**

My Beloved Jesus, You live in the garden hearts of all of Your children. Each garden is beautiful and unique. Each heart garden is a special place that You have created for Your own pleasure. It is a place where You come to walk and talk with Your chosen people. Just as in the days of Your first creation when You came in the cool of the day and fellowshipped with Adam and Eve, You now come to dwell in the garden of our hearts.

We sit and meditate upon the fountains and streams of the water of Your precious Word. We talk about the development of my fruits or lack thereof. You sometimes dig around the roots of unforgiveness and bitterness. You sometimes prune a branch of dried up service, so another fresh ministry is allowed to sprout. You have surrounded my garden with Your protection. You cause the Holy Spirit to seal my heart so that no predator is able to invade and steal the fruit.

You have called and spoken to my companions, the other members of Your Church, just as You called me. You love each one of us the same because You are no respecter of persons. When I see You leading them into a closer walk with You, may I not be jealous or envious of their call. Only let me listen to Your call upon my life. Draw me closer, and draw my companions closer to You in fellowship and love.

My Beloved Jesus, Your voice is sweeter than anything my ears have ever heard. Cause me to always recognize Your voice and to respond quickly. You are my shepherd, and I will trust no other. Though the voices of this world try to deter me from Your paths, I always come home to rest in the green pastures of Your love.

Jesus, I love You above all this world has to offer. Please continue to dwell in my garden and in the gardens of my companions. I look forward to the day when I will join hands with all of the saints around Your throne and sing the NEW SONG that only the redeemed are privileged to sing.

COME QUICKLY

Make haste, my beloved, and be thou like to a roe or to a young hart upon the mountains of spices. Song of Solomon 8:14

The Bride is climbing one more mountain. How many times she has climbed the mountain of myrrh – self-sacrifice? It seems to be a never-ending battle with her will, pride, and selfishness. Then she remembers that time-after-time her Beloved has come to her skipping upon the mountains of her distress turning them into mountains of victory. The spices of frankincense and praise begin to flow from her lips.

Thank You, Lord, for saving me from my sin and backsliding. Thank You, Lord, for healing my body. Thank You, Lord, for saving my sons and daughters. Thank you, Lord, for Your patience with me. Thank you, Lord, for counting me worthy to work in Your harvest field. Thank you, Lord, that You have promised: "Behold, I come quickly; and my reward is with me, to give every man according as his work shall be" (Revelation 22:12).

As the Bride of Christ sees the day fast approaching when her Lord and Savior will return, she joins the Holy Spirit in making one last plead to the world: "Come. And let him that heareth say, Come. And let him that is athirst come. And whosoever will, let him take the water of life freely" (Revelation 22:17). I pray that if you have read this book and have not yet decided to come to the water of life that you will make that decision right now. Please do not wait another moment to make Christ your Lord.

May I encourage you, my fellow believers and companions in the Bride, "Look up, and lift up your heads; for your redemption draweth nigh" (Luke 21:28).

My Beloved King says, "Surely I am coming quickly."

From the very depth of my soul, I respond to my Beloved:

"Even so, Come, Lord Jesus!"

Revelation 22:20

264

The End

Intimate Moments with My Beloved King Order Form

Use this convenient order form to order additional copies
of
Intimate Moments with My Beloved King

Please Print:

Name_____

Address_____

City_____ **State**_____

Zip_____

Phone( )_____

_____ copies of book @ $15.00 each $_____
Postage and handling @ $4.60 per book $_____
HI residents add 5% tax $_____
Total amount enclosed $_____

Make checks payable to: Virginia Ah Yee

Send order to: Virginia Ah Yee
95-460 Kaelo Place • Mililani, HI 96789

Discounts are available for orders of 5 or more books.
Please email for rates to ahyeer001@hawaii.rr.com